STRAIGHT TALK ON CAREERS:
80 PROS TAKE YOU INTO THEIR PROFESSIONS

by

Mary Barbera-Hogan

2311409

ABOUT THE AUTHOR:

Mary Barbera-Hogan is an honors graduate of the University of California at Berkeley. Her first exposure to writing and interviewing came as a result of her work as Sports Editor of the Berkeley annual, *The Blue and Gold*. After graduation, she was hired by a state agency and assigned the job of interviewing its personnel to determine how their work affected the functioning of the department as a whole. This lead to an interest in the realities of the working world, specifically the relationship between education and day-to-day job activities.

Ms. Barbera-Hogan is the former Feature Editor of *'Teen Magazine* where she researched and wrote about career trends and preparation for different professions, among other topics relevant to the high school crowd. She is now an Assistant Editor at *New Woman* magazine.

In compiling information for this book, Ms. Barbera-Hogan interviewed over 80 men and women currently working in their chosen professions. Their profiles provide the inside view of working life at the top, middle, and bottom of their fields.

Ms. Barbera-Hogan currently lives in New York with her husband, Robert Hogan, a well-known television actor. She has also written a novel, screenplay, and several short stories.

Library of Congress Cataloging-in-Publication Data

```
Barbera-Hogan, Mary.
   Straight talk on careers.

   Bibliography: p.
   Includes index.
   1. Professions--United States.  2. United States--
Occupations.  3. Professional employees--United
States--Interviews.  I. Title.
HF5382.5.U5B29  1987   331.7'12'02373      87-80809
ISBN 0-912048-48-4
```

ISBN 0-912048-48-4
Library of Congress No. 87-080809

Published and distributed by the
Garrett Park Press
P.O. Box 190B
Garrett Park, MD 20896

DEDICATION

Dedicated with love to
Robert Hogan
My husband and my best friend.

INTRODUCTION

The lights dimmed and the curtain rose. The quartet of chamber musicians began to play. I was particularly fascinated by the violinist. He was in love with his instrument, and looked as though he would rather sit on that stage and play than do anything else. "How very special," I thought, "to do what he does for a living."

As the evening progressed, I began to wonder what it was really like to be a professional musician. How long did he have to practice each day? How many football games and dances had he given up in exchange for the mastery of his instrument? How many young violinists would embark on a career based on what they thought his life was like?

My curiosity was piqued. Our high schools and universities offer superior education, but how many students really know what it's like to live the life of a doctor, a lawyer, a fire fighter? What are their days like? What are the stresses and rewards accompanying their work? What realities should young adults know before making decisions about their future?

These questions started a chain of inquiry that led to this book, *Straight Talk on Careers: 80 Pros Take You Into Their Professions*.

Straight Talk is a career book with a difference: professionals themselves talk about their jobs—what they did yesterday and today. And their hopes for tomorrow. In a conversational style, men and women share their inside knowledge with a directed purpose: to help young people make intelligent career decisions based on realistic expectations. For example, a female surgeon talks of dating difficulties due to her professional responsibilities. A veteran baseball player discusses the stress related to the constant demand for top performance. An Air Force Captain cites the difference between flying for the military and a private airline.

Straight Talk was written for readers in high school and college. The style and content are geared for accessibility without condescension. The interviews provide information with a human touch. Noted lawyer Melvin Belli does lose a case occasionally. Irving Wallace had four unsuccessful novels before he made it big. Joan Jett does, at times, lie awake at night thinking that her success is all a dream.

Straight Talk is not a book of celebrity interviews, but a profile of professionals at all levels of their chosen occupation, from rookie to veteran. The selection of careers was based on research in high school and university counseling centers which indicated the most frequently chosen occupations today.

Studies show that most educated young adults aspire to the top levels of a profession, then filter into different branches as they continue on their career path. For example, a freshman may enter college as a premed major and eventually choose to work as a medical laboratory technician. Consequently, *Straight Talk* presents the major occupational headings, with a few variations in the field.

Each section opens with a brief introduction to the profession; current statistics on the field, and a summary of applicable educational requirements. Some introductions include quotes from experts offering memories and advice to help the newcomer avoid common educational pitfalls.

In addition to dispelling some of the myths about their fields, the professionals offer advice on how to best prepare for the real demands of their work. Some of the advice may surprise you. Some may be a confirmation of what you already know. But, all of it comes from professionals currently working in their fields—in the middle of the action. Success through knowledge and preparation is the underlying theme of this book.

Straight Talk is not a compilation of colorful biographies—although I hope the readers will find them as interesting as I do. It seeks to provide the realities of a profession, not the wacky and wonderful peculiarities of a person in the field.

Straight Talk is not an exhaustive outline of the working marketplace, but an inside view of selected professions of particular interest today.

Straight Talk does not intend to sway the reader in any one direction. The professionals were given the opportunity to say, "This is what it's like to do what I do for a living. If you want to get into the field, here's the benefit of my experience." For instance, a private in the army describes her experience as one of the worst of her life. The interview before her profiles a career soldier who can't imagine happiness outside the military.

Straight Talk refuses to dwell on the negative odds, but concentrates instead on methods to better your chances. If a person wants a career in acting, for example, this book will tell how others have moved from desire to reality—their techniques and trials, their successes and sorrows.

The interviews in this book were collected over a number of months. Some of those interviewed have since changed jobs—such as the professional baseball player who has been traded to another team, or the other who is now one of his team's coaches. Others have expanded into double careers, such as the rock singer who has now made a motion picture. But, their views on their careers are as valid now as then.

The interviews in this book present information gathered from the professionals themselves and reflect their opinions of their work and sometimes their lives. Two of the names have been changed at the professional's request.

No introduction would be complete without expressing, once again, my deep appreciation to wonderful working people who contributed their career profiles. Thanks to them, *Straight Talk* can help solve the single biggest problem facing newcomers to today's job market—a lack of realistic information about their future working world.

TABLE OF CONTENTS

ACTING

MUSIC

DIRECTING

JOURNALISM/REPORTING

MEDICINE

SPORTS

EDUCATION

COMPUTER FIELDS

Twenty years ago, the thought of purchasing a computer to track the inventory in a small business was dismissed as "futuristic." Now, the topic of conversation around the family dinner table might be how soon the little one should be exposed to the PC.

The computer field is one of the fastest growing areas of our economy today—science fiction turned into reality. Micro computers, the type that most people are familiar with today, have flooded the market with such speed and force that many business people, artists, and homemakers can't imagine life without them. Several technical colleges already require each entering freshman to acquire a personal computer and use it as confidently as one uses a fountain pen and notebook.

Today, doctors puzzled by a patient's ailments can punch the symptoms and medical history into a computer to see if other physicians have treated patients with similar complaints. This new technology is invaluable in improving diagnosis and treatment. Manufacturers of hot dogs look at the prices of various cuts of meat and use their computers to determine the best formula for blending today's products. Investors in the securities market trace prices, returns, and develop investment strategies. High school students with competent computer skills develop term paper outlines and final drafts on the family's PC, while at the same time, use computer files to keep their social calendars intact.

The 80's has been called the "Information Age" and computers are its key tools. The first modern computer was built in the 1940's and its 18,000 vacuum tubes occupied several large rooms in a building provided by the University of Pennsylvania. Today, computers come in more handy sizes—there are desk top models and systems so small that they fit easily into briefcases for immediate use anywhere.

Computers have created the growth field of the last 25 years. In 1970, computer occupations accounted for over half a million jobs. This rose to nearly one and a half million by 1980, and is expected to jump to over two million by 1990. Additionally, the number of bachelor's degrees awarded by colleges in computer and information science fields increased from about 2,300 per year in the early 1970's to approximately 25,000 today. There's no question that computer know-how is a valuable asset in the current job market.

Employment in the field can be broken down into five major types:

- **Systems Analysts** determine the machinery (hardware) and instructions (software) best suited to process and produce the needed information.

- **Application Programmers** prepare instructions based upon the system analyst's recommendations to make the computer perform specific tasks.

- **Computer Operators** enter data into the system, operate the equipment, and retrieve the results.

- **Computer Technicians** install and repair computer systems.

- **Data Key Entry Operators** operate keyboards which enter information onto magnetic tapes, disks or cards. However, in recent years, different techniques for entering data have reduced employment opportunities in this area.

One authority has estimated that by the year 2000, 75 percent of all jobs will require computer skills. Assembly line staff in modern factories use computers to direct assembly and inventory activities. Modern supermarkets no longer rely on the memories of cashiers or printed prices on products to determine amounts owed. Military service members use computers to guide missiles, aim cannons, and predict weather, as well as plan recruiting needs, inventory medical supplies, and keep up-to-date on scientific research. Libraries are rapidly replacing card files with computer terminals. In short, computers are everywhere, and are here to stay.

All of this suggests a highly favorable outlook for professionals in computer fields. It's a field that offers room to grow and, with constant advances in technology around every corner, provides exciting and stimulating new challenges to meet and conquer.

MICHAEL ATI

Systems Analyst

Different brands of personal computers line the walls of Michael Ati's fledgling company. A coffee machine invites you to help yourself while multi-colored ads for different computer manufacturers invite you to sit down and sample their machines. The wood paneled setting is a computer smorgasbord where you can taste everything the micro computer world has to offer.

Michael is a systems analyst and a partner in one of the hottest entrepreneural businesses of the computer age. Narrow tie, linen suit, his style matches his expertise. As technical director, Michael is in charge of the engineering and software[1] aspects of the company, and has been since its birth in 1981.

> *A person who is deciding to computerize his or her business will come to us to talk about needed applications—what needs to be done. I listen, then give advice on what to buy and do. If he or she takes that advice, the company can also provide the hardware and software, integrate them, interface them, install them, and train the client to use it. If necessary, we support the client later by maintaining, upgrading, and repairing the system.*

Michael Ati knows computers. After graduating from college, with a bachelor's degree in electrical engineering, he landed a job as hardware engineer for a large electronics company. Shortly after, Michael became interested in learning about software, or programming, and attended a training program offered by the company. The seeds were planted, and he set his sights at continued growth.

> *I decided to go back to school, and got a master's degree in computer science, which is really about software. Later, I went back to school again and received a master's degree in electrical engineering, in hardware.*

Now, Michael is involved with micros—the newer, smaller generation of computers—and has worked with them for the last eight years. With the vastness of this relatively new field, he sees a need for specialists. However, the people who know *both* hardware and software are in greatest demand. And, while large companies with extensive personnel may seek experts in one narrow field, the entrepreneur must know both.

> *Computers have become small enough to be handled by one person, so it doesn't make sense that you should be blind to one part of it. When computers were huge, there were usually three or four people taking care of the hardware, and three or four other people taking care of the software. It's wise to specialize in a particular part of either hardware or software, but you'd have a big boost with a general understanding of both.*

In a business such as a systems house, the largest percentage of the company's work involves software. The software portion of the job is essentially software selection and analysis.

> *For example, I talk to a person who is in charge of a company and she tells me what she wants to do with a computer. I think about the software and programs that are available in the market, and try and match it. I may be able to find software that can do perhaps 85% of what she wants. At that point, a decision must be made. If the person wants the computer to do exactly what she wants, I design a system for her, then a programmer writes a program using my design specifications. The other option is to find software in the market and modify it for the client.*

Typically, Michael's working day begins at home. Most of his clients don't come into the office in the early morning, but they may call. So, before heading out, he phones the answering service. Often, it's necessary to

---

[1]Hardware, in the computer field, refers to machines and equipment. Software includes programs to work with the equipment.

return calls and solve problems before he steps out the door. "I can be on the phone from minutes to hours, depending on the problems."

When he does arrive at the office, the process repeats itself. Round two is returning the phone calls that have accumulated for him in the office.

> *Most of the (calls) are from ongoing clients. They already have a system and either need something more, or have a question about how to do something they haven't done before. They usually need some kind of technical support. I try to give advice over the phone, or I or one of the programmers or technicians will take a trip over there. Sometimes clients prefer to come into the office because it costs them less if the work is done here.*

Other calls concern consultation. Some haven't bought a computer yet. Some are expanding their systems. They need professional advice. In some cases, a client will request a specific number of consultation hours and, for a fee, Michael will examine their needs and prepare a report with his recommendations.

Most of the working day, however, is spent with systems design and programming. About half of the day is spent in the office, the other half is outside at various businesses, running errands, trouble-shooting.

> *About 40 percent of my day is me and my computer, 20 percent is me and my mind—in front of the computer, thinking, laying down by the beach, whatever—the final 40 percent is in communication with other people.*

In any entrepreneurial situation, the business day rarely ends at 5:00 p.m., and the thinking process and worries of the day never end.

> *Very few people have my home number, but those who have it, do call me at home. I tell my clients that if they have a complaint or an argument, keep it for my office hours. If they want to talk about something interesting, I don't mind calls at home.*

In the world of computer software, there is a hierarchy. The top rung of the ladder is the systems designer, followed by the systems analyst, programmer analyst, senior programmer, junior programmer. The person at the top spends most of his or her time with people, and the least amount of time with the computer.

If the company is large the systems designer may never do any programming. He or she simply talks to the client, understands the application, and designs a system. The systems analyst then analyzes that design and translates it into computer terms.

The programmer analyst is the interface between the programmer and the systems analyst. The senior programmer supervises the rest of the programmers in their writing of the program. Together, this group creates a system. Along the way, there is feedback throughout the chain to insure that the system is being written according to the designer's specifications.

When all of this is done, the system must be tested, installed, and described to the client. Then, the client is trained to use it.

By contrast, in a small system, company, or chain, a few of these jobs may be done by the same person.

> *Most of the time, our team consists of two or three people. I do the system design, the system analysis, the programmer analyst's job, and a little of the programmer's job. Then, most of the programming is done by a second or third person in the company.*

Many aspects of the computer profession are still considered "state-of-the-art." The excitement of riding the crest of a wave is a major high to the profession. But, to a certain extent, the size of your company will determine your freedom of movement and your ability to continue to ride on the tip of change.

> *It isn't a rigid profession like civil engineering, for example, where the rules were made 50 years ago. You can be very creative and go many different ways.*

> *Since the field is state-of-the-art, it's important to be fast—you don't want a big bureaucracy on top of your head. An advantage as an entrepreneur is that when you know something is right, you don't have to wait or be discouraged by the manager or your manager's manager. You can go ahead, if you can afford it.*

IBM, a great company, didn't have any micro computers until 1982. By that time, some companies had already been in the micro computer market for 6 or 7 years. All of a sudden, IBM discovered that they were missing out on a big market so they jumped in. They bought most of the important components of the computers and software from other companies, put it together, and put their name on it. Then, their master salesmen and their advertising went to work. It took a long time for IBM to gear up and enter the field. A smaller company can move much faster.

A negative aspect to any entrepreneurial venture is the uncertainty of income.

You have to think ahead and say, "I'm going to be in the red, the black, then the green." I'm going to lose money, break even, then make money. Unfortunately, you may be a great scientist, but if you don't have money, your landlord is still going to throw you out in the street.

The average pay for a person with Michael's education and experience is about $40,000–$45,000 per year if he worked as an employee in a company. Conversely, the entrepreneur cannot be certain of any income for a few years.

Most possibly, at the beginning you'll make much less, and most possibly you'll make much more later. Not a few months, but several years later.

To be successful, begin by setting specific goals for yourself. See a clear reason for everything that you're doing.

In my heart, I never though about quitting at all. To be a successful entrepreneur, especially in this field, you have to go in with all your heart. If you are building bridges in the back of your mind for going back or quitting, most possibly you will. You must spend all your time thinking about how to make it rather than how to quit.

The computer field, especially micro computers, has and is changing rapidly. Preparation for the current marketplace is essential.

If you were starting in 1976–1981, you needed a good technical background. In 1982, you needed a lot of money and good salesmanship. Now, you need technical background, financial ability, and marketing ability. You either have it yourself, or you form a team where each person is the complement of the others. If you don't have all three, it's going to be very tough on you. But, if you do have these three things, do it. Don't even think about it. It's a great field to jump into.

WAVERLY HAGEY-ESPIE

Computer Programmer

She likes to solve things, always has. Waverly was a school teacher who enjoyed her profession until declining enrollments wiped out her job. She was handed her pink slip and a huge career problem. So, instead of searching for another precarious teaching position, she decided to see what the rest of the world was doing—now Waverly Hagie-Espie knows she's found her niche.

For the last four years, Waverly has worked for AT&T Bell Laboratories as a computer programmer, one of the company's 5,000 employees. To prepare for computer programming, she returned to school. After previously obtaining a master's degree in education, she took two years to complete an associate's degree in computer science.

Essentially, programming is the process by which a person provides a computer with a set of instructions. Waverly's current assignment involves software integration.

I make the old programs work compatibily with new programs that have been developed.

Unlike a retail customer where you distribute the software to a company and people come in and buy, my customers are people who will be using my software to develop on top of it. Our responsibility is to develop software for our international customers, right now we are in The Netherlands, Korea, Saudi Arabia, Egypt, Taiwan and Singapore.

Waverly works on a deadline—one that she formulates and meets on her own. With each assignment, she assesses the difficulties and complications and sets her own benchmarks. "Then, I do what I have to do to meet those deadlines." As she has discovered, experience is the only way to accurately determine how long something will take.

We also have to meet the customer's deadline for the software delivery. There is some negotiation involved. If, for example, I had a very complicated assignment, and based on my experience I knew that I needed two years to do it, but had to deliver the product within 18 months, then I really couldn't set my own benchmarks. My supervisor would negotiate to have more individuals put on.

Every assignment has its own requirements—some are less time-consuming than others. Currently, Waverly starts her day at about 7:30 a.m.

Yesterday, for example, I had to do a lot of research on a particular file to find out how it could be integrated into the software that currently exists. That meant talking with the people who had written the file, in some cases to make sure that I understood the interfaces between the file and the rest of the system. Then I came back to my desk to determine how I was going to put it in.

After you understand the code and the interfaces involved, you want to determine how to option the code into the existing development.

I also had to modify several other files because of the interfaces that were associated with the file that I was integrating.

Though it may *sound* complicated, after four years, Waverly doesn't need to spend much time discussing specifics with colleagues. More importantly, she uses her time to confirm her perceptions of how the file is supposed to operate, then carries on with her work.

It's not something that you know right away. With the new people in my organization, it takes about four to eight weeks to bring them on board so that they understand what integration is, what conversion is, and what software optioning is.

Waverly shares an enclosed office with one other person. Most often, there are just two individuals to an office with a door that can close out the sounds of the hallway. Seated in front of two computer terminals, she works steadily until the program is ready to be tested in the lab.

The lab is a simulated environment in which the programmer can test the software. The testing process allows you to see that the software logically performs what you thought it would perform, and doesn't do anything that you don't want it to.

I've had the kind of job where you come home and your work is over, 8 to 5, period. This job is not like that. You do what you have to do to meet the benchmark. I like the challenge, but sometimes, it does interfere with other aspects of my life. The interference can be huge if your planning isn't very good. Still, even if you plan well, you'll have to put out brushfires.

To meet her benchmarks for this particular assignment, Waverly works more than an eight hour day. The lab hours vary: it's open 24 hours a day and you can come in any time you like. This is an advantage in planning more daylight time to spend with family or do other activities. With a company the size of AT&T, Waverly enjoys the fact that she will always be working with the state-of-the-art equipment.

Since Bell Laboratories is an innovator, some of the information obtained through the work there is new to the field. This information must be documented and generated. Therefore, for this job, you must know how to write and effectively present information.

You need a good foundation in English, and a technical writing course would be very helpful. Technically, all of the information is documented: the requirements and the design. The requirements state what your customer wants. The design states how you plan to give the customer what he wants. You also have documents to verify that you have achieved those things.

Learn how to give an oral presentation. You will frequently find yourself in a position where you must communicate what you're working on. "Present your capabilities to others so that they have confidence in what you are doing."

Although debate continues over the issue of academic study versus practical "hands-on" experience, Waverly feels that a combination of the two is the most valuable background for a career in computer science.

In the computer area, you have to maintain a level of technical expertise. A lot of it comes from current higher education. A lot of it is going on in institutions such as Bell Laboratories where many of the new things are coming out.

Innovations are occurring because people are trying to apply theoretical knowledge. It's really the intermingling of knowledge and experience that help you develop the innovations.

I would encourage individuals to take in-house courses, or if they so desire, go back to school. But most definitely, part of our job is to keep up.

A big plus to a career in computer programming is the future of the field. Computers are here to stay. Programmers are needed everywhere.

I know I will have a job in computer science as long as I am able to keep up with the technology.

DAVID GROSS

Personal Computer Salesperson

In a tidy, expansive room dotted with computer keyboards, display screens, and disk drives, David emerges looking sharp in a three-piece grey business suit. Stylish. Professional.

"Coffee?"

"Please."

David Gross has come a long way in a few years. His brand new wedding band marks the end of an era and the beginning of another. He is settled, happy, and has found a comfortable and lucrative runway for his ambitious future.

Computers. Sales.

Unlike computer whiz kids or PC connoisseurs, David's entry into the computer field was a mistake. "It was the best mistake I ever made." He had always been good in math. While attending a two-year college, the time came to decide on a curriculum. The school offered a computer technology program which included logic and arithmetic and basic electronics, "mathish" types of things. Sounded good.

The training was geared toward repair of mini-systems. It was specialized training for the marketplace.

He was on his way. David got his start in the computer industry with prestigious Hewlett-Packard. After graduation with an associate degree in computer technology, he was interviewed on campus by several companies and was offered a job as a customer engineer on HP's large business systems. Essentially a technician, he did the installations and emergency repair on the systems.

Once you're in a company, there are a lot of different avenues open to you: one is software, another is management and another is sales. At that time, I was too young and restless to sit down and become a part of management, so I chose sales. I let my intentions be known. They told me what to do and I did it.

Accounting classes. On-the-job exposure. David frequently rode with salesmen to find out exactly what he was getting into. It was a major transition.

To tell you the truth, I was not successful at that transition.

In my eyes, Hewlett-Packard was the greatest company that you could work for. When I was a customer engineer, we were all friends and supportive of one another. Well, when I moved up to sales, it was a different world.

The world of sales is the world of self-motivation. *You* determine whether you will be successful or not.

There was no one saying, "I have a trouble call, go out." There is nothing tickling you.

Salesmen get paid by what they do with their time. They didn't have time to help another salesman outside of their territory. Now that I have been in sales for over three years, I can see that. Then, I felt very alone. I did wade through, however, and eventually was successful.

A retail computer company called Businessland was changing locations. It sent out headhunters to find specific types of computer salesmen. They were looking for men and women who could sell solutions, not just sell computers. The opportunity arose, and David grabbed it. He was hired in 1983 and is now a senior marketing representative.

I am very senior and I have a lot of good accounts. I am presently up for promotion as a marketing consultant which is the next step up. I have earned that because I have sold my numbers. Promotion is based on performance only. You can make or break the career on your own.

Businessland's clients are mostly small businesses. It provides personal computer systems for companies that need a computer, but don't have the money or the need for a system the size that Hewlett-Packard offers. Businessland is a chain of retail stores. People come in off the street, ask questions, and sit down with a personal computer to see what it can do.

By 8:30 a.m., David is at the office—a half hour before the store opens to the public at 9:00. Once a week, all the salesmen meet for an early morning sales meeting, but normally, David finds that the half hour of calm in the morning allows him to get a few things done before the store opens. He checks his phone messages, goes over the mail, and calls his major accounts.

I want to touch base, make sure everything is going well, and—heaven forbid—they might want to place an order. My accounts are basically friends, we have already worked up a friendship. We'll chat, have some small talk, see what's going on. I just got married last May, and everyone wanted to know about my honeymoon.

You want to make sure that everything is going smoothly. It's very important to not let things get to a critical point. It's important to stay on top of it, and maintain control over what is happening.

The next action is to handle the floor traffic. When customers enter the store, they approach the marketing assistant who is situated at a large, circular desk. Of the sales force of 14, three are scheduled to handle the floor traffic at any given time.

When he's not assigned to the floor, David calls new leads. New leads range from "cold call" names in the telephone book to new businesses he notes as he drives around.

Even when I am not working, if I am in an area and see a potential business, I'll go in, introduce myself, and see if anything is possible there.

I see a new little retail store with inventory all over the place. I ask them how they track it. Many times they will say, "I'm thinking of getting a computer." I say, "Let's talk."

Each salesman must go through a month-long training program to learn the five-step sales process, how to configure a system, and the major software that they will be selling and supporting.

The first step in sales is to introduce the client to Businessland. You walk the customers around the store, offer some coffee, allow them to feel comfortable. Many times customers are nervous. They want a computer. They've never used a computer. They're expecting a car salesman to greet them at the door. To put them at ease, Businessland salesmen explain what they will be going through.

Step two is to find out what customers plan to do with the computer.

Until I have that information, I can't offer a solution. I sit down and find out what the customer's needs are.

Step three is discussing possible software.

Software is the only thing that is worth anything on a computer. All computers basically do the same things. They all have disk drive, they all have memory, and they will all do what they are told. Software is the vehicle that tells them what to do.

A successful sale fits customers to the proper software. You don't want them to overbuy or underbuy.

Once the software is selected, the salesman knows the required minimum hardware requirements—step four. Step five is implementing everything.

We have a minimum amount of software, we are not a software house. What we do have, and what we train on, is software that we can support. I would say at least one quarter of the day is spent being supportive of my customers.

Though the center closes at 6:00 p.m., David's day could end anywhere from 5:00 to 8:00—often he doesn't get away until after 7:00. Business comes from existing accounts, there are mailings, calling, and paperwork.

We have to generate quotations and registration forms so that when our technical staff configures the systems, they can serialize the numbers so we have a record of it.

The salesmen lead fairly autonomous working lives, when things are going well. If you are not "doing your numbers" the sales manager and the general manager will help you out, and keep a closer watch on your work.

When we sell a system, we don't just release the system that day. We put in the configuration. Our technicians then configure it the way the customer is buying it, and test it for 24 to 48 hours to make sure it all works. Then we rebox it.

Everyday there is a tracking of all the numbers—what all the marketing reps are doing. We have weekly sales meetings and we talk about what our projections are, what business we have, what we need to do to close.

We are a retail store and have to get the dollars in—now. It's month by month. A new month starts every single month. It's always go, go, go! You can never just relax and say, "Ahhh, I've made it for this quarter." Forget it.

The stress inherent in sales work is understood by all the sales staff and dealt with accordingly. Everyone feels the tensions of the business, and everyone recognizes it. "Sometimes you blow up, or whatever. We all realize that it's going to happen."

One of the most difficult transitions that David had to make when working as a salesman, was accepting a "No" without taking it personally.

It's very hard for people to accept rejection day in and day out. I like when people say, "Yes" and give me my pats on the back. You have to realize that they are saying "No" to the business deal, not to you.

A lot of customers come in with the attitude, "You are the enemy, but I need this. Help me!"

However, a tangible reward to sales is that you are specifically compensated for the amount of successful effort you put in. Even though he is paid a salary as well as a commission, David's salary would never increase if he didn't perform.

If you are doing the numbers, you can make quite a bit of money.

To prepare yourself for the computer end of the business, get involved in the sciences, electronics and math. See if you have an aptitude for it.

I think by the time you are in high school, you should have an idea if you can stomach sales or not. You need the type of personality that can get along with people.

When you are in a group and no one knows what to do, are you the person who guides them? If you can never persuade your friends, sales is not your vocation.

BUSINESS

Pioneer auto maker Henry Ford once said that business is the oldest and most useful of all the professions. In the same era, President Calvin Coolidge commented that "the business of America is business." Granted, both men were practical and conservative, but the fact remains that business affects your life everywhere. The clothes you wear, the food you eat, the magazines and books you read, and the movies and TV shows you watch—not to mention where you live and how you get to work or school.

More than any other field cited in this book, the general area of business offers the widest range of employment options. Here are a few cross-country examples:

- Clothing store owner in Bismarck, North Dakota
- Life insurance salesman in Miami
- Public accounting trainee in Salem, Oregon
- Discount record store manager in Pasadena
- Plumbing contractor in Nashua, New Hampshire
- Securities sales person in Toledo, Ohio
- Airline reservation agent in Chicago
- Executive search recruiting specialist in New York City
- Marina manager in San Diego
- Employment agency counselor in San Francisco
- TV advertising sales worker in Los Angeles
- River boat manager in New Orleans
- Credit collections worker in Brooklyn
- Executive secretary in a Rahway, New Jersey chemical company
- Real estate agent in Lowell, Massachusetts
- Beauty shop operator in Cleveland, Ohio
- Assemblyline supervisor in Louisville, Kentucky
- Appliance salesperson in Atlanta

Jobs in business are varied—they also are changing. A hundred years ago, most Americans were employed in farming and manufacturing. Today, fewer than two percent work in agriculture and around nine percent in manufacturing. The big shift in recent years has been to business in service fields which handle the products of farming and manufacturing, as well as a thousand new kinds of businesses dealing with everything from credit cards to personal services.

The range of opportunities in business is no mystery to today's college students. The number of business majors has jumped sky-high, while the traditional liberal arts majors of English, history and foreign language, to name a few, have shown significant declines. One fourth of all bachelor's degrees today are awarded in business fields. And, the most significant shift in a student's preparation for a business career involves higher education, specifically in the rapid expansion of master's programs in business leading to the MBA degree. In 1960, only 4,800 MBA degrees were awarded. This number increased to nearly 33,000 by 1974, and over 71,000 today. At the same time, the number of institutions offering the MBA degree increased from 389 in 1974 to over 600 today.

Women have contributed greatly to the soaring statistics of business students. In just 10 years, the number of women in executive, administrative, and managerial jobs has increased from 18.5 to 30.5 percent. A recent study of women who graduated Harvard Business School with MBAs found that most met with success in their careers. After ten years, some were earning salaries ranging from $80,000 up to $200,000 a year. In the early 1970s, women accounted for only 5 percent of Harvard's business students. Today, they make up about 30 percent and that figure continues to climb.

As America revives the work ethic, business fields are once again moving into the spotlight. Both men and women share the family work load as never before, working toward filling their days with stimulation as well as above average financial rewards. For many, working hard to play hard is the common goal, and business is their means of achieving it.

TOM RUFFINO

Advertising Account Executive

The receptionist sits, illuminated by a single light, in the corner of a massive, mauve-colored room. One wall is lined with a single row of miniature international flags. The gray furniture declares a designer's touch. It's not a room for pizza-on-the-floor gatherings, but an elegant waiting room—a quiet separation from the activity on the other side of the door. A room where big money deals are about to happen.

Tom Ruffino enters and welcomes the guest into his spacious office. The lines are clean and sharp—the feeling modern. High on the eighth floor overlooking a busy boulevard, he views the changing traffic patterns from the wide picture window. Tom's been in advertising since 1970. His demeanor is calm and confident, his conversation laced with humor.

When I graduated college, in 1969, I started looking for a job in advertising. I had the names of eleven agencies, two in Chicago and nine in New York, and I sent them walnuts which I had hollowed out. There were three walnuts in a little box. The middle walnut had my cover letter in it, and the two side walnuts had my resume. I put a little strip across them that was taped onto the walnuts and it said, 'I hear advertising is a hard nut to crack.'

Eleven agencies responded, five arranged for an interview and Tom ultimately landed a job. The tensions of his tense business have not taken him. He won't allow it.

There is a funny thing about agency people. If it were Wednesday and someone came into my office and said that they needed a major presentation done by a week from Friday, we would probably sit around until Wednesday of next week to start. Somehow, the juices don't get flowing until the pressure starts to build. Somehow, the pressure propels us.

An account executive since 1972, Tom was adamant about receiving his advertising training in New York or Chicago. In his mind, other cities simply don't provide the same formalized training, the breadth of experience, or the varied accounts. "I finally decided that I would treat going to Chicago like going to school, and work there for four years". That's exactly what he did. But, in 1982, after obtaining the solid background he was seeking, he accepted a job offer in the west coast office of an international advertising agency, Needham, Harper, World-wide, Inc., where he works today.

In addition to his practical training, Tom has an undergraduate degree in business administration and an MBA with an emphasis on marketing.

For my job, if a person doesn't have an undergraduate degree in business, I recommend they get an MBA. If you graduate with a BA in business administration with an emphasis on marketing, I don't think you need an MBA unless you want to open up more doors later.

Essentially, an account executive for an advertising agency is the channel of communication between the client and the agency. Visualize a wheel. The spokes of the wheel are the creative people of the agency: media, traffic, sales, promotion, and public relations. The account executive is the hub of the wheel. He or she directs all of the other areas. While other people in the agency have specific functions, the account executive is more of a generalist.

I am the constant. Depending on the subject matter, the other departments will be there or not be there, but I would always be there.

I represent the agency to the client, and I represent the client to the agency. The key thing, I think, is that the account person should not be an order-taker. He or she should hopefully lead and direct the client.

Tom's training included experience as a junior account executive with two years in the media program before taking the step up the ladder to assistant account executive.

You are an assistant for about ten months, then promoted to account executive. After that it's account supervisor, then management supervisor.

In an advertising agency, a 9 to 5 day is the exception rather than the rule. "We were just involved in a new business pitch, and for the last couple of nights I worked until 1:00 in the morning." Generally, Tom gets to the office around 9:00 am and leaves about 7:00 at night.

On a daily basis, I deal with clients—talking with them on the phone. Basically, you talk about the business in general and specific projects anywhere from creative development to media planning.

Tom is assigned two clients that are his responsibility exclusively.

The client wants my personal attention. He is spending his money with the agency and wants a person that will be there when he calls, come and visit him, and get into his business. One of my clients is in San Francisco and I go up there about once every two weeks to see him.

Travel varies with the location of the client, but usually travel is a part of every account executive's job. As an agency grows, the client list often spreads further and further from the location of the agency.

Travelling is a pain in the neck. It gets old after the third trip—and I took the third trip 12 years ago.

The advantages to a job in an advertising agency include a nice salary and the stimulation of working around creative, exciting people.

It's not only the day-to-day running of an account, but the thinking of and generation of new ideas.

The stress in the creative area of the agency involves the pressure to consistently come up with brilliant new advertising ideas. The account people deal with the stresses of handling the business analysis and planning the strategy.

My stress is one of being the key interface with the client. I have to bring bad news, but I also bring the good news.

Tom sees a disadvantage to the profession in the fact that you are working for clients rather than for yourself.

Since they are spending the money, it is ultimately their final decision. Sometimes you have to execute things that you wouldn't necessarily agree with.

In the field of advertising as a whole, misconceptions abound.

I am still looking for the nymphomaniac model or the boss's wife that is hot after me. Advertising has a glamorous image, a lot of entertaining, little work, sitting around creating things. The truth is, it's a business. It's very much like being involved as a consultant with various businesses.

Contrary to many other businesses, Tom finds that there is an abundance of qualified young women rather than men entering the field. It is, however, a difficult field for anyone to enter. The number of men and women applying for positions in advertising far exceeds the available positions. Prepare yourself with a solid education.

Get a liberal arts undergraduate degree then go and get an MBA somewhere so you have a nice balance. I would say that as you are going to school, try and get as interested in advertising as you can. Look at commercials, ads, think about the strategies behind the advertising. Those are things that you can't force or teach someone. Either the interest is there or it isn't.

Get yourself noticed. Stand out from the crowd. And perhaps most importantly, show creativity in helping yourself break into this creative field.

ZABELLE BEDROSIAN

Interior Designer

An air conditioner blows cool relief through her spacious, white office. A Christopher Pratt print of a rocking chair on a veranda overlooking the ocean evokes memories of the calming sea. Color coordinated fabric swatches and paint chips hang in the hallway—some of the tools of her trade.

She's on the phone with a client, another is on hold, a third line rings. With several waves of her hand she says, "Have a seat. Make yourself at home. Nice to meet you. I'll be off the telephone soon." Professional and confident. She does good work and knows it. Few people intimidate her.

Zabelle Bedrosian has been an interior designer for the last twelve years. Her jobs range from individual doctor's offices to high rise office buildings. She's the boss, charged up by her profession and very glad to be on her own.

I worked as an in-house designer for a company that was building hospitals left, right, and center. It was a good experience. I set up a library, did everything. After five and a half years, I felt it was time to leave, but had become very complacent.

Then, I went on a vacation to see my sister in Berkeley. I walked into her room and saw the cover from a Berkeley newspaper that said, 'And the day came when the risk to remain closed in a bud became more painful than the risk it took to blossom.' I went back to my office and gave three months notice.

Years earlier, out of high school, unsure of her direction, Zabelle spent two years in a junior college. "I was a bit good at everything and not really great at anything." History and art were her major interests, and interior design seemed the perfect blending of the two. Three and a half years later, Zabelle graduated Woodbury College with a Bachelor of Science degree in interior design. Woodbury College combined the artistic side of interior design with the business end. She covered all the angles.

Also, I was lucky to be working as a designer, while finishing school. I got a lot of experience, much more training while working than I did in school. Doing both at the same time was fantastic.

Of her formal college education, certain classes provided essential training. However, Zabelle feels that a solid foundation in basic design concepts, combined with personal talent, are more valuable in the working world than a formal degree.

Her first step into entrepreneurship was taken with a partner. He had been hired as her assistant when Zabelle worked in the salaried position of in-house designer. Two years later, he was laid off. In the following year, Zabelle left to go out on her own. The time was right. He needed help, she said, "Sure," and their business began.

For six months, we worked in my partner's apartment until we felt solvent enough to take on what seemed like big rent. We did start getting busy. We look back and laugh at how excited we would get about a $500.00 retainer check.

As the business grew, differences in philosophies developed over marketing, clients and design. When their design tastes began to differ substantially, the partnership weakened and, after four years, dissolved.

All the daydreams I had about being on my own were suddenly a reality. I thought, 'Can I do this? Boy was I dumb!' I was scared and I was thrilled.

Now, Zabelle runs her business her own way. The shaky feelings at the outset melted into confidence. After a few weeks of separation anxiety, she began to feel her oats and realize the advantages to working for herself.

I knew that the day I put flowers in the office was the day that I really felt like I belonged here by myself. It took about a month.

Generally, by 9:00 a.m., she's in the office listening to the answering machine messages, making and returning phone calls and going through the mail. After that daily routine, each day is different.

There might be a color board to do, or a proposal to type, or a meeting. I do whatever I have to do, and go home anywhere from 5:00 to 7:00 in the evening.

A color board is a visual representation of design concepts. In essence, the designer compiles samples and pictures of the intended interior design and organizes them artistically on thick white cardboard suitable for presentation to the client. The proposal is essentially a technical statement of the job specifics and the costs to complete the job.

For Zabelle, and most other entrepreneurs, the biggest fear is the generation of steady income. There is no guaranteed paycheck every two weeks. In addition to the fixed costs of rent and utilities, there's general overhead which includes stationary, advertising, office supplies, and office furniture. The small "out-of-the-pocket" expenses can eat up any limited income.

When you go into your own business, you work your own hours, and take whatever money you can out of the business. You find out that your hours are 94 hours a day. You don't just go home and not think about it. You are always positive that at the end of a job, it will be the last job you will ever get.

Clients generally come through referrals. It is a networking process. A physician will see another physician's office and ask for the designer's name. At parties, through conversations, names and business cards will be exchanged. It is simply a case of putting your name and face out and meeting people.

The one thing I've learned is that the minute I let go of the frenzy and the 'Oh God, I don't have any business', the phone will ring.

The initial meeting with a prospective client is a time for professional charm and an air of confidence. At the first meeting, Zabelle brings color boards and photographs of past jobs to present as a design portfolio. At this point, it's important to get a feel for the client's tastes and desires, and stress that the samples reflect the previous client's tastes.

I also want to find out who I will be dealing with. Will the wives be involved?

After receiving the green light to submit a design proposal, Zabelle takes the necessary time to complete it, returns to the client, presents the information, then waits hopefully for the phone call that will initiate the job and income for her business.

Generally, when designing a client's office, an average of five months will pass from the first stage of color boards and proposals to the final stage of the unveiling. A semi-social relationship develops between client and designer. They have lunch together and communicate by telephone regularly. However, the fine line between social behavior and professionalism must be maintained.

You are treading on your client's vulnerable points, their tastes, their pocketbook, and the very nature of their business. You are spending their money and clients can be on your back.

The stresses of the business center around the fact that the designer must rely on everyone else to do his or her job. The designer is the liaison between the client and the supplier. After the initial design has been worked out and the items ordered, Zabelle has to wait for shipment and absorb the stresses of delays. "The client has to open in three weeks and you know you can't get the furniture for eight weeks."

The bonuses to the business include the sense of satisfaction that comes with completing a job successfully.

When the furniture starts coming in, and it looks incredible and everybody is happy, I literally jump up and down. I get so excited. That is the payoff. Opening night.

In the business of interior design, it is essential to begin by working for someone else, "unless you are some heck of a person, an heiress, or very precocious and have a million leads and incredible talent." Get experience, and learn the business of interior design while you still have the security of a salary and the guidance of more experienced designers.

A lot of designers are artists, but if you are just an artist, you'll never make it. If you are really good with your color boards and your work, it's great, but you have to get the business. If you're going out on your own, you have to have either a really good marketing and sales person in the office, or be a combination yourself.

Most designers I know are adequate, but it's the responsive people who are number one. You have to get information back to the client quickly. If someone gives me something to do, I do it right away. So, if you're responsive, you get back to people and you're honest, you're going to do well.

BARBARA BEMISTER

Branch Bank Manager

Barbara Bemister is a self-starter. Her career in banking is a testament to that fact. As a young woman, she began as a bookkeeper with the intention of working only a short time. "I think when you're younger, your goals are more short-ranged. After a while, I got into long-range goals." Barbara's pride in her work shone a spotlight on her potential for a supervisory promotion. She is now a branch manager for the Bank of America and has been since 1978. Her recent promotion to branch vice president is as high as you can be promoted in a branch bank.

Of course, you can go into various departments like administration, corporate banking, national division. I see a lot more possibilities than I did 15 years ago.

Barbara has two years of college and she successfully completed the extensive courses offered through the American Institute of Banking, as well as Bank of America management training. College and training courses are essential for a career in banking.

In her branch, Barbara manages 28 employees. In many ways, her job is quite unlike a typical 9 to 5 job. Her day usually begins before 8:00 a.m., when, with the assistant manager of branch operations, she opens the interbranch bag that contains all of the work to be distributed during that day.

Inside the bag are teller reports that we have to do, the status statements of customer's accounts, all of the activity from the prior day's work and anything that flows through our branching system. We are responsible for distributing the work to various departments.

Barbara is also responsible for all of the staffing.

My operations manager does the hiring and firing and I am responsible for the planning, organizing and control of the branch, and the profit plan.

The profit plan is made up on a yearly basis, and it states where we are and what we anticipate our goals will be for the coming year.

On paper, the working day ends between 5:00 and 5:15, but Barbara may be required to go out on a customer call at any time. She's responsible for business development—arranging financing for new businesses, expanding businesses, or getting new major accounts. Depending on the customer's needs, she may go out to see them at their business address.

Along with the specifics of the day to day running of a branch bank, Barbara is responsible for the people who are under her.

I am responsible for career guidance and morale. I am also responsible to the customer, seeing that the quality of service is maintained at a very high level.

There is constant interaction with the customers, both pleasant and otherwise. The general public is rarely aware that the operations manager can handle any problems or praise regarding employees, but they know that there is a bank manager and will frequently come into the bank and ask for her. A positive and accessible public person is essential.

For Barbara, the advantages to a profession in branch banking can be summed up in dollars and cents. Aside from an attractive salary, "regardless of what they say about women being behind men in salary", the compensation and benefits are excellent. To its employees, the bank extends a preferred loan rate, also a break on checking, savings, and trust accounts—all a part of the benefit package.

After an employee has been with the bank for one year, he or she is eligible for a preferred rate on a home loan. It's in conjunction with the existing rate, about a difference of one percent. "That can amount to quite a bit over a thirty year period."

A disadvantage is that the profession can be time-consuming.

As a woman, you must have an understanding and supportive husband. Many times you are involved in long manager's meetings that may last into the evening. It is a part of your job, it's your responsibility. I do a lot of planning for the future growth of the bank.

The right educational background is very important for anyone thinking about a career in branch banking. Business administration is a necessity when you're going into the finance business.

We are looking for people with MBA degrees. In branch banking, we certainly wouldn't pull back if someone were an undergraduate. We have programs available within the banking system, tuition assistance, where you can hire in as an undergraduate and get your MBA while you are working.

Also, for students, we make available the privilege of coming in to observe and be banker for a day.

Additionally, Barbara is continuously looking to promote from within the bank. She is always on the lookout for people with management potential.

Some people do their job and leave. Then, there are people who do over and above what is required. I look for those qualities to see what someone's future will be.

HARVEY A. GOLDSTEIN

Certified Public Accountant

Handsome and slick, he dresses, walks, breathes, and does business with pizzazz.

The profession is changing drastically. It's becoming highly competitive. We suddenly find that the introvert who sits in the corner doing some phases of accounting and taxation is no longer desired. We now need people with personality, people who can relate to people.

Harvey Goldstein is a CPA. He has been a Certified Public Accountant for the last 18 years. At the time he was certified, the requirements included an undergraduate degree in almost anything, though the examination required a certain number of credits in business. You took the exam, then had to work for an established CPA for two years to become a public accountant.

In the certification exam, there is a section on law, on accounting theory, auditing, and a section on "problems", where you work out actual accounting problems.

Let me set the record very straight. There is no requirement, and no real strong need, to have any kind of special interest or background in mathematics. There are times when we may have to come up with an idea or a formula for problem solving, but we rarely have anything to do with math.

People say to me, 'I've got a son and he's a brilliant mathematician. He should be a CPA!' My CPA math is this adding machine right here on my desk.

Harvey does not consider himself a typical CPA, and contends that many people harbor a misconception as to what a typical CPA is really like.

Accounting firms are interested in the guy who can spend 25-50% of his time out there schmoozing with business people, bankers, lawyers, and insurance people, so they can bring in business and continue to expand the business.

My success is my people skills, not my accounting skills, although I do have good accounting skills. People skills are becoming far more important than ever dreamed of or imagined in this profession. We are business doctors. We have to have a bedside manner just like any other doctor.

Typically, accounting firms that are not national or international in scope work with mostly small businesses. The clients in Harvey's firm are small businesses ranging from zero in sales to 30 or 40 million dollars in sales. Most of them fall between the 5 and 15 million dollar mark.

Harvey was promoted to partner with a speed that could qualify him for the Business Olympics. He made partner in four years. As the managing partner of the firm, with a staff of 85, he spends his day doing things that most accountants would not do.

For example, he might get up in the morning and head over to a chamber of commerce meeting to speak to a group about maximizing the profits of their businesses. After that, he might go to the office, check the mail and return phone calls before setting out for a luncheon meeting with a banker. He may spend the afternoon with a prospective client talking about how to save money in income tax, how to improve his profit picture, how to help in different areas of his business.

To paraphrase baseball Hall of Famer Yogi Berra, the day is over when the day is over. There is no such thing as 9 to 5. Harvey must also stay current on changes in Washington, DC.

It changes all the time. I always have to do reading at home to keep up with everything.

I've been married to the same lady for almost 23 years, and we have two children. The family learns the routine. I see them, and have quality time with them, but nobody becomes successful working 9 to 5.

In contrast, a typical CPA spends more time doing the detail work for the client. They do more pencil pushing, dealing with numbers and filling out forms.

The basic CPA is either in his office or the client's office most of the time. The job requires judgement and a knowledge of the rules involved in the practice. There are accounting rules, tax rules, and legal rules. Accountants must maintain a body of current knowledge to function effectively. A typical CPA will spend his or her day carrying out those aspects of the practice while Harvey is off on speaking engagements, maintaining positive public relations, managing the practice, and solving people problems.

> *As you move up the ladder, you do less and less of the detail work, and more of the supervision and people work.*

Clients come into the practice after you go out and get them.

> *You have to make your own way. Opportunity knocks on your door when you tell it where the door is. Consequently, you have to be out beating the bushes.*

> *Clients come from speaking in organizations, getting people to know my name and the name of the firm, getting them on our mailing lists and bombarding them with mail. Eventually, they succumb to the propaganda and say, 'I need you. I need you. I need you!'*

In a firm like Harvey's, handling client taxes is an important part of the practice, but it's not the only part. The firm also audits financial statements—a function that CPAs alone are licensed to do.

> *When a company puts out its financial statements to secure credit, or investors, or just to inform the public, some need a CPA independent of the company.*

> *In effect, accountants pass on the financial statements saying that they are O.K. Accountants keep the companies honest.*

Harvey is in contact with clients on a regular basis, all year long. Depending on the client's requirements, they may set up regular meetings or solve minor problems over the phone.

> *We want to guide them significantly, to help them become profitable and efficient operations.*

However, in any accounting firm, there will be long hours at certain times of the year. Specifically, tax time. "But, it depends on who you work for and what you do."

Harvey's firm operates on a fee-for-service basis. He sees that the biggest complaint people have when they change accountants is that their accountant didn't service them. They can't get them on the phone, things like that. As far as the fees go, most people don't object to paying the fees if they are getting the service.

> *When you take your clothes to the cleaners, you know they've done a good job if it comes back clean. If it's dirty, you know they've done a bad job. But, how do you know that the guy down the street couldn't do it better?*

> *There is nothing unique. If the client is happy and comfortable, the fees are reasonable, and the service is good, they are going to stay.*

Occasionally, Harvey is a guest lecturer at a university, and he tells people who are going into accounting to take two courses:

> *Speech and English. Most accountants are derelict in that area. Learn how to communicate verbally and with the written word. You will learn the other knowledge you need along the way, but those are the two things that nobody will teach you and you'll need to know.*

CAROL PHELAN

Wall Street Bond Broker

Wall Street, New York City. The hub of the capitalist wheel. Noontime brings out the business suits. In the evening, when trading has stopped, the streets clear and it resembles a skyscraper ghost town.

Carol Phelan was studying commercial art and advertising as an undergraduate student. To support her education, she got a job as a waitress in a restaurant on Wall Street. Each day, she waited on business people with their credit cards and their money. She was in the center of things, but far outside the inner circle.

> *I said, 'Wait a minute!' I was frustrated in school because I saw that the best people, people I thought were 20 times better than me, weren't getting jobs.*

It was time to change her life. A friend in the bond business got her the interview, Carol got herself the job. She was hired as a United States Bond Broker. "I guess I am what you would call a rookie."

In contrast to a stock broker from whom you would buy stocks, the bond broker is the middleman between the bond traders who buy and sell the bonds.

> *For example, if Paine Webber wants to buy a certain bond, and Merrill Lynch has that bond, either Paine Webber or Merrill Lynch will come to me as the middleman. I work on Wall Street and deal with companies rather than individuals.*

Bonds have different coupons, different ratings. An AAA bond is a highly rated, premium bond. Single A bonds are not as good. So, each bond has a coupon and a maturity date. The broker takes a bid and an offering for a particular bond and tries to barter it.

The corporate bond market moves more slowly than the government bond market. There isn't the screaming and yelling on the trading floor.

Bond brokers were formed because when companies knew who they were buying and selling bonds to, there was a great potential for dissension among companies who might have some sort of a grudge against another company. It upset the entire balance of bond trading. Now, no one but the bond broker knows which companies are involved.

There are approximately 40 people in the company that Carol works for. Everyone from the Chairman of the Board to the newest broker does exactly the same thing.

> *It's not like you move up in the ranks to more responsibility, but you move up to more money. You are paid by the amount of business you do. If you are new, you get the little customers, as you build things up, you start getting bigger customers.*

Unlike stock brokers who must go out and get customers by calling them and saying, "I'm working at this company now. Call me if you want to buy stock", bond brokers are given accounts. Experienced brokers within the firm will introduce you to your accounts over the phone, then you're on your own.

The working environment within the office is fairly easygoing and relaxed. Trading generally starts about 9:00 a.m. "I like to get in a little early because some guys ring in before 9:00."

About half of the brokers sit at a large round desk in front of computer screens. The issues of bonds are on the screens. Each person has a telephone with the phone numbers of their accounts on it. The numbers ring right through. The busiest hours are between 9:00 and 11:00 a.m.

> *You start calling your customers, 'Hi, how are you?' 'How was your weekend?' You get as friendly as you can with them. It's the same kind of deal on the other side. There is a big desk with screens and telephones.*

> *I sit there all day. It slows down as the afternoon goes on, and picks up again around two or three.*

There is no lunch hour. The brokers must stay at their screens all day. "We can get out sometimes to take a customer out to lunch. But most customers can't get away from their desks either because the trading goes on while they are away."

The company buys the broker's lunch.

In the office we eat like kings, and order out everyday. Plus, we have a stocked kitchen. There is a shower and sauna, shampoo and conditioner, toothpaste, everything you need. You don't pay for anything.

Entertaining the customers is a big part of the job. The company wants each broker to have personal contact with the person they talk on the phone with daily. Wining and dining.

It's the name of the game.

When you go out with customers, you hand in a check for three hundred dollars, the company won't ask why. They expect to see the business back with the customer. We get theater tickets, take them around in limousines.

Now, I'm not embarrassed about it at all, but I felt funny in the beginning because I knew that he knew that the only reason I was taking him out was because I wanted his business. But, that's how everything goes.

I say, 'Let's get together one of these nights and go out and talk about business.' He says, 'Sure. When?' Sometimes you send a cab for them. For big accounts, you wine and dine them in limousines. We talk about business, people we know. You find a common ground. They have four other brokers doing this to them, too.

Most frequently, the day in the office ends at 5:00 on the nose. If it's very slow, you can check out at 4:45 or so, but generally, you stay to make sure no calls come in at the last minute.

Mistakes are made occasionally. Some of them are very costly.

One guy didn't check out with a customer at the end of the day. You are supposed to say, 'O.K., I bought this from you at this price, I sold this to you at this price', so you avoid mistakes. He cost the company $150,000.

Training to be a bond broker is a process of immersion. You pick up what you can, then you sink or you swim.

When I first started, I felt really stupid because I was actually there for six months not doing anything. You ask questions, but you really just have to listen and catch what is going on. Finally, they'll see a wire ringing in, everyone will be busy, and they'll say, 'Pick that wire up!' So, you pick it up and the guy on the other side will give you an order.

Find out about getting registered. A government bond broker does not have to be registered, however, a registered broker has an advantage. A registered broker can be a stock broker, bond broker, or anything.

The RR test (Registered Representative) is difficult. You must take a class and study the entire stock and securities market. Facts and formulas. The company will pay for the class which may last one week, 9:00 to 5:00 each day, or two hours a night over a three month period. After the class is completed, the exam is a six-hour test on a Saturday.

It's important to get registered. When you get into a firm, ask about it.

As soon as she passed her registration exam, Carol was given accounts and her career as a bond broker began.

The stresses of this kind of profession are client-related. You may feel that they are not giving you what you think they have.

I know it's not me. My guys are small, so the little bit they have, they have to also give it to other brokers. They can't give me everything.

Additional stress revolves around entertaining. Carol goes out two or three times a week. The more you build your clients, the more you go out. It's fun in the beginning, but can wear on you, especially if you're a woman.

> *Two guys that become friends will take their wives out. For me, it's strange to take a guy and his wife and my boyfriend out. We aren't pals.*

> *I also had a problem with one of my guys. He wanted to take me home when there was no reason for him to. So, I had to set it straight, I had to deal with him the next day in business.*

Carol sees the biggest advantage in terms of the amount of money you can make. The sky is the limit. Each broker is on salary, with a raise every six or seven months, and a good bonus at the end of the year.

When she first thought about working on Wall Street, Carol imagined that the complications of the business would be too much for her. "But, just like anything else, it becomes easy once you stick with it a while and learn."

Ten credits short of a bachelor's degree, Carol cautions that her background is the exception. Without a college degree, jobs on Wall Street are rare. Finish college. You'll be much further ahead.

HOTEL AND RESTAURANT MANAGEMENT

A more mobile and affluent America has helped the hotel, motel, and restaurant field expand rapidly in the last two decades. Providing away-from-home lodging and meals has created an industry employing over six million workers.

The lodging industry features three different types of accomodations, each with a distinctive market.

- **Hotels** are generally located in metropolitan areas and cater to business or personal travellers who generally stay no more than a few nights. The exceptions are residential hotels for semi-permanent residents who desire the kinds of services only found in a hotel setting.
- **Motels** operate much like hotels except that they cater to motorists and are generally located on or near major highways or roads.
- **Resort hotels** are usually located in popular vacation or recreation areas and cater to the traveller who wants recreational facilities operated in conjunction with housing. The typical guest at a resort hotel checks in for longer periods of time than regular hotel or motel guests.

Hotel and motels may be mammoth city enterprises, often operated by national chains, or they may be small family business motels in sleepy rural areas. Regardless of the size, hotel and motel staff perform the following duties:

- Front office (direct contact with guests including reservation assistance and registration)
- Service (handling luggage, room keys, etc.)
- Accounting (billing, credit, collections)
- Food service and Preparation (preparing, and serving meals, drinks, and other food related items within the hotel)
- Housekeeping (maintaining rooms, ordering and laundering supplies, etc.)
- Sales (developing new business, including working with groups planning conventions)
- Other (security, repair and maintenance, fire protection safety, etc.)

One aspect of hotel and motel work, as well as restaurant and other food serving occupations, is the need for extensive evening and week-end work. The most popular check-in time in hotels and motels is from 3 to 8 p.m. And, hotels and some restaurants are 24-hour operations.

Statistics report that in the average American household one of every five meals is eaten away from home and one of every three food budget dollars is spent on restaurant meals. All of this has not escaped the attention of thousands of entrepreneurs whose enterprises range from ethnic (Chinese, Mexican, French) restaurants to fast food takeouts, pizza parlors, or night clubs where entertainment accompanies a meal.

Some say the three most important ingredients to operating a successful restaurant are location, location and location. However, employees who can provide the supportive skills needed to run the restaurant are in keen demand. Chefs, cooks, waiters, maitre'ds and managers—each staff member plays an essential role in contributing to financial success in this potentially risky business.

There are over 400,000 commercial eating and drinking places in the United States today with an annual sales business of over $63 billion. The resulting effect on the job market is the creation of close to five million jobs with a wide potential for movement and growth.

ROBERT MARSILI

Hotel Manager

It stands pink and pretty on twelve acres of one of the wealthiest communities in the United States. There are 325 rooms, individually decorated, and the exclusive privacy of The Beverly Hills Hotel bungalows. Verdant shapes and colors fill the lobby, resembling a classic extension of the outdoors. Banana-leaf wallpaper. A trademark.

Young, sharply dressed employees smile with the pleasure of being a part of the tradition. It is a place where movie stars, business executives, and Arab sheiks stay with their accompanying eccentricities. The hotel has been host to guests that have ranged from Marilyn Monroe to the Shah of Iran. The pink facade appears regularly in films and on television. "One of the world's great hotels and a California landmark."

Robert Marsili has managed The Beverly Hills Hotel for five years. He is a well-dressed man with practiced diplomacy. Patrons wave hello as he walks through the grounds. Special guests call him directly for the reservation of a bungalow or their favorite suite.

In college, Robert double majored in political science and history, with a teaching minor in German. He began graduate school to obtain a teaching credential in history.

> *At the same time, to finance my graduate work, I worked part time in a hotel as a desk clerk. After I got my teaching credential, I still maintained a part time position as a night auditor in the hotel.*

Robert taught for nearly three years before deciding that teaching was not his cup of tea. He enjoyed his work in the hotel and embarked on a new career.

> *I enjoyed interfacing with the guests everyday, meeting new people all the time, and hosting them in 'my house'. At the time I was working in a 1200 room resort, convention hotel. There was always a lot of activity going on, people coming and going.*

Eventually, the young, ambitious man worked his way up to a chief clerk position and was offered a job as night manager in a hotel in San Diego. After a period of about five years, in that and other hotels, Robert had worked up to the resident managership position. It was time to move on. The next step was in a national chain, supervising about 15 properties.

> *I was offered a position as manager at the original hotel I started in. I accepted, and went there for five years. Then, I decided it was time to look for something else, for my own personal growth. I was offered a position at the Beverly Hills Hotel and here I am.*

There is an inner circle of hotel managers which can provide the flexibility to move all over the country in various managerial positions. Word is spread that a manager is looking to relocate, and offers come in.

> *Through annual meetings, associations, and different types of civic groups, we see each other and keep in contact.*

> *It's very important to keep the network going. Not only for my own growth, but for other people I know that may be seeking employment. For example, if a wife, whose career is as important as her husband's, accepts a position in Chicago, her husband can begin to make contacts with people he knows in Chicago.*

Robert Marsili believes that personal drive rather than a formal education is the determining factor in the direction of a career. In hiring employees, he feels a college degree is unimportant unless the position to be filled is of a specific nature such as the controller. The hotel business is one of working your way up. Experience versus education.

My education provided me with the basic tools of how to go about finding information, where to research something. Methodology rather than actual knowledge itself.

Hotels are 24 hour a day operations. Guests come and go constantly, and require certain services at all hours of the day and night.

Robert arrives at his office in The Beverly Hills Hotel between 7:00 and 8:00 in the morning.

I come in earlier than most of the office staff, and most of the other department heads, because it affords me the opportunity to have quiet time.

I generally can have my desk cleared of the things I have to take care of by 8:00 or 9:00 in the morning. Then I wait for the gun to go off. When it goes off, it's going to be firing at me from all angles.

He reviews reports, talks to the personnel, and has the opportunity to see the graveyard shift before they go home. The day is full. He sees the daytime shift arrive, and generally doesn't leave for the night until the evening shift has begun. "I have contact with people working the full 24 hours."

Robert's working day ends when the work is through.

On days when things are running smoothly, I can go at 4:00 p.m. Other days it may be 7:00 p.m. On the average, I get in at 7:30 in the morning, and leave at about 5:30 in the evening.

Since the operation of the hotel is a 24 hour business, Robert institutes a firm policy against continuous calls to his home when he's off work.

In my absence, the assistant managers have my full and complete authority. They have the authority to make the decisions, and the knowledge to make those decisions. If I am there everytime they need to make a decision, they are going to call me every time. I would rather have them make 100 decisions, 99 of them right, and one really bad, than make no decisions at all.

The job of hotel manager is basically one of monitoring the costs, levels of service, and general running of the hotel. Ninty percent of his time is spent delegating responsibilities and clearing his desk as soon as possible.

I have assistant managers who work when I am not here. Basically, when I am ready to go home, they are already here, functioning as supervisory people monitoring the operation. The communication goes in a circle, we are constantly in touch with one another, and handle the hotel through each other.

There are certain projects that I maintain myself, like capital investments for new projects. My job is to know what is going on in every department at all times.

As manager, Robert hires and fires supervisory people only. It has been his experience that people tend to be more responsive to the people that hire them, so he hires the supervisors, and they hire their staff.

Within the Beverly Hills Hotel, there are several businesses that cater to the guests, a hair salon, boutiques. Some of the shops lease the space, but all of the food and beverage operations belong to the hotel and require the manager's involvement.

My secretary said to me the other day, 'You've had over 100 phone calls today.' It's true. There are two minute calls here, one minute calls there, someone needing a direction for something that is out of the ordinary, or just to apprise me of something that has happened.

Most of the guests are return guests. Many recognize Robert as the hotel's manager and drop by his office, or approach him to chat. A major portion of the job of manager is maintaining good public relations.

I make a point to call guests everyday, new guests to the hotel, and return guests, welcoming them back.

I have employees that will take reservations, register the guests, make their beds, and serve their food. That's not my job. My job is to make sure that they are doing all of those things, and get feedback from the guests that everything is acceptable.

Daily room inspections keep the manager in touch with the day to day workings of his staff. It is an essential aspect of maintaining a high level of service, and insuring that the management responsibilities are completely carried out.

I have a terminal that keeps me abreast of which rooms are vacant. In a matter of seconds, I can see which rooms are vacant, grab the key, and go check the room. I check a minimum of 5 or 6 rooms a day, sometimes more.

A guest can ask for anything. Specifically with The Beverly Hills Hotel, the expectation of service may be higher than in many other hotels, and although the staff may not be able to grant a specific request, they always approach it with an alternative.

In a hotel such as this one, the one thing that I became aware of very quickly is that any change made in the hotel is immediately sensed by the guests, and we are made aware of it.

For example, we remodeled the lobby about four years ago. We had to take down the banana leaf wallpaper and replace it. It had deteriorated, the color was gone. We stripped the paper off, repainted the background, and had to hand cut the appliques of banana leaf. So, during a period of about five days, there was no wallpaper. We had many reactions, most of them positive. But, there were traditionalists who had been coming here for years and thought we were ruining the hotel, they were panic-stricken that we were getting rid of the wallpaper. In another hotel, people might say that there was a lot of noise, or dust, and that would be the end of it. They would come back next year, and there would be no comment.

Guests feel that it is their private club, and it is their privilege to tell us what we can and can't do with the hotel. But, I see that feedback as an advantage.

A disadvantage of the field is that, at most levels, hotel management is not the most lucrative of careers. Additionally, the manager must ride the fine line between friendliness and professionalism.

We are a service industry, basically an outgrowth of the household maid. We are here to serve people. We are to be available when they need us, and not interfere in their life.

You are a part of their life, but really just on the edge of it. Friendly, but not familiar unless you are invited past that.

The days and nights are filled with the excitement of hustle and bustle. Things are happening at all hours. The profession can be stressful if you allow it to be.

There are certain stressful situations, certainly, whether it be internal within the organization, or dealing with guests. Confrontations will happen. I am not aware of tension and stress, but it may be the way in which I have learned to handle it.

Get as much exposure as possible in a variety of hotels. Hotels range from commercial properties, such as airport hotels catering to the overnight business patron, to convention hotels, to resort and vacation properties. Secondly, get as much experience as possible in different operating departments of the hotel.

Not only the white collar, but the blue collar. Try working in the food service department, front desk, sales. Within one building, there are so many different types of work to do.

Many large hotel chains offer a "Manager of Tomorrow" training program. These programs look for entry level people who have excitement, enthusiasm, and aggressive learning capability, and exposes them to all the areas of hotel operations. Obtain your experience as early as possible.

As far as formal education goes, it helps. Probably one of the best things is to have good communication skills. You can study business and marketing all you want, but if you can't communicate, it won't do you any good.

College is not essential, but I think for ultimate growth, and if you want to move a little more quickly, a degree is good. It doesn't have to be a degree in hotel administration. The degree shows someone that you have the ability to learn and the incentive to go past the required, to try something past the point where the law says you have to go to school.

Most importantly, early working experience will provide a realistic view of the profession at all levels. You can have the opportunity to see, firsthand, if the fast-paced world of hotel management is for you.

I can honestly say that there has not been one day when I have woken up in the morning and said, 'I don't want to go to work'.

BEVERLY KIRKHART

Inn Proprietor

As advertisement for The Villa Rosa Inn states that Ernest Hemingway, Henri Matisse, Carmen Miranda, and Errol Flynn never slept there, but would have if given the chance. This sense of humor and style is exemplified by the staff and the Inn's proprietor. The hotel, with its 18 rooms, considers itself, "A small inn that has the amenities of a fine resort." The grounds are quiet and peaceful, with arched patios, a pool, and swaying trees. The inn was carefully designed to include the comforts of home, and is successful. The lobby resembles an elegantly comfortable living room, the grounds, a well-kept backyard.

Ms. Kirkhart and her partners have owned the Inn since 1981. They tackled the massive task of renovating an old Spanish colonial revival building, and opened for business in 1982. The partners are two couples, friends, and Beverly enjoys her responsibilities as proprietor. The long hours are a labor of love.

> *I am a very dedicated person, and to me, this is an exciting project, and I am going to make it work. The hours that I have to be here aren't as intense as when we first opened the doors. One of my main goals was to get a good staff that could run the hotel without me.*

Beverly spends five days a week at the hotel, Monday through Friday from 9:00 in the morning to 7:00 in the evening. She is in and out on the weekends, but close to a year passed before she felt comfortable enough to leave the running of the operation to the staff.

> *When we first began the operation, none of us knew anything about running a hotel, so I found a gal who had worked at the Biltmore, here in town, for six years. She was ready to make a change, so she joined the ship. She is considered the general manager, and she runs the day-to-day operations. I oversee what is going on.*

The Villa Rosa's busiest time is during the summer months. The daily activity centers around the guests from the minute they check in, to the minute they check out.

> *In this kind of operation when you are an owner, and there are only 18 rooms, and a staff of thirteen, you pretty much have to be a jack of all trades. In the summertime when we are moving so quickly on a day to day basis, if a housekeeper is sick, there is nobody else to make the beds, I'll make the beds. During the summer, I make myself available when I am needed.*

During the winter, when business has slowed down a bit, Beverly concentrates on marketing. A large portion of her day is spent with the telephone on public relations.

> *I work with different corporations to try and get corporate people into the hotel, and put together a marketing package.*

> *We don't do much advertising on a regular basis, as far as the newspaper, or different magazines go. I promote through direct mail or through personal contacts.*

> *We have a critique sheet in each room. When we first opened, the purpose of the critique sheet was to find out what we were missing. Now, we use the critique sheet to more or less find out where people heard about us. It is usually repeat business, word of mouth, relatives, and people in the area.*

At the beginning of the day, Beverly checks the daily financial report to see that it matches the tape, and that the deposits are correct. She acts as bookkeeper, insuring that the night audit is accurate, and the finances are running smoothly.

In the evening, from about 5:00 to 7:00, she spends time meeting guests, making sure they are comfortably checked in, and making herself available to deal with whatever comes up.

Also, it's good for the employees to know that I am watching what is going on. Not that I have any employees that would take anything away from us, but it's good to have them aware that you are keeping watch.

Beverly graduated college with a degree in business administration. Her concentration was on marketing, and it has proven invaluable in dealing with the financial aspects of running the Villa Rosa.

Before beginning this business venture, the partners talked to several people in the hotel business to get a clear picture of what lay ahead. There were still some surprises.

I think that the most difficult problem that I have is when a guest can't accept what we have here. They are obviously the type of person that belongs in a Biltmore where it is larger. I have a real hard time accepting the fact that they don't like it here. I take it personally, but through the years I have become a little harder, and have learned how to deal with it.

I think that working with the staff has been a little surprising to me. I am a real softy, and I have a hard time accepting the fact that some of them would take advantage of my kindness.

As Beverly sees it, there are only limited disadvantages to owning and running a small inn. You can't just go home and leave the business behind. You are continuously wondering if the staff is all right, or if there are any problems that they might have difficulty handling.

As in any beginning business, finances are always a concern.

I must bring in the income to meet the expenses. I want to always make sure that I can pay my staff and my bills.

We worked very closely with a local accountant who has had experience with other hotels. He had a better handle on what type of expenses I would be looking at for this type of operation. We had to develop goals for what we wanted to accomplish as far as our type of market, and prices we had to establish to make it work for that market, then look at the expenses and juggle as we went along.

For the first quarter, the hotel didn't break even. It was a very difficult time, but the second quarter, we broke even, and we've done better than that ever since.

Advertising expenses include theft of the hotel's supplies.

Our rates are such that people respect what we have in the room. However, there are things that people do take. For example, we have acrylic glasses that we serve around the pool. They were beautiful, and people liked them so much, they took them without realizing that they were not to be taken. This summer, I put our logo on them. They cost me a bit more, but now when people have them in their kitchen, they can see where they came from.

The excitement of seeing a project that you initiate grow from the bottom up and become a success is the best reward for the many hours of working and planning. As guests repeat visits, there is tangible proof that you are providing the type of service that you aimed for.

As the hotel becomes more known within the industry, there is the opportunity to work trades or reductions with other hotels, providing an advantage to travel and take a look at other operations.

Before thinking about opening a small hotel, take a hard look at the numbers.

Get an accountant that really understands this kind of operation, and have a fairly large pocketbook behind you that can help float you through the lull months.

ROBERT MANDLER

Restaurant Owner

It began with a plan for a small take-out styled Chinese restaurant. Some people could stay and eat, or wait at the counter nibbling on a dumpling or two while the chef packed their meal in white chinese cartons. It grew. It expanded. The dine-in demand exceeded space and they added a downstairs space for take-out alone. Tables and chairs were moved outside in the warm sunshine, the small interior dining room a marvel in the maximum utility of space. Where the indoor tables had once been towered-over by crowds waiting for to-go orders, they now are elevated, placing the seated patrons on par with the standing customers.

Chin Chin is a success story. Robert Mandler, a successful restaurant owner. The business is, in his words, "a mid-life crisis acted upon."

Robert Mandler had been a practicing lawyer for 15 years, but the frustrations of law practice were mounting, and he grew increasingly more impatient with the stresses and tensions of being a lawyer.

I cooked as a hobby. I started cooking Chinese food in 1972 or so, experimenting on my own, for myself, my family, and so forth. I took Chinese cooking lessons from all the people in Los Angeles who give them, Madam Wong at UCLA, and Madam Wu, at Wu's Garden. The more I did it, the more I enjoyed it. I began giving dinner parties on my own.

As time progressed, Robert talked more and more about opening up a restaurant. He kept his dream alive, and took steps toward finding out exactly what it would take to make Chin Chin a reality.

I took the steps that would cost nothing but time. It didn't cost me anything to go out and look at locations. It didn't cost me anything to interview potential investors. It didn't cost anything to fool around with the recipes. Little by little I became more serious, then all of a sudden, some guy said, 'You've got the money.' Then I really said, 'This is it'.

Chin Chin has been in business since 1983. Having continuously heard of the risks in the restaurant business, Robert believes the field has gotten a bum rap.

I can't think of many restaurants that have been properly planned and adequately financed, that haven't made it, given the time. The statistics that you hear on restaurants are terribly misleading because they include all the little mom and pop places that open up on a shoestring and are out of business in three months.

To insure his success, Robert took several steps to reduce his risk. He knew how to cook, but knew nothing about the restaurant business. The first step was to pick the brains of everyone he knew in the business. He hung around restaurants, spoke to managers and owners, and made a conscious effort to find out why restaurants had succeeded or failed.

The second step was professional financial assistance.

I went to one of the largest accounting firms in the world, number one restaurant specialists. I spent $2,000 to have them study the concept of Chin Chin. They did a feasibility study based on the information that I gave them, and plugged in a lot of expenses that I hadn't thought about. They gave me an education.

Generally speaking, you have certain costs that vary per square foot. They figured what my energy costs would be. For three days they interviewed me, and I interviewed them, and they taught me restaurant accounting. They taught me what my percentage should be in terms of food costs, labor costs, and advertising budget.

33

The restaurant business is basically a 10-15% net profit business, sometimes 5%. You must keep a careful watch on the cash, because it can vanish quickly. Robert's feasibility study came to the conclusion that Chin Chin needed to pull in 81 customers a day to break even.

I remember being scared. Where am I going to get 81 people? I remember waking up in the middle of the night seeing a bare room with 81 people in it, 8 rows of 10 plus one, 10 rows of 8 plus one. I kept picturing how that looked. I kept wondering, are they going to find their way to Chin Chin?

With the magical 81 figure in his mind, Robert went to every operation that was similar to his vision to ask them about their daily customer count. Most of the businesses did at least 81, and it was time to proceed.

By that time I had my investor. He encouraged me, and I encouraged him. The day I went around to look at locations, it was pouring rain. I was running around with my little notebook, and I decided to swing through here and take a look. It was a blank space, but I liked the location.

Chin Chin was born.

Robert Mandler is a working owner. He gets to the restaurant by 8:30 in the morning, has a cup of coffee, and starts work at 9:00. At this point, he is the bookkeeper. He counts the money from the night before, and makes certain that the register receipts are correct, and the register is ready for the day's business.

I have basically two managers, a kitchen manager, and an upfront manager, and I serve as the financial manager. The kitchen manager takes care of preparing all the food, getting it ready for cooking, and making sure the inventory is there for the cooks. He also helps with the catering as well. The whole (kitchen) area is his responsibility.

The upfront manager hires and fires and trains the waiters, busboys, and foodrunners. He helps with splitting the tips, money matters, and all sorts of on-the-job types of things that need to be taken care of.

From 11:00 in the morning onward, Robert makes phone calls, oversees the operation, deals with employee complaints and scheduling problems that the upfront manager can't handle, and keeps a close watch on the costs.

For example, if payroll is too high, I figure out how to deal with it. I make sure that the economics of the restaurant are sound, and various percentages don't get out of hand.

I try and do as much observing as I can. I work one or two nights a week to try and stay in touch. Sometimes, I act as a host to help out. I try and pitch in wherever I'm needed. The take-out area is an area that usually needs help, so I help organize that. I do a little of everything. I observe and try and see if the system is working properly.

The most difficult part of making the restaurant a success has turned out to be the personnel. Getting, keeping, training, and sustaining the right people to put your carefully thought-out operation into effect. Personnel problems are a major part of any service business, and must be handled effectively and efficiently.

The biggest thrill in owning your own restaurant is the opportunity to work for yourself. Robert spends his day in contact with customers. He enjoys the feedback and interaction with people.

Of course, it's been a successful restaurant. I'm sure if the business is not successful, there are no advantages.

In contrast to the law business, where everything is relative, a transaction in the restaurant has a beginning, a middle, and an end. It's either good or it's not good. The customer is happy or he's not happy.

I like that kind of certainty. If he's not happy, you generally know what to do about it. I don't have to compromise, I don't have to negotiate. I know what to do, and if I do the job, the return is there, monetarily, psychologically and emotionally.

The stress involved in owning and working in your restaurant is an immediate stress. It goes up and down. Robert doesn't find himself taking long-term worries home with him. "You deal with it, and you go on to something else."

There is also the chance to take time off, and leave the business to the trusted staff members.

I didn't want this to be Bob's Place, where everyone who came in knew me. I decided that after a certain period of time I would cut the cord, so I went to Hawaii for two weeks. This place has run itself. I have been on three vacations so far, and that's the way I want it.

Robert's advice to potential restaurateurs comes from the perspective of having changed careers.

First of all, don't stay in a profession you don't like. You have heard all the stories of what it can do to you. You spend more time in your profession than you do with your family.

If you are thinking about changing, don't listen to people who are telling you the negatives. Keep talking about it, keep romancing yourself, keep kidding yourself, keep it alive. Do all the things that you can afford to do time and money-wise which are a part of the dream. Don't worry that you are taking the cart before the horse, because that will keep the ball bouncing.

Do all the corny things. I went to UCLA and took a course on restaurant management. I probably prepared myself for this (restaurant) for two or three years. Cook for people. Do the things that will give rise to encouragement from people.

Do the specific nitty-gritty things that you need to prepare. Do all the things that occur to you quite naturally. Take the courses, pick the brain of everybody you know, go to a restaurant, sit down and talk to a manager, pick his brain, maybe steal him away from somebody.

The money spent for the feasibility study was a wise investment. It gives you the bottom line, and tells you precisely what you have to aim for.

Subscribe to the restaurant industry's magazines. Immerse yourself in the feeling of being a restaurateur.

Obviously, you have to get the money somehow. You need to talk to people. If you talk to enough people about your dream, you'll be surprised the things that happen and the people that come to you. The other end of the deal is out there looking for you too!

You will hear more negatives than positives as you talk to people about opening your restaurant. Listen, absorb what they say, and find out where you don't fit into it.

TOM KAPLAN

Restaurant Manager

One of the dining rooms overlooks Los Angeles's famous Sunset Strip. The coffee is served in dainty porcelain, the white linen is smooth and pressed. The chef, Wolfgang Puck has become a celebrity. Photographers ask to use the restaurant's garden patio for magazine shots. It is perfect for a wedding reception, a tete-a-tete, or a clandestine rendezvous.

General manager, Tom Kaplan, is the epitome of professionalism and style. His relative youth exemplifies the upbeat nature of Spago. After three years as general manager, he has the experience to handle any problems with the staff or the diverse clientele with confidence.

Generally speaking, I have to be responsible for all areas of the restaurant from the kitchen to the dining room, to the business. It's a triangular effect to make sure all is working well.

Tom has a BA in art history and studio art. He originally wanted to be an architect, studying architecture at a college in Maine. An architectural job brought him out to California, where he worked on a design project for a restaurant and met Wolfgang Puck.

I think a liberal arts education is very important, whatever field you go into. If you have a good education, it exposes you to so many different areas and disciplines. There's an awareness, not only of the technical, but of the social aspects of a restaurant. You need to be able to communicate, not only with the workers, but with the clientele who have diverse backgrounds.

Each day is different. At times, Tom arrives at the restaurant early, at about 9:00 a.m. and leaves in the early evening. Other days he stays until closing at 2:00 a.m. Generally, Tom's working day begins at 10:00 and ends at about 9:00 at night.

The environment is such that it's not the intensity one might have in the stock market or in the banking world. During the day at least, it's basically a calm environment, busy, but calm in the sense that it's not rigorous exposure to the public.

The job of general manager involves coordination of the three areas of the restaurant (food and drink, service, and financial). He must maintain constant communication, knowing costs at any given moment, current price trends, and availabilities. This is not only for food, but wine and liquor also.

We serve a tremendous amount of wine here. There has to be a lot of creative buying, inventory, storage, things like that.

Another important factor is dealing not only with customers, but with employees. Tom is responsible for the hiring and firing of everyone but the kitchen personnel. He works very closely with waiters, waitresses, hostesses, cashiers, bartenders—training and scheduling, and dealing with problems they may have with customers or each other.

There's somebody here they can talk to who won't dismiss anything that might happen.

I think the hardest thing is dealing with the staff. You are working with people on all different levels, different educations, different ethnic backgrounds. Sometimes it can be very frustrating for me to try and enforce ideas and theories, and get cooperation. I think that is true in any management situation. It's sometimes been quite disillusioning for me to spend a lot of time doing very basic things, and have it not really catch on or work, or having to spend more time than I anticipated trying to make something work. It's very important that everyone work well together.

As general manager, Tom looks over the reservation list to insure that they have been booked carefully, utilizing all the tables. He checks for special parties, or special people, and is involved in the actual reservation if it's someone that they know.

There is a lot of phone work, public relations, handling promotions and the media.

There is a lot of coordination in terms of discussing projects with people. Wolfgang also uses the office spaces for other projects that he has above and beyond the restaurant. He consults for hotels in Texas and Los Angeles, various cookbooks, and various cooking demonstrations.

Tom is involved in the restaurant's finances all the way up to profit and loss and distribution. He has learned a lot along the way.

A background in business would help, certainly. Understanding finance is first and foremost in any restaurant. We do have accountants that work with us on advanced levels.

I think that far too many restaurant people get involved on a level of either being a waiter or a maitre d', and not in terms of understanding the business end. A restaurant background is helpful to a certain extent, but I don't think it is imperitive that somebody spend five years in restaurant school to become involved in the restaurant business. A good business sense is important.

The restaurant business, by its very nature, requires long and irregular hours.

It's very difficult to enjoy a normal life. Management practices and techniques are changing so that if things are done well and efficiently, it still won't be a nine to five job, but it won't be a 10 or 11 hour job.

The stress can be high at two different levels. In the daytime, there is stress involved in the preparation for the opening at night, and maintaining a tight control on the business aspects. At night, it involves the public.

There is a lot of stress particularly with this type of restaurant in this kind of city. We do extraordinarily well. The clientele is so diverse in terms of the Hollywood, movie, television, music, and theater industries. Not to mention lawyers, and bankers. There is the big game of having to be able to serve everybody and keep them happy.

On the positive side, it's like having a dinner party at your house every night. There is an opportunity to make a lot of friends, and meet different people from different businesses.

It's a lot of fun, and it exposes you directly to all sorts of different things.

HENRI ABERGEL

Restaurant Maitre'd

La Serre is French for "the greenhouse", and the restaurant is a lush green and white representation of its name. The walls are lined with white trellises, and the many hanging plants weave themselves throughout the latticework. It is delicate and simple, the refined atmosphere of one of the most expensive and successful restaurants in Southern California.

Henri is the maitre'd, exuding the elegance and French refinement of his working environment. He began as a waiter, nine years ago. In two years, he worked his way up to maitre'd and manager.

Simultaneously, when I was asked to take the job, I was asking to leave. I wanted to go into advertising. I left for about six months, and came back to that job.

Henri's varied educational background ended at UCLA just short of graduation. His last major was economics, though he started his education as a premed student. He had always worked in restaurants to support his education, starting as a busboy at 16 and a half.

I had six and a half years of restaurant work behind me, a good attitude, and I wanted to work. A friend of mine was working at La Serre, and I made an appointment with the owner. She gave me a one-week try-out period.

There were a few things I didn't know about this kind of restaurant. I had been working in a family restaurant, and it didn't have all of these sophisticated foods, sophisticated wines, sophisticated service. But, I was willing to learn. I had a week, and I guess I showed promise in that week.

Until recently, Henri had worked Monday through Saturday, with Sundays off because the restaurant was closed. He has since pared his schedule down to 5 days a week, with the owner and himself handling the restaurant's night business.

Somebody of responsibility has to be here. People don't like to take responsibility when they work for an hourly wage. They say, 'This is my job and I do it'. If the guy comes with the meat, they aren't going to make sure that all the meat is there. If the linen company isn't here, nobody is going to notice until the busboy comes in at 12:00 and then it's too late.

I have to make sure the chef takes care of his responsibilities, and check to make sure everything is alright. My main responsibility is the night shift. Basically, I am supposed to be here at 4:00, but I come in the morning just to follow-up on the night before, to make sure that I won't have any surprises.

At 4:00 in the afternoon, Henri returns to the restaurant, dressed in a suit and tie. He makes sure the rooms are set up for dinner, checks to be sure the chef has prepared all the specials for the evening, then gets ready for the night's patrons.

I am on the phone a lot. People like to talk to someone in charge when they call, even to make a reservation. If none of us are here, they are disappointed and they say that they will call back.

As the guests enter the door in the evening, Henri greets them, seats them, and makes sure they have a nice dinner.

I see them throughout dinner. I recommend wine, I recommend food. I make sure they are happy. This is like a home for us. It's a very personal business. It's not like a restaurant owned by some corporation. I create a personality for the restaurant.

We get people at their most relaxed time, and they are very demanding, they want to have everything just perfect. You cannot forget anything when you are serving people, when they are spending that kind of money. These are people that run big corporations, multi-million dollar corporations. They are very responsible during the day. They are under stress themselves during the day.

Henri feels the stress of his profession, but does not consider it a negative factor. It's part of the job.

As a young boy, I always wanted to have the responsibility of being in charge, of dressing up to come to work. I have that, and I am very happy. When I took the job, I left school. I wanted to be a big business executive, then the opportunity came and I thought, 'This is what I want. This is management.'

In a restaurant the caliber of La Serre, where a dinner check might run into hundreds of dollars, an advantage for Henri is getting to know the people that he sees each evening. With many patrons, he insures that they are well taken care of in the evening, and reads about them the next day in the morning newspaper.

Henri is totally in charge of the hiring and firing of the waiters and he looks for the same professionalism that he exhibits.

It used to be in the restaurant business, you could ask a waiter, 'What do you do during the day?' and he would probably have an answer for you. 'I play guitar, or I want to act'. But now, I have a crew of waiters here that do this as a living, solely. They have no other aspirations. This is their business. I like that professionalism. I want them to learn about wines, I want them to learn about food. I try and push them to go back in the kitchen and see how the food is prepared so they will be able to explain it to people who have no idea what a dish involves.

I am a buffer between the owner and the employees. I make both sides happy. They both come to me.

Again, the hours are long and late. "I usually close the place up. Of course, I could leave it to someone, but I am usually here until 1:00 in the morning." Another aspect of the management of La Serre is the ordering of wines and liquor which Henri shares with the bartender.

Management makes the decisions about things that need to be bought. With the chairs, for example, I had a say in picking the fabric and the style of the chairs.

Henri advises education for a career in the restaurant business. Conversely, if someone has no hope in school, he can work his way up from busboy.

School gives you a discipline, it gives you a method of thought. You can break down things more easily than a person who didn't go to school. You approach problems differently because you have read examples, you have read about other people's lives.

For this profession, you can study business, economics, public relations. My position is very delicate. You need to have the personality to do it. You can be very good at working in an office, you can be the best administrator, and could flunk on the floor of a restaurant.

Your personality and nature are very important in determining how far you will go in the restaurant business. You must be friendly, understanding, and maintain a strong sense of yourself. You will come across all sorts of people, and must be willing to treat even the most difficult with respect.

If some guy comes in, snaps his fingers and says, 'Get me a table and two bottles of champagne,' you can't say, 'Who does he think he is?' He is paying for that, and some people have that type of personality. It takes the flexibility to deal with the good and the bad. There will always be more good than bad.

Get to know everything about the restaurant business. You must know how a busboy works, how a waiter sets up tables, and the process inherent in the supply industry.

You cannot start out in a restaurant of this sort. You need a lot of experience. The clientele may be more difficult to deal with, much more knowledgeable, and they are paying for a certain level of service. They want professional waiters. They want someone who knows and can discuss wines and food with them.

Work hard, and whatever you do, do it well.

Someone will always notice a good worker, even if he is quiet. You don't have to go up and say, 'Hey! Look at me. I am the best!' If you do the job right at any level, somebody will notice it, and eventually you will move up.

ENGINEERING

Engineering is the application of scientific principles to practical purposes. Engineers design roads, bridges, and subway systems. They develop and test plans for automobiles, airplanes, and missiles. They build electric power generators, reservoirs, and waste disposal systems. They design buildings, develop equipment to probe underwater, and produce machinery for manufacturing. They create radios, television, and telephone communications systems. In short, much of what we take for granted in our everyday lives is a direct result of the work of engineers.

Engineering is one of the oldest professions, aided by recent major advances in technology. In the numbers employed, engineering ranks second today, behind teaching. Within the field, there are a number of specialities. For example:

- **Aerospace Engineers** design, develop, and help produce commercial and military aircraft, missiles, and spacecraft. Most of the 48,000 aerospace engineers work in aircraft and missile jobs.

- **Chemical Engineers** design and produce chemicals and chemical products. Two-thirds of the 56,000 chemical engineers work in manufacturing.

- **Civil Engineers** design and supervise construction of roads, airports, tunnels, bridges, water supply, sewage systems, and buildings. Around half of the 175,000 civil engineers work for a governmental agency or for a contractor serving government.

- **Electrical and Electronics Engineers** design, test, and supervise the manufacture of electrical and electronic equipment. This is the largest branch of engineering with 390,000 employed.

- **Industrial Engineers** determine the most efficient and economical method of using people, machinery, and energy to produce goods or processes. Most of the 125,000 industrial engineers work for manufacturing firms.

- **Mechanical Engineers** design and develop power-producing machines such as engines, turbines, and jet and rocket propulsion systems. The occupation employed 237,000 in a recent year.

- **Metallurgical, Ceramic, and Materials Engineers** develop new types of metals and other materials to meet specific requirements (weight, heat resistant, etc.). There were 19,000 in these fields in a recent year.

- **Mining Engineers** find, extract, and prepare minerals for manufacturing industries to use. There were around 7,200 in a recent year, most employed by mining firms.

- **Nuclear Engineers** design and operate nuclear power systems. Most of the 9,700 nuclear engineers work for a public utility or military service.

- **Petroleum Engineers** explore and drill for oil and gas. A major employer of the 22,000 petroleum engineers are oil companies.

The basic requirement for employment as an engineer is a bachelor's degree in one of the above specialities. Many also go on for master's or doctor's degrees.

Since the Russians launched the first space vehicle in 1967, national attention has focused on the need for international leadership in science and engineering. Despite the strong demand for engineers over the last 30 years, the percentage of college seniors majoring in engineering actually declined from 9.6 percent in 1960 to 6.4 percent in 1980.

The decline would have been even greater if women hadn't entered the field.

In the 1950s, only one or two percent of engineering students were women. Today, the number has increased to around 10 percent.

For technically-oriented people with a mind for math, the field of engineering can offer job stability as well as exciting challenges.

KEVIN KERR

Computer Engineer

They placed a big ad in the city's primary newspaper. "Job Fair This Saturday". He had the background—a bachelor's degree in computer science and engineering, a master's in computer engineering, work experience. He knew how to talk to people, knew how to conduct himself in an interview. He could compete. Kevin Kerr arrived at the job fair, resume in hand, and waited with the other hopefuls for an interview. He went in, talked about what he knew and shortly afterward, was hired by Hughes as a computer engineer.

They asked me a few technical questions, but it was mainly simple stuff that I learned from my classes.

Hughes, in general, likes education. They view a master's degree as one year of experience. They like you to be as technical as possible, so a master's degree shows that you're more technical.

Now, after four years with Hughes, Kevin's job title is Group Head, a position he defines as "the lowest level management." His group is responsible for designing a land-based computer for air defense systems. They use integrated circuits to put together the logic required for the computer.

Basically, there are three components. There is the processor, the I/O (Input/Output unit), and the memory. The I/O's responsibility is to talk to the outside world. The I/O is like the keyboard, he's what we all see. The processor is the main thing. He does all the calculations and computations, executes all the instructions. The memory is where you store your programs.

Essentially, you load your programs into the memory through the I/O, and then the processor executes those instructions.

As the group head, Kevin must oversee the design of all three components.

Typically, there are two guys who design the memory, four guys who design the processor, and another two guys who design the I/O.

Kevin learned much of his programming knowledge through his formal education. Programming classes are readily available in most universities and many high schools. However, the most essential background qualification needed is the ability to think with the kind of logic that is required for computer engineering.

For example, when interviewing prospective entry level engineers, Kevin doesn't expect new graduates to possess a complete understanding of everything they will need to know for the job. University classes teach much of the basics and the theories behind what you are doing, but lack the practical, "real world" experience.

When we get someone new, we show them all of the shortcuts they never learned. If they have a good logical mind and basis, then they pick them up and understand them and go from there.

We have designed computers over and over again, and have learned simplifications. You learn ways to make good approximations about the hard parts of the design. They work, and they cut down on a lot of the time it would normally take.

At Hughes, Kevin works a basic eight hour day, beginning at 8:00 in the morning, ending at 5:00 in the evening, with an hour for lunch.

The work flow is as follows: Kevin and his boss work out a schedule for the tasks that need to be completed. Based on that schedule, Kevin assigns tasks, delegates work, and sees that everyone stays on time and gets everything done. If there are problems, a shortage of equipment or parts, Kevin takes the necessary steps to correct the situation.

An advantage at this level of management is that Kevin has the opportunity to involve himself in design as well as management.

The tasks that I do can range from getting involved in a study on a new design while overseeing the current design, to actually doing the design. It's the kind of position where you have enough power to have some say in what's going on, and you can also determine your own destiny to a certain extent. If you want to do the hardware design, you get in there and give yourself part of it. If you just want to oversee, you sit back and oversee.

Conversely, a difficulty inherent in a first line management position is the fact that you sit between the workers and higher management. You strive to support each side.

You end up getting caught in the middle a lot. The people below you think you should be doing one thing, and the people above you think you should be doing another.

Another difficulty lies couched within the nature of a company the size of Hughes.

You end up with too many chiefs. They can't make a decision as to exactly what they want to build. Everyone wants to get their finger in the pie, and try and make their one decision. By the time you get down to the real workers, we end up getting bounced around all over the place.

A major difference between a large company like Hughes, and a smaller engineering firm, is the distance between management and the technical work of their employees.

In a small company, even the President of the company is only two or three levels above the actual workers. He is tightly in touch with what is going on. He directs the entire machine.

Here, the guy who is two levels up from me is knowledgeable in our area, but he has three levels above him to deal with. And, those guys are totally out of touch (with the technical).

Kevin has been working on the same design project for the last four years. Although it varies, an average design for a computer will take approximately two years.

The shorter time the better. The actual design of this computer could probably be accomplished in about a year, if we had good direction up front and they weren't going to change any of the ground rules.

So, since I have been working on this for four years, what have I been doing? I have either been misdirected because requirements change, I have been doing things twice, like I design one part they totally change it and I have to start all over again, or I have been off studying other parts of the machine that we might change, and we end up not changing it.

In a small engineering company, the projects move more quickly for two reasons. First of all, the projects are more directed because the head of the company is closer to the action. Secondly, a smaller company can't afford to waste the money that a large company can.
However, engineers in smaller firms tend to work much longer hours.

You can get burned out working in a small company, but often, you get more experience because things are moving more quickly.

An engineer who works for a small company in the early stages of its growth has the potential to receive substantial financial rewards if the company succeeds.

You can make good money at Hughes, too. The bigger companies have to be competitive.

Typically, as a general point, if you stay at a company for any length of time, you are going to drop behind what you might earn. The people who make the most money are the people who jump jobs, at least to a point. It has to do with demand. If there is a high demand for engineers, and you look like you've done a good job, people will pay you more money, to a point. However, Hughes isn't going to be far behind because they don't want to lose their good people.

Technology in the computer field is racing ahead. Everyone wants a faster computer than the one they have. You must stay on top of the technology to remain technically competent.

In our project, we changed things halfway through to speed it up because we found out it wasn't fast enough. You can't stop learning when you get out of college. Computers are faster and more complex.

Go to college and take classes that will give you knowledge in both hardware design, electrical engineering, and software design, programming.

That is crucial. So much of what we are doing now, and where technology is going, is a real mix of both. Get a strong math background, and strong physics. Don't specialize in either. When you get out into the real world and go into computer design, you'll need both. You may find that you want to do one over the other, but you will also find that the most valuable people are those that know both. They are like the hand and the glove. When we go to design a computer, it's very important that we understand what kind of software is going to be running on it. When you are designing software, you really have to understand how the hardware works, and how to take advantage of it.

There have been so many times in the check-out of our computer that, because I understand software, it was easy for me to get into what they were doing, find out where they were having a problem, and then trace it back and find the problem on my end. It's all interrelated. You can't just look at it from one point of view.

In the job interview, show the interviewer that you can communicate with people as well as with a computer.

For me, I want to see if a prospective new-hire can work well with other people and communicate well.

I can tell if someone can communicate if his resume is done well. I get resumes from people and there are misspellings, for example. I think that with a resume, you should take the time to do it right. Have someone check it out if you are a lousy speller.

The bottom line is knowledge and how you convey it. If you don't have the work experience, then you should really understand what you are doing in school and be able to talk about it.

RICHARD HUBACH

Chairman of the Board

Richard Hubach is Chairman of the Board of View Engineering. At 45 years of age, his life is set up just as he wants it. He is a risk-taker with the unshakable belief that he will always land on his feet. His company's financial statement tells him, and everyone else, that he's right.

Richard briefly attended the University of Oklahoma on an athletic scholarship. "By brief I mean one semester." After transferring to the University of Illinois for three semesters, he completed his education at the University of California, Berkeley, eventually obtaining a bachelor's degree in engineering physics, and a doctorate in physics.

I worked at Rocketdyne for a year on a propulsion system for transport vehicles in deep space. Then I went to Hughes Aircraft and worked in a lot of different divisions for 15 years, mostly missile guidance.

For the first couple of years, I was a member of the technical staff, which includes anyone who has a bachelor's degree. I quickly found out that I wasn't very good at technology, but better at managing things, so I went into system and programs managing.

The practical advantage to an advanced degree in the engineering field is specifically related to research. Richard could have done the things he did at Hughes without a PhD.

I once looked at a study on the pay of people with various degrees in the engineering industry. If I take the four years that I put into my education, and count what I would have been paid if I had gone directly into industry, I would be repaid for that amount at the same time I retired. As far as the financial end goes, (a PhD) is of no value.

Many successful people had no education, they were dropouts. If you have that sort of direction, I wouldn't say it's necessary to have an education. However, the average person has a far greater chance of success if he has an education. In doing business, it's very important to have a good cultural background as well. Can you talk to people? Are you limited by only saying equations in physics, or can you talk to them about other things.

After 15 years at Hughes, Richard left the company. He was then managing 250 people, and ran into a problem.

I always dress casually. Most of the management felt that it was O.K. because I did the job and there were no problems. Eventually I went to work for a guy who said, 'You will never get promoted again unless you dress according to the way I think you ought to dress.'

He named a promotion level and told me that he would promote me in six months if I would buy suits and ties and wear them for that period of time. I thought about it, and I decided to do it.

At the end of five months I went into his office and said, 'We really ought to talk about how we are going to make this transition.' He looked at me and said, 'What was your understanding of our agreement?' Well, I told him in a lot of four letter words to take his job and shove it. I quit after 15 years with no place to go.

Dressed as he pleased, Richard Hubach and two friends put up $5,000 each to start View Engineering. The company was his second attempt at starting his own business. "Some people are natural entrepreneurs, I wasn't." A few years earlier, he and a partner started a corporation.

Mercifully, it failed very fast. If they linger, you can lose everything for years and years. We simply lost everything we had, and lost it very quickly. But, I did learn about business and how not to do things.

A self-proclaimed "totally secure person", Richard Hubach smiles and points out that you have to be secure to start a business like this. "You really can't have any fears."

With that in mind, View Engineering was born. They were the first people doing what they do, about three years ahead of anyone else. They developed a system by which "with high-resolution television cameras and a powerful user-programmable microcomputer, the View-719 automatically takes measurements, checks orientation, and verifies specifications on each part coming through the production line." Essentially, the system allows the elimination of manual inspection of random samples, providing instantaneous and automatic process and quality control.

A friend let Richard and his partners use space in his office building in exchange for payment of half the secretary's salary and the promise to do some sales work for him. They didn't take a salary and didn't have any overhead expenses. After about nine months, they were each able to put another $5,000 into the business and it continued to grow.

As president of the fledgling company, Richard's role was minimal. He chose the products and the people. In the third or fourth year of the program, the 20 hour working days began. He was the chairman of the board, chief executive officer, president, vice president of sales, vice president of engineering and ran the whole operation. As the company grew, their needs changed.

The kind of management that is required to start a company is very different than the kind of management required to run a 100-200 million dollar company. I simply didn't have the experience to know how to handle the complications that accompany such growth.

Now, in our fiscal 1983 year, which ended in July, we did fifteen and a half million dollars. Our profits were about 9% after taxes. The company did very well, and we were lucky in the industry.

You work your tail off and have all kinds of things that you think are going to happen. They rarely do, but you keep your eyes open and some ancillary thing happens and you take advantage of it. If you're lucky, it turns out to be right.

With the company firmly on its feet, they hired a new president, a new vice president in sales, a new chief financial officer, vice president in finance, and a new vice president of operations. The whole management structure was different. Also, for the first time, the company got outside capital into the company through a venture capital group.

Today, eight years after the company began, View Engineering employs nearly 200 people. Richard is now chairman of the board.

It means that you have a card that says you are the chairman of the board and when you talk to someone who is a major executive in another company, you go with credibility. Usually, the chairman of the board is the largest share holder, which I am, or plays an active role in the management of the company, which I still do. The chief executive officer is the guy who really runs the company. Everyone reports to him. The board is responsible for replacing him if he's not doing his job, checking up to make sure things are right, and planning strategic advances in the corporation.

There is no typical day. "We are about to sign a big deal with General Motors so we have literally three inches high of paperwork that we have to go through. Today, for example, was spent reading legal documents, and this afternoon will be spent the same way."

Arriving at work by 7:30 in the morning, Richard seldom leaves before 6:30 or 7:00 in the evening. But, his day is a lot shorter than it used to be.

When I was the president, the whole thing was on my shoulders. I didn't sleep well, only 4 or 5 hours a night and I would make it up on weekends. Sometimes I would get to work at 2:00 or 3:00 in the morning and work to 7:00 at night. I was lying in bed worrying about it. I might as well have been at work.

It's a matter of commitment. The more time you put in, the better your company is going to do. If you are going to start a company, and really make a success of it and go for the big banana, not a mom and pop store, your competition is immense. Our company is now worth 50 to 60 million dollars, and it started with 15 thousand dollars. If you are going to have that kind of growth, it requires a serious commitment on your part. You have to be ready to do it, or you're not going to succeed.

From his varied and experienced view, Richard Hubach sees a widening need for engineering managers who understand engineering.

The problem is, engineers don't like to be managed by accountants or anyone other than engineers. They're very egocentric that way. In fact, most people don't like to be managed by people who don't talk their language. There is a real need for engineers who don't have a tremendous ego tied up in their own engineering skills. Managers can't be writing codes or designing circuits. There is a need for people who are engineers and who can manage engineers. It turns out that I am relatively good at that.

Consequently, Richard spends a lot of his day doing just that: talking to engineers about their programs, helping them schedule their programs, calling meetings so that they can coordinate well together, and making sure everyone has the equipment that they need.

While I don't do technical things, the technical people respect me because I have a number of patents and a PhD, and they can't fool me very well.

One of the problems lies in the American tendency towards striving for promotion, with industry management as the root to making money.

If you don't get promoted into management, you feel as if you've failed. There are very few people who feel that if they stay a technologist all their lives, they have succeeded. These people demand to be promoted, but they aren't trained to be managers. In fact, most of them don't have the skills to be managers anyway. Eventually, they fail.

If we could clearly distinguish between those who have good technical capabilities, and those who have management capabilities, root them properly and reward the technical people appropriately, we would have a better system.

At View Engineering, Richard sees the opportunity to put his theories into practice. The good engineers in his company, and the engineers who have been with the company for a long time, receive stock in the company and a percentage of the sales of the systems that they have helped design. "There is a premium to stay at engineering rather than go into management."

The stress of starting your own business, and of starting a business of this type is high. It can be a serious strain on relationships, family, and friends.

I've had an ulcer, and been through the whole business. Most of my personal friends have now left, don't talk to me anymore for one reason or another, I came very close to ruining my relationship with my girlfriend. It basically ruins your personal life. You have to be able to dedicate your life to it, or you're not going to make it.

It's much harder than you can imagine. It's the worse thing to be boss and to have the ultimate responsibility for the lives of the employees, the suppliers who depend on us, and all the customers who support us. That responsibility can never be shared with anyone. There is no way for anyone to understand it until you've borne that pressure.

Another thing that I discovered was that an enormous amount of financial understanding is required. Cash flow problems, inventory problems, keeping track of where all the parts are all the time. You have to understand how all the key elements play together. I couldn't keep track of what was going on in the company without all that knowledge.

Conversely, there is nothing like taking a risk and succeeding.

So many people are afraid to try things. That's terrible. The reward is commensurate with the risk. If you take a lot of risk, you'll have a lot of reward. If you don't, you don't. If people could be more secure in their own beliefs, and confident in their capabilities, then the sort of thing that I've done, would be a lot easier. You have to fail a few times and understand that you're not going to die.

DEBBIE MAH

Civil Engineer

A professional-looking woman with jet black hair and straight posture, Debbie Mah smiles as she remembers high school and college.

She had always liked science and math and subjects that involved numbers and calculations. Engineering was a natural flow from study to work. Civil engineering was the branch in which she felt most comfortable. Her choice, she feels, was the right one.

Debbie received her bachelor of science degree in civil engineering and went to work for the California Department of Transportation (Cal Trans) shortly afterwards.

As far as the field goes, most engineering firms only require a bachelor's degree. Some will ask for a master's, but with a BS, and your registration, you can go pretty far. An MBA would help if you want to move up into management.

The state Board of Engineering licenses those who seek to practice under the title of "engineer". Each state handles the registration of its engineers. Currently, in California, obtaining your registration is not mandated by law, but required by many companies and engineering firms. Without your registration, you may not legally call yourself an engineer, though you may practice engineering. The examination fee is $85 to $100. Military engineers and some state and federal agency engineers are exempt from registration requirements.

Five years earlier, Debbie Mah joined the hundreds of other engineering students in her university for the on-campus recruitment conducted on engineering career day. Engineering firms interviewed the future engineers. Debbie talked with many before deciding that she wanted to work for the state of California.

I had worked for the state before, as a student assistant during the summer. The state has a special two-year rotational program for the entry level engineer once you have your degree. You work in different departments within Cal Trans—design, construction, surveys, traffic, different branches, etc. The rotation program has a very good reputation. They get you involved in whatever they are doing. You get a chance to really see what type of work is being done there. The rotation program has a very good reputation.

Now, a licensed civil engineer, Debbie Mah is at work by 7 a.m.

Our hours are flexible. We can start anytime between 7:00 and 9:00 in the morning. Once you set up your eight-hour workday, that's what your regular schedule is.

The day begins with continued work on her current project. About 50 percent of her time is spent out in the field where she does field drilling or investigative work.

I like it because it is varied. I'm not cooped up in the office all day. My office work is actually an extension of field activities. I write reports and make recommendations based upon what we found out in the field. Those results are incorporated into our project reports and designs.

It's an active, eight-hour day, ending at 3:30 in the afternoon. Debbie's classification is Assistant Transportation Engineer. She reports directly to an Associate Engineer.

He is considered the project engineer. He has given me a lot of freedom to do whatever I feel is necessary for a job. I have the tools to use. I have a drilling crew and testing facilities and can order the test I want. I am lucky that he has given me the responsibility to make the reports on the job and to talk to other project engineers so I can work with them on a one to one basis.

It took Debbie about two years to reach her current level of autonomy. For the initial two years, she rotated through different departments. Then she was assigned a permanent position with one branch, working for one associate.

> *That's when I gained independence and the responsibility. After two years in the assistant position, you are eligible to take the associate exam to become a project engineer. Engineering offers job satisfaction that is tangible. With the design work we do in civil engineering, I actually get to see results. I make a design, can see it being built, and feel a sense of accomplishment.*

Stress levels on the job are not too high. There are reasonable deadlines and although you do have to get the jobs done, there is not a sense of deadline pressure.

Get experience while you are a student. Many firms hire students, during the summer. You have the opportunity to see if that's really how you want to spend you life, while you still have the time to change.

> *If you are going to enter the profession, and want to plan ahead, there's an EIT (Engineer In Training) exam that you need to take. You usually take it in your last year in school. I would say to make sure to get that out of the way. Once you pass that, within two years of graduation from school, you are eligible to take the exam for your registration. Your registration and your degree will get you very far.*

Debbie heard about the exam while she was working, the other engineers advised her.

> *While I was in school, a lot of people had never even heard of the exams. Some professors aren't working out in the field so they are not as able to tell students what to look out for once they start working.*

HOWARD SIMONS

Structural Engineer

In a large, cool office, housing countless blueprints, Howard Simons sits behind a white drafting table. On a bulletin board, 9 x 10 color photographs of his baby daughter bring splashes of color into the room dominated by the pale blue of his structural designs. It is quiet. He is alone.

I am a corporation. I am an employee of that corporation. The only employee.

Howard is a structural engineer in business for himself. "I went through a number of firms, worked for a contractor, before I started my own business." He shares offices with another structural engineer, and they have an arrangement whereby they use each other's services.

Structural engineers design structures of all kinds. Howard is a structural engineer who designs buildings.

In a house, for example, the wood framing, joists, the stuff you would cover up and never see, but will walk upon, is the structure. The structure is the reason you would presume that the building isn't going to blow over in the wind or topple in an earthquake.

A graduate of UCLA, Howard earned a bachelor's degree in engineering, period. He learned of the special aspects to structural engineering through working.

You come out and work for a large office. In essence, you get lost in the office, and you absorb what other people know.

Howard never intended to go into business for himself. He merely backed into it.

I had one client, went into business for myself, and as the years went on, didn't get very many more. At this point, I have one or two extremely good clients and they provide me with everything I need. We do office buildings, parking structures, things like that. They are good-sized projects.

I happen to be extremely fortunate. Most people have to spend time hustling, talking to people, taking them out to lunch, playing golf, the usual type of thing. I don't. I spend most of my time producing the work.

With the birth of his two-year old daughter, he revised his working schedule. Where nights and weekends were once the norm, he made a specific effort to complete his work within the confines of a nine to five day, and succeeded.

It takes months to do the calculations and the drawings (for an average job). I go out to the job site on occasion. I go to the building department on occasion. I see the contractor on a weekly basis and have job meetings. Predominately, I am here doing the work.

The calculations are done by hand, totally. Each building is a unique entity, a set of plans for one building cannot be used for another. It doesn't work. There is a tremendous amount of work to be done.

Structural engineers can be hired by architects, by an owner, a developer, or a contractor. Their job is to do all of the necessary calculations and drawings for a particular structure. The drawings go out to the contractor, he bids on them and builds a building from them.

If Howard found himself in a position where his basic client dried up and he needed a job, he would begin by calling architects.

An owner hires an architect and pays him sufficient money to hire all of the sub-consultants out of his fee. He will hire the structural, mechanical, electrical, landscaping, and all of those guys. The incentive for the architect is to hire the cheapest guy. The less he pays someone, the more he keeps.

So, if I want a job, I would call up an architect and tell him, 'If you are very happy with your engineer, fine, I will say goodbye. If not, consider me on your next project.' Then, I might get a call, they would send me a set of plans and want a bid. I, in turn, would bid the job and try and get it.

That is the cut-throat nature of the business unless you can deal with people who know your services and want to pay for them at a fair price.

The expenses for running his own structural engineering business include books on building codes and regulations, rent for the office space, and malpractice insurance.

Doctors are very vocal about the big crisis in malpractice in medicine. Let me tell you some statistics. In one year, out of 100 physicians, 8-10 will have some sort of a claim for malpractice. Out of 100 engineers, that number is 39.

If you look at a set of plans, there are literally thousands of words. So, it's hard not to make mistakes. You are liable for what you do, and you are liable if a mistake causes something. Right now, things are going berserk. People expect perfection. When they open their door, they don't want it to stick or anything like that. The suits are getting unbelievable.

For a one-person office, I paid $17,000 in insurance last year. And, I have never had a claim against me.

Buildings do fall down. They fall down for a number of reasons, physical things happen to it. The wind blows. An earthquake rumbles. The structural engineers job is to design a building in a coherent fashion for those complicated physical effects. No one knows exactly what goes on, but they do have approximations. They know what happens when you shake things—the laws of dynamics.

Through the years, people have formulated procedures. If you want to design a column for a certain amount of load, you go to the steel book, and there's how to do it, and the rationale behind it. That's what we do.

Now, God may, for some reason, want that column to fall down, and it falls down. After it collapsed, I would come back and say, 'I can't help what God wanted to happen. I have carried out that procedure correctly, therefore, I did my work correctly.' That's the approach.

A malpractice claim against a small engineering business can be devastating.

Here's an example of what can happen: suppose you hired a lawyer to sue me for half a million dollars. To begin with, I have already insured myself against something like this. I have paid my $17,000, and I have malpractice insurance. My insurance has a limit to it, and a deductible of $10,000.

The deductible applies to legal defense. Therefore, the minute I get the letter that says you want to sue me, I call my insurance company and they say, 'Fine. Just send us the letter.' From that minute on, they have their legal department or a law firm they have hired incurring expenses in my defense. Nothing has happened. I haven't gone to trial, I haven't admitted any wrongdoing.

When the defense gets over $10,000, I don't care in any case. It can get over $10,000 very, very easily. So, you know that the minute you get that letter, you are going to pay $10,000 without even knowing how it will wind up. The defense could cost $50,000 and you could settle for $2,000.

After a claim has been made against you, the insurance company may not want to renew your insurance. Consequently, a lot of small offices are forced to close down.

Also, if you have been in business for ten years, and you have been doing all these buildings along the way, and they are out there doing their thing, wearing out, whatever they do, you could be sued for something happening on a building that you did years earlier. If you decide to get out of the business, you could still be sued ten years later.

It's a mean business. If someone was injured on one of your jobs, it could be limitless. This is the kind of business where it's unlikely that a catastrophe will happen, but it can happen. We all can make mistakes, but if I made a mistake, people could potentially die. It's the kind of thing that you keep in the back of your mind. It makes your stress level very high.

Faith in his competence and a sense of pride about what he does for a living are the satisfactions that Howard pulls from his profession. Additionally, there is a strong technical aspect to the job.

If someone gets their kicks out of the technical aspect of the profession, wants to work at a desk and hide from people, I would say, fine, this is the thing to do. The best way to prepare yourself is to get to be good at it. It takes a hell of a lot of work. There are a tremendous amount of books. My advice—don't be a lousy engineer.

LAW

America has been called a country of law and, naturally following, we are a country of lawyers. In contrast to the 15,000 lawyers in Japan, America has 600,000 lawyers and law schools continue to produce new graduates in record numbers each year. In fact, law was one of the most rapidly growing occupations in the 15 year span of 1970-1985.

Perhaps one of the main reasons for the popularity of legal careers today may be the variety of options open to those who have earned the LLB (basic bachelor's degree in law) or the JD (doctor of jurispudence degree). Among the fields open to the approximately 36,000 person who finish law school each year are the following:

- **Trial law**—Handling civil and criminal cases that go to trial before a judge or jury.
- **Criminal law**—Dealing with cases involving offenses against society or the state—such as those concerned with theft, arson, or murder.
- **Labor law**—Handling wage-hour disputes, strikes, contract negotiations, and other employee-employer relations for labor unions or industrial organizations.
- **Family law**—Specializing in such legal matters as annulments, separations, divorce, adoptions, and child custody.
- **Real estate law**—Working on transfer of property via deeds, leases, and mortgages.
- **Tax law**—Advising clients on matters related to state and federal taxes and representing them before special tax courts.
- **Patent law**—Preparing and filing applications for patents for individuals or corporations.
- **Corporate law**—Representing legal concerns of employer organizations through review of potentially liable activities, providing legal advice on issues before organizations, and representing organizations in trials and other activities.

While many lawyers, such as Abraham Lincoln, prepared for their job by interning with a lawyer or judge, that practice is rare today. Most lawyers begin by earning a bachelor's degree followed with three years of law school—four years if the course is done on a part-time basis. The American Bar Association has accredited around 170 law schools to provide superior legal training. In addition, a number of unaccredited institutions offer regular law school programs.

More so than most other fields, rank in law school plays an important role in the type of job offer received upon graduation. Many of the big city law firms only hire top graduates, those with ranking grade point averages and those who have demonstrated sufficient prowess by qualifying for a place on their school's law review. Salaries of up to $65,000 may be offered by these firms—but once again for only the very top of the class at some of the most prestigious law schools. The average for all new law graduates is closer to $25,000 a year.

Throughout most of our history, a high proportion of the members of Congress have been lawyers. In a recent year, over 300 of the 535 members of the House and Senate held law degrees. Legal training provides good background for the complexities of studying issues and passing laws. Another factor which encourages lawyers to run for Congress is the fact that a high percentage are self-employed or members of private law firms which offer considerable flexibility to its partners. They were able to take time off to campaign in primaries and general elections—an often difficult task for persons employed in key positions in other types of organizations.

The law profession has been attracting women in growing numbers over the past three decades and recent figures indicate that close to half of the students in law school today are women. But, only around one-sixth of the practicing attorneys and judges today are women. Many who study law decide to enter other fields. Law provides a good basic background for a wide variety of activities ranging from business to teaching.

Attending and completing law school can be a trying experience.

When you go to law school, they take your brain apart and put it out for the audience to watch while you put it back together. It's hell. It's a way of learning, a way of analyzing—there are no right and no wrong answers. They teach you to be paranoid and you never lose it.

Patricia Brady, Probate Attorney

Traditional law school education consists of three years in an accredited law college. An undergraduate degree, or its equivalent, is generally required before you can begin studying law. Any type of degree is acceptable, but the general consensus favors a liberal arts education with a strong emphasis on both written and oral communication skills.

The entrance test for any law school in the United States is called the LSAT (Law School Admissions Test). It is similar to the college entrance test, the SAT (Scholastic Aptitude Test), but is geared specifically towards the skills required for the comprehension and study of law.

It tests your ability to comprehend and conceptualize from basic facts, and to use the analogy which is one of your basic tools in practicing law.

Leslie Swackhammer, Copyright Attorney

There are study courses and books available to assist you in preparation for the LSAT. The classes provide the opportunity to familiarize yourself with the format of the exam and to bone-up on specifics such as the math portion of the test. You can increase your competitive edge by joining the other students who are rigorously studying for the exam.

The LSATs are very important. Individual law schools put different emphasis on them, but the score you get is really going to determine where you get in, even if you have really good grades, you need a good score also.

Leslie Swackhamer

Applications for law school differ with each institution, but most require essays describing the reasons you would like to attend that particular school, why you close the legal profession, and your unique qualities and special interests that will help you in the pursuit of a law degree.

One interesting application is Yale. They ask you to write a two page essay on anything. You could write about why you think the Rolling Stones is a great band, for instance.

Leslie Swackhamer

Although the essays are merely a portion of the complete application package, which includes undergraduate grade point averages and LSAT scores, it is important to present a well-thought out essay that is well-written and free of all grammatical and typographical errors. Develop a feeling for the psychology of a reader. Hundreds of applications will come across that desk. Remember that excellence in content and execution will stand out more than purple ink.

Most applicants apply to several law schools in an attempt to minimize their risk of rejection. A lot of law schools reject a lot of people. The cost per application is generally in the range of $30 to $50.

Once in law school, the true test begins. The first year is an ego-breaking process, and a strong sense of yourself is necessary.

Everyone who goes to law school is very smart. And 50 percent of the class is going to end up in the bottom half of the class. This 50 percent is composed of people who had 3.6 averages in college and good LSAT scores. People can't feel bad about themselves if they don't do super well. It's hard.

Leslie Swackhamer

Grades in law school are vitally important. The job you land upon graduation may very well be based upon your grades in your first year. These grades will determine whether you will make "Law Review", the legal magazine each law school publishes.

Most often, a law student will interview for a job in his or her second year. In a law firm, the entry level position is associate. Associates are most often hired right after graduation before they take the bar exam. If the associate does not pass the bar, the firm has the option of termination or allowing another attempt at the next opportunity.

Bar exams differ by state. Essentially, they are two to three day comprehensive examinations, using multiple choice questions, essays, and performance. Attorneys must also pass an exam of professional legal ethics which is a separate, but important, test before they begin practice.

> *In the bar exam, we were tested on 23 subjects representing all of our legal training. It's very important, for literally two months before the test, to study very, very hard. I studied harder for that test than I ever studied in my life. It pays off, but I wouldn't want to have to do it again.*
>
> *Leslie Swackhamer*

There is a threshold for passing or failing the exam, and if you do not pass, there is the opportunity to take it again. Different states have different rules about retests. In some you may take the exam as often as you like. In others, such as Washington, DC, three times is the limit.

Upon passing the examination, you will be granted a license to practice law in your state, and you are on your way.

MELVIN BELLI

Tort, General Lawyer

Melvin Belli is at the top of his profession. He remembers wanting to be an attorney in grammar school. The feeling never faded.

A native Californian, he received a bachelor of arts degree from the University of California at Berkeley, his law degree at the University's law school, Boalt Hall, and set up his law practice in the heart of downtown San Francisco. Dynamic litigator. Prolific writer. Melvin Belli brought the concept of demonstrative evidence, the graphic use of physical evidence, into courtrooms all over the country. He showed the jury photographs, recreated situations, brought graphic understanding to the laymen in a jury box. His innovative advances and published works on personal injury law motivated his peers to crown him the "King of Torts".

I'm not a personal injury lawyer, I try everything. I've tried and written so much about personal injury because that's where the action is. There are more personal injury cases than any other.

Seven days a week, including holidays, Melvin Belli arrives at his office to read law, work on his cases, and talk with people. Generally, he is seated at his massive desk before 8:00 in the morning, and leaves for home about 6:00 in the evening.

I am here because I like what I do. I am tremendously interested in it. I can't find anything else that I like to do more.

At least once a week, he heads down to the courthouse for a variety of reasons. On the average of three times a month, he is in court trying a case. There is nothing in the world he would rather do. During a trial, there is nowhere else he would rather be.

I just can't imagine how someone wouldn't be interested in the law. It involves everything—surgery, airplanes, domestic relations, children, capital punishment, politics, everything under the sun. We get every kind of a case, about 50 new cases coming in a day. But, we take about five cases each day.

Melvin Belli doesn't feel that an attorney has to exhibit his kind of obsession to be successful. He does feel, however, that they won't have as much fun, or like the profession as much as he does, without committing themselves totally.

In the office, potential clients go through a screening process, and he makes a determination as to which cases he wants to handle personally.

It's pretty easy to see me, but if I saw everyone that came in, I wouldn't be able to handle anything else.

A big advantage to practicing law is the opportunity to live your life in the center of all the action.

It's current, it's paramount. You have to know what is going on in the legislature, what is going on around you in your city. You are not in the past. You are very much in the present and the future. You are up to date on everything, and you are dealing with people.

The many uncertainties to the profession only make it more interesting.

You can never be sure of what the jury is going to do. I lost one last week. The newspapers and everybody thought I was going to win. I had four Mexican clients. I was down in Santa Ana, and they didn't like Mexicans. You run into stuff like that. You see some of the petty jealousies, some of the ethnic problems in the world, and you see them acutely, better than anyone else does. We are right in the middle of them.

Stress. It is a factor in the life of all trial attorneys. Melvin Belli doesn't consider stress a negative aspect of the profession, however, because to be interested in something, you must be actively involved in it. Active involvement in the process of the law and the human involvement in each case produces stress. There is no way to have one without the other.

Melvin Belli has written 62 books. *Modern Trials* brought him royalties of over a million dollars.

I think I've done more writing than any lawyer practicing today. I enjoy it very much. Usually, I write on weekends, sometimes I get in early in the morning to write.

Admittedly, the lifestyle is hard on family life.

It's just like an obstetrician who has to be on call at the hospital and has a cot out in the hallway where he snatches a few hours sleep a night. It does take away from a family.

Imagination. To achieve the level of success that Melvin Belli experiences, use imagination.

Imagination and thinking things through, following things through—that's what demonstrative evidence was, a lot of imagination in preparing things.

The way to develop imagination is to find out what life around you is really about. Take one course, it can be paper hanging or embroidery or physiology, and carry it through to its conclusion. Don't jump around and be a dilettante in ten different things. By sticking to one thing, you'll learn the modus operandi, to exhaust, where to go to research, how to find things.

I was never in a firm. I always had myself, and I started in immediately because I became the lawyer for the priest at San Quentin. I didn't get much money, in fact, it was several years before I really got any money, but I got more than enough cases to try. One case got another, and before I knew it, I was on my way.

LESLIE SWACKHAMER

Copyright Law Associate

In life, as we pass through experiences and encounter hundreds of people, we are occasionally struck by a person who transmits the spark of success. They are not the people who were voted, "Most Likely To Succeed," for while Ms. "Most Likely" was out canvassing voters, Ms. Successful was out succeeding. Simple, satisfying success.

Leslie Swackhamer is a successful person. She does not own a summer house on the Cape or instruct the chauffeur to wait for her outside. She lives in a Washington D.C. apartment with her new husband and old Wheaten Terrier. Leslie's success can be measured in simple terms—she sets goals and achieves them.

I targeted my career. I decided that I really liked copyright, it's so interesting. I took a lot of courses that were relevant, and when I wrote papers for different classes, I wrote them on aspects of copyright law. For example, when I took computer law, I wrote about copyright and computers. When I took communications law, I wrote about cable copyright problems.

By picking my career area, I feel I now have more control over what I'm doing. That's probably a big gripe that first year associates have, they don't have control. I have more control, because I have an established area of expertise.

At Emory University in Atlanta, Leslie began as an undergraduate premed student. Her plan to be a brain surgeon shifted after the first year, and she graduated with a bachelor's degree in history.

I discovered that I had a lot of verbal skills and writing skills that I wouldn't be using if I went into medicine. I found that I enjoyed things that were more conceptually oriented than a lot of areas in medicine tend to be.

I am probably the only history major who has full credits in biology, calculus, and chemistry.

Leslie was pleasantly surprised to receive acceptance notices from most of the law schools she applied to. Based on the school's reputation and location, she picked George Washington University.

Law school was not the most enjoyable of experiences; the similarities to the movie, "The Paper Chase", were all too evident.

In my law school, for the first year, everyone is put into sections which are determined by where you sit on the alphabet. There are about 110 people in your section and you go through the whole first year with them.

In your first year, the classes are huge. Professors get you to stand up when they call you. They have you recite cases and ask you ridiculous questions. Everyone gets very intimidated until, one day, you learn that saying, 'I don't know', is O.K.

It takes a lot of time to get used to the way the law is presented. In America, we study cases more than we study a textbook that talks about the cases. A lot of them are written really horribly. They take a long time to comprehend. I found that in my first year, I was really studying from 9:00 in the morning to around 11:00 at night, including class each day.

Job placement for summer associate positions begins in the first year of law school. The summer associate is basically an apprenticeship, and the firm uses the summer work experience to determine if they will want to hire you after graduation. Generally, the permanent associate job placement interviews begin with second year students.

The employment process follows a standard set of steps. Dozens, potentially hundreds, of law firms announce that they are going to conduct spring interviews and invite students to sign up.

They can ask you almost anything. Since we are in Washington, firms will often ask about your political affiliation because a lot of law firms are also lobbying groups. They ask you things like, 'What can you do for us? What kind of firm do you want to practice in, large or small?' They are trying to see if you are going to fit in with them. They also ask a few strange questions to test your composure.

Bypassing the interview "cattle-call" entirely, Leslie chose a non-traditional route to getting a job. She stresses that you don't always have to play by the rules to achieve success.

First, I did not write on "Law Review". When you write on "Law Review", you wind up editing a bunch of other people's articles. It's a lot of hard work, and I didn't feel that I would learn that much. I came from a college background where I knew how to write, so I wrote my own article, sent it out to law journals, and got it published.

The article that Leslie wrote dealt with an issue that a motion picture association was very concerned about. She sent the article to them, and they in turn forwarded the article to the law firm that represented them. The law firm called Leslie and offered her a job.

I don't think that this is your usual story of how to get a job, but it is certainly one way. Guerilla tactics in the job market. Go out and market yourself. Don't go through the usual channels.

Currently, Leslie is a first year associate in a relatively small firm of 20 attorneys. The firm specializes in communications and copyright law. It also practices aviation and energy law, serving as counsel and liason to many out of town corporations and law firms and represents them before Federal agencies.
As a first year associate, there is no typical working day.

If I am working on a long range project, and there is an emergency or something, I am yanked off my ongoing project to work on that.

Leslie's office is a pleasant, enclosed space with a window. She shares a secretary with a senior partner. In the morning, generally between 8:00 and 9:00, the usual stack of mail awaits her review.

I get a lot of what we call 'trade press' which are little magazines of the industry, and I skim through those to see what's happening.

A legal "brief" is a formal written argument that one presents to a court of law. It is only filed in the context of a trial.

Basically, a brief summarizes the history of the case, and argues our position; based on the precedent of case law. You have to go and research a lot of cases, make your arguments, and support them with your cases. It's usually about 25 pages long, but it can be longer.

Currently, Leslie is preparing an "amicus brief," a brief that the firm will file in a court where it is not a party litigant in the case, but interested in the outcome. The firm wants to write a brief about its position, educate the court on the issues, and hopefully influence the outcome.

I have been working on (the brief) with the name partner of the firm, so I have been a little nervous about it. This morning I made the final corrections, discussed them with the partner, gave them to my secretary, then went to research another issue for a different client.

In firms that specialize in litigation, for example, an associate might spend her day going to hearings or making an argument in court. Leslie's firm prepares a number of position papers and briefs, and good writing skills are essential. Trial lawyers need good speaking skills, but they also must have the skill to convey their position effectively in written form.

If you go in to argue a case, the court has already read your brief. If you have written a good brief, the court is going to be predisposed to your position. The things you say only strengthen your position and you won't be building your case on what you say alone. Of course, the opposite applies. If you are a bad writer, the court is going to say, 'I'm not going to listen to this joker. How can they argue orally when they can't argue on the written page?'

It's important to take a break when you are using your mind in such an intensive manner. Leslie lives three blocks from her office, and usually returns home to take a good solid hour for lunch, without working on law. It is a necessary time to relax and reduce the stresses of the day.

An influential tool for building respect from clients and colleagues is appearance, in the office as well as the courtroom.

I think it's important when you are going out to see a client, or going out to a meeting, to put on that 'mannish look', but I also think it's important for women to retain their individuality.

One of the partners in our firm is a woman, and she is a dynamic litigator. She specializes in going into court and making the arguments and planning the strategy of a trial. She's really hot, and she wears dresses more than she wears suits. She will always wear a suit to court, but around the office, she wears a really elegant dress. I advocate that. I think it's important for women to have their own style.

It is important to put yourself together well. Even if you are wearing a dress, accessorize and package yourself. People are looking at you as a first year associate, and seeing if you've got what it takes to get to the top. One of the things they look at is what you look like.

In many respects, law school doesn't teach you how to be a lawyer, it teaches you where to find the information you need to be a lawyer. It is more of a theoretical atmosphere than a practical one.

As an associate, I am as much an apprentice as anything else. I really don't know anything. I can go out and find facts and apply them, but every time I get a new project, I am operating from a base of ignorance until I go out there and research and find out what I need to know.

Now, after working for eight months, I am experiencing the joy of attacking projects where I know something about them because of the work I have done in the past. It's great because it really cuts down on time. I was spending a whole lot of time learning, one thing I wasn't prepared for.

The second aspect of practicing law that Leslie wasn't prepared for was the realities of practice. She began to see the effect of the work she was doing. "Some of the things I have worked on have affected millions of dollars. That's a little nerve-wracking."

In the private sector of law practice, you may not always believe in who you are defending.

If you happen to be a crusader, you can go into public interest law, or you could be a public defender. There are a couple of cases that I didn't enjoy working on because I really didn't agree with the position of our client.

I hope I don't get over that. I am learning how to separate my private thoughts from my professional duties and obligations. Hopefully, I will fulfill those duties and obligations and still retain my moral integrity.

A major advantage to the law profession is the financial compensation. The pay is good, and the more you work at it, the better it gets. As an associate in this type of firm, Leslie is on salary.

It means that often I work very long hours, weekends, and this year I worked on Thanksgiving and Christmas. That's the big drawback. When you are an associate, you are slave labor. I am lucky to have found a firm that doesn't want to work its associates too hard. There are firms, especially the prestigious firms, where first year associates work until 11:00 every night.

A law degree in and of itself can lead to a number of careers. Practicing law in a law firm is not the only working situation available. You can go into the corporate sector, associations, many different areas.

Also, as a woman, a petite woman, the law degree gives me instant clout and prestige and authority. It's rather bogus in my mind, but it's very real to many people. They automatically respect me.

I have been very pleasantly surprised by a lot of the older males. They treat you with a great deal of respect as long as you are intelligent and back up what you say. If someone doesn't treat me well, I simply overwhelm them with logic.

In most law firms, promotion is based on performance as well as the length of time you have been practicing with the firm. You will not be considered for a partner until a certain number of years have passed. It varies from firm to firm, but is generally around seven years. There are raises in pay along the line, and after the prescribed years have passed, your performance, in terms of work and the number of new clients you have brought into the firm, will determine promotion to partner.

Leslie cautions all potential law students to be very certain that they indeed want to be an attorney.

A lot of people go to law school because they can't figure out what else to do. They should look at all of their options. Talk to lawyers. If they have friends whose parents are lawyers, go through a day with them. Talk with younger attorneys also. Find out what it is all about.

Once the decision has been made to enter law school, get as much practical experience as possible while still in school. There are clinics in law school where you can involve yourself in a law student support program. For example, every school has a moot court program where you learn how to brief, and how to argue in a competitive situation.

For me, doing practical things during law school made it more enjoyable. Otherwise, it's just a paper chase and you don't feel connected to what you will eventually be doing. You don't see the meaning of it. When you don't see the meaning of something, it's hard to do it. When I started doing practical things, I said, 'Ah, now I see why this is important. I guess I can put up with it.'

Plan ahead toward the type of law practice you want to eventually enter. Think about the size of firm you would like to work for. Different areas of law attract different kinds of people. You must make a decision as to where you will feel most comfortable.

I personally like the size of this firm because it's flexible. It doesn't have hierarchies and bureaucracies that are cast in stone. It doesn't need to be. If I wanted to, I could come in at 10:30 in the morning and leave later in the evening. Nobody is watching me, as long as I get my work done.

The flexibility is really nice is a smaller firm. I can walk into the name partners' offices anytime I want and sit down and start talking to them. It's a big benefit to be able to gain from someone else's knowledge. In the larger firms, a junior associate really doesn't have that access to the senior partners. You are really pigeonholed into one little niche that you have to work in.

Larger firms may have more prestige, and they pay more, but you also work a lot harder. I didn't want to have to work so hard that I would have no personal life.

Leslie's third piece of advice is to maintain a positive personal life. Be happy outside of your profession.

It's important to realize that your personal life is as important as your career, because without a good personal life, your career is not going to be good.

SANFORD GAGE

Personal Liability Lawyer

Seated behind an enormous desk in front of a panoramic window is a man who truly enjoys human beings and all of their differences. People fascinate him. He listens with genuine interest. Within the minds of men and women are worlds that will never cease to amaze him. Sanford Gage has been a practicing attorney for the last 26 years, and he loves his work.

Generally speaking, Sanford is a personal injury lawyer, representing injured victims, the plaintiffs to a lawsuit. The defendant is the person or company being sued. He sees himself as a modern day Robin Hood taking money from the rich insurance companies and distributing it to the poor, keeping a bit along the way to allow him to continue on a regular basis.

A senior partner in his private law practice, Sanford's days are divided among the court and the office. The days in the office begin at 8:00 in the morning, an hour before the phones start to ring. The peace and quiet provide the perfect atmosphere for concentration on matters that have accumulated overnight.

Sometimes there are memos from other lawyers to review, sometimes there are files for me to look at. Generally I organize materials that I want to cover on the cases that I want to work on.

A good portion of the day is spent on the telephone with clients, other attorneys, and matters in the courthouse. The firm institutes a careful screening process when interviewing prospective clients.

We do our initial intake by telephone. If it sounds as though we might be able to help them with (their case), and might be interested in pursuing it, we will either have them come in, or if they are unable to come in, an investigator or lawyer will go to their home or the hospital.

Sanford will personally see a client if he feels there is a special reason to, or simply because he has the most time to do so. Otherwise, a law clerk or other attorney will initiate the interviewing process.

We listen to the client on two levels. One level is what they tell us. The other level is testing it against what we think we will be confronted with. Does it sound logical? Does the client sound accurate and honest? Is the wage loss provable? Did they get to a doctor promptly, or are they stopping here before they see a doctor? Will he or she make a good witness? Right at the outset, we want to feel good about representing the client, and have them feel good about us.

On occasion, a verification of the client interview is needed before a decision can be made to take the case. Generally, however, the decision is made during the interview, and the terms are discussed.

The cases in a personal injury practice are handled on a contingency basis. If the attorney recovers nothing, the client pays nothing. Conversely, when they do recover, the attorney's share is usually a third of the collected amount—determined by the type of case and whether the case is concluded early in the litigation or only after trial.

The fees are based on results. It is the inherent risk to the business and increases the lawyers need to select cases likely to be successful.

Technically, the client is obligated to pay costs. Attorneys are often called upon to advance the costs of litigation. This is understandable because if it is a severe injury, the client will not be working and will have increased medical or hospital expenses and can't pay the bills. Usually, it's impossible for the client to handle the expense of investigation or of getting experts lined up. The lawyer will often take this risky responsibility. The client is obligated for it, but frequently, if the case is not successful, they simply cannot pay the lawyer back.

A continuing aspect of the practice of law is the handling of the case itself. In Sanford's practice, the initial steps often include filing the lawsuit and undertaking "discovery". The discovery phase is the process of obtaining information from the opposition.

We may take a deposition, which is testimony under oath, in our office or the other lawyer's office. Everything that is said is recorded, then typed up. It has the same legal force as if they were testifying in court.

Again, the attorneys make an evaluation on two levels: what is actually said, and the credibility of what is said. Additionally, the attorney submits written questions to the other side, and they in turn submit questions to him. The opposition answers their intentions and their witness statements, and the attorney follows up on the information received.

At this point, the case is reviewed, and the attorney advises the client of the information he or she has learned. The ensuing step is to document the file and reassess the client's position.

In rare instances things will develop during the handling of the case that may suggest that we shouldn't represent the client.

It is an ongoing, time-consuming process occasionally involving legal research. In a law practice where the concentration centers on personal injury cases, much of the research is medical in nature.

If we are involved in a medical malpractice suit, we want to understand what the treatment was, and so on, so we can translate it into money damages. Witnesses aren't going to cooperate by giving nice simple answers in simple terms. You have to be able to understand it, and come back with even tougher questions.

Sanford's working day ends when he has put out all the legal fires for that day. As he makes each move, he will always have an opponent whose job is to tell him that he's wrong.

It is not uncommon for me to leave at 6:00, or return and do additional work at night and on weekends as well. It's enjoyable, though, like a contest.

Some cases are settled out of court, some can only be presented effectively in a trial. Many cases are settled because the economics of litigation require settlement. Expenses in taking a case to trial include the time necessary to present the case, the expense of presenting expert witnesses, and jury fees. A delay of several years is not uncommon. "Obviously, with a badly injured person, it doesn't do much good to get the money seven or eight years later."

There is also pressure from the court itself. Judges realize that if every filed case went to trial, there wouldn't be enough judges and courtrooms in the world to handle the litigation in a city the size of Los Angeles or New York alone.

A day in court. Young law students dream of the day they will be let loose to sway a jury. There are two types of court days: actual trials, and other types of court appearances. Non-trial matters include requests for court orders, settlement conferences, or motions to dismiss the case or obtain an early trial date.

Trials are the reason many attorneys seek a personal injury practice, one of the more interesting aspects of law, with the greatest opportunity to excel. Modern cases are fraught with intricacy and complication. There are expert witnesses and a great number of bright conflicting lawyers and parties involved. The average case may remain in court for three to four weeks.

An enormous amount of skill is required to be a successful trial attorney. You must have the communication skills to elicit convincing evidence from the witnesses as well as present that evidence effectively to the judge or jury.

There's a little bit of the actor in each of us. You have to be able to present things in an interesting fashion. Although we like to feel that the judge and jury will understand the merits of the case and make an appropriate award, justice is far from perfect. The skill of the lawyers on both sides has a lot to do with the outcome of the case.

Sanford prefers to try a case before a jury. His experience indicates that a jury is more likely to listen to a case in terms of the dollar evaluation.

If we have a serious case, the jury will give us the current market value of those injuries. The judge often has to overcome a built-in feeling. How can he or she give you what you are asking for, when five years earlier, in a similar case, they awarded less money?

Another reason is that we try a fairly large number of insurance cases involving punitive damages. On the question of punitive damages, judges are innately conservative on awarding substantial amounts.

Intellectually, the practice of law is continuously stimulating. Sanford cites this stimulation as the greatest advantage to his profession.

It's constantly interesting. It astonishes me each time I find a legal point that I am learning for the first time, or a new point that is being raised for the first time. I am a student. I like the learning process.

For the outgoing person, the law profession offers the chance for flamboyance, the visibility of newspaper and television coverage, and the excitement of courtroom drama. Another advantage is the opportunity for enormous financial rewards. The reverse, however, is also true. Competition abounds within the law business. In many areas of the United States, the profession is over-populated.

At the entry level and in the earlier stages of law practice, it may not be particularly financially successful. It takes a lot of money to research cases, and for beginning lawyers there is a lot of risk. You need a very strongly developed sense of self, and a fairly good ego. It can be very time-consuming and stressful because your payment is tied up in the results.

I've often said that every family of four should have at least one lawyer in it. There seem to be a lot more legal issues than are currently being addressed. More people are willing to hire a lawyer and stand up for their rights.

When setting up a private law practice, it is essential to understand that aside from your mastery of legal concepts, the practice of law is a business. Realities in the day-to-day running of an office must be faced.

Nobody in law school taught us how to set up forms and procedures. Nobody told us how to organize material. Nobody taught us how to handle the accounting function, or to be sure that we properly kept records and accounted for things. The complicated matters of running an office, the hiring and firing, ordering of equipment, the practical business end of it was never part of our theoretical law course.

You must learn how to evaluate a personal injury case, how to go out and investigate it, and select experts. In law school, I never learned how to go about getting clients, how to keep them satisfied, or how to map out my daily activities.

Preparation and faith in your abilities are essential tools in exploring possibilities in the law profession. "There are still good opportunities, still good earnings, still good potential. And at the top, there is very good potential."

PATRICIA BRADY

Probate Lawyer

Patricia is 62 years old. After twenty two years as a legal secretary, she took the plunge and became an attorney. Now, her three year old practice is flourishing, sooner than the generally accepted time period of five years to set up a solo practice. She is an intelligent, competent women, with the determination to go after what she wants and obtain it.

People take a look at these wrinkles and assume that I have been in practice for many years. I would never lie to anyone, but it has worked out beautifully.

At 17, Patricia got her first job in a law office where she kept three sets of books and did all of the legal secretarial work. She made $45 a month, and stayed at the attorney's office for two years gathering invaluable experience. Patricia witnessed firsthand the ins and outs of an attorney's life. As a legal secretary, she picked up skills in tact, spelling, and the oral and written skills necessary to be a successful practicing attorney.

Lawyers didn't feel threatened by a secretary who remained in the background and kept her ears and eyes open. Because you can hide as a secretary, attorneys under pressure would give a little bit of their strategy in discussions, so I learned about strategy from working as a secretary.

Patricia landed her next job in a criminal and family law firm. Then, she learned how to do a divorce.

During World War II, I was doing five and six divorces a week on my own where I even signed the lawyer's name to all the pleadings. That was a great opportunity.

The firm had the second largest probate case in the state, providing the perfect opportunity to learn about federal taxation in probate estate. That is Patricia's current specialty. She was 20 years old when she first learned about probate.

In her job, Patricia Brady became editor of *The Legal Secretaries Handbook*, a reference guide of legal procedures, directing legal secretaries and new attorneys how to get the paperwork to the courthouse without getting it kicked back. Attorneys know the theory of law, but many don't know how to get it out on paper, and correctly to the court. She continued her career by conducting educational programs, teaching adult education and legal procedures for legal secretaries.

One day, an attorney and educator contacted Patricia to see if she could gather some legal secretaries together for a seminar aimed at explaining exactly what one did when one studied law. Patricia got about 300 legal secretaries together and sat with them in the audience. After hearing what the study of law was all about, she decided that she would go to law school. "I felt I had done my share of working all those years, and it was a good time to study law."

Each morning at 4:30, Patricia was awake and reading law books before putting in a full day at the law firm. Four nights a week, she attended a university on her way home from work. She took the accelerated part-time course of three and a half years, and made "Law Review" her second and senior years. The extensive experience as a legal secretary was immensely helpful.

I typed the bar exam, and I was thanking God as I was typing. I was so relaxed watching everyone get hysterical. I could type a hundred words a minute. It gave me a lot of time to pour it out through my fingers. I got calmer, and kept thinking, gee, even if I don't pass, it is such a thrill to actually know after all these years, what all these lawyers had gone through to take the bar. It was really quite exciting.

Before entering law school, Patricia knew that she would practice probate law. She had done probate for the last ten years, and had been answering lawyers' questions for years.

I knew what I was doing. It was a matter of getting the actual license to practice law. The courses they teach you in law school don't give you that information.

The minute Patricia opened her law practice, the phones began to ring. Legal secretaries have referred clients that their bosses couldn't or didn't want to handle, other attorneys associated her in on federal court cases because it is another area that she knows well. People have picked her out of the yellow pages. "I don't have a display ad, but being close to the beginning of the alphabet helped." She knows probate, and other attorneys know that she does and call her for assistance.

From the age of 17 to her graduation from law school, Patricia always worked for someone who told her when she could go to lunch, when she had to be in the office, and when she could go home.

I never thought of myself as being independent, but the minute I was sworn in, I realized that I wasn't going to throw away that part of me that went into studying law.

Her days are erratic, and she deliberately keeps them that way. If she should chose not to come into the office some mornings, she will make it up on the weekends when there are fewer phone calls and interruptions. At least twice a week, Patricia goes to the courthouse for hearings or filing. She arrives at least an hour ahead of time.

Since the hearings are usually in the morning, and I cannot stand the thought of being late to court, I plan to eat breakfast downtown.

Patricia does her own courthouse filing. She has to be at the courthouse anyways, so brings a briefcase full of filings with her. An advantage to doing your own filing is that you have a firsthand opportunity to stay on top of new filing procedures.

Upon her return to the office, there are telephone calls to return, mail to open, and letters and other matters to dictate into her Dictaphone. Occasionally she does her own typing, but has a secretarial service for the bulk of the work.

Normally, people are not coming in and out of the office. The initial contact is generally made by phone, and Patricia tries to stack all her office visits into one or two days a week. For the remainder of the week, she is reading or researching.

I do a lot of reading. Most lawyers have to. I read all the appellate cases in the legal newspaper, and read and clip anything that has to do with probate or taxation. I go to several bar associations. I go to a lot of continuing education of the bar matters. I may spend an average of two hundred dollars a month on education.

Continuing education is only one of the expenses that a private, solo practicing attorney must incur. Patricia spent $5,000 for books that barely fill four shelves. "Some of them you can just throw away at the end of the year and get a new one, $50 each."

There is a two-year lease on the rental of her office space, and the monthly payment is $610. Rent includes a receptionist to answer the phones and greet the clients, distribution of the mail, and a message service when she is not in the office.

It cost me about $1,000 or so to get my lines through their switchboard. I had to buy my own phone. I spend $250 to $350 a month on telephone bills.

As a legal secretary, Patricia had worked her net income to over $2,000 a month, plus the extra benefits available to employees, insurance, sick leave. As a practicing attorney in a solo practice, she didn't take home that kind of money for the first couple of years.

I would have to get a $200,000 estate every month to make that fee. But, I figured that if I was going at this late date, I would have to see what I could do all the way. If I joined a firm, or became a partner, I would never know.

For a beginning attorney without the background and experience that Patricia Brady had, she advises taking the exact opposite route than she did. "Get with a firm, get a salary, and get trained."

Attorneys pay malpractice insurance just like a physician does.

For example, if I am preparing a will and my client tells me, 'Look, I have three sons. The one no-good who is on cocaine, I don't want him to have anything. I want him cut out of the will, and the other two kids to inherit.' If I somehow word the will improperly, the third kid could come back at me.

You must keep reading and keep up with the law. In probate law, for example, there are certain cases where notices are required to be sent to particular people. If the attorney doesn't research and find out all of the little things, each time, she might find herself up against a malpractice suit.

It's very important. If you don't have integrity, you really shouldn't be a lawyer.

In law school, I used to giggle to myself when the rest of the students and I were scurrying under the impossible time demands they made on us. Students would say, 'It's ridiculous that we have to do research now. When we're lawyers, we'll hire someone to do the research.'

I always worked for the senior partners in large firms. The associate attorneys would have to do research, but the senior lawyer never relies on their research. They do it themselves, too. You have to research yourself or you can't argue effectively. You have to be sure your reasoning is right, based on the law.

An advantage to the practice of law is that the attorney can truly help people in an effective way. He or she can really make a difference.

A disadvantage to the profession is that once you get into a case, you can't get out without your client's consent.

Sometimes you get in, and it turns out not to be so good. You don't dare give away the fact that your client has a lousy case. So, you are sometimes stuck with some less-than-beautiful cases.

Prepare yourself for the time pressures that will constantly be upon you as a practicing attorney.

You want to turn out a perfect product that has all of your marvelous thoughts. You write and rewrite, edit, but there is a time barrier. I worked 18 hours one weekend for something that was due Monday morning. I got to the point where I had to say, 'That's it. It has to fly.' That's what the other side is doing.

There is the pressure of thinking against time, and the mechanics of getting it out. So, if you can't take the pressure, you shouldn't get into this kind of work.

JOSEPH GUTIERREZ

Public Defender

A quiet man, well-dressed and groomed, extended his hand in a firm greeting. Born and raised in a tough neighborhood, he was no stranger to the workings of the legal system—from the other side of the law.

I had a couple of contacts with the law, and my brother had a couple of contacts with the law. A couple of times my brother was represented by a public defender. He was a balding guy with a corduroy jacket, with something like 10 clients that day. Still, he managed to have enough time to sit down with my brother and me. He showed a lot of interest in us. I admired that and thought that if I ever became a lawyer, I would like to be a public defender.

Joseph Gutierrez has been with the public defender's office for four years. During law school, he clerked with the office to insure that he would be hired after graduation. He has always had feelings for the underdog, and finds the public defender's office the perfect place to please his social conscience. He tends to represent a lot of minorities, indigent people, and people that have never had much going for them. There are, however, frustrations inherent to this type of client list.

Sometimes you'll represent a client who's indigent. He'll be charged with a felony. Bail is set at such a high amount it's like no bail at all. It will take you five or six months to get to trial, and I believe that he's innocent. A young man will sit in jail for six months when he's innocent.

Joseph's established office hours are from 8:00 in the morning to 5:00 in the evening. Quite often, the working day extends beyond 5:00. He has his own office, "It's a little cubicle, fairly private." A legal secretary is assigned to six or seven lawyers, or more, depending on the work load.

He spends nearly every day at the courthouse, appearing, filing motions, discussing case settlements. A lot of his time is spent at the county jail discussing cases with clients who are in custody.

I try and take one day off to go to the jail. Many times I'm not able to, so I spend my afternoons, an hour or two, at the jail.

Supervisors look into each attorney's work, occasionally sit in the courtroom and watch the progression of a trial. For the most part, however, the attorney is free to represent his or her client.

Joe's office handles only criminal cases. He is not allowed to handle any private cases, and when hired, signed an exclusive contract.

In most instances, a public defender has a very heavy case load. The Constitution guarantees each citizen the right to a speedy trial. In a misdemeanor case, if the client is in custody, he has the right to trial within 30 days of his arraignment (when the client is called before the court to answer to the charge against him). In a felony trial, after arraignment in superior court, the client has the right to jury trial within 60 days of his arraignment.

I am assigned to a felony courthouse, so all I handle are felony cases. I average about 24 cases a month. These are cases that I will handle from the prelim to the jury trial, if there is a jury trial.

Before the preliminary hearing, Joe interviews the client. A preliminary hearing is the municipal court hearing designed to determine if there is a strong suspicion that the accused committed the offense. In cases that are very involved, Joe might discuss the possibility of continuing the preliminary intake with the district attorney.

If a strong suspicion is established, the next step is to go to superior court.

We are arraigned in the superior court. That's where the process of motions, court trials, jury trials, plea dispositions, and hearings start.

For Joseph Gutierrez, the most interesting part of his profession is the trial. In his four years with the public defender's office, he had tried approximately 60 jury trials. The trial experience is unequaled in the private sector. There is the additional advantage of learning about different judges, their idiosyncrasies, which judges are good on particular cases, and which judges are difficult.

If every case went to trial, the system would break down. So, it's important to have a good rapport with the district attorney and the judges so that you can dispose of the cases that should be disposed of. You need the judges and they also need you, so it has to be a working relationship.

Unlike attorneys in the private sector whose business fluctuates, a public defender receives a steady paycheck. Other advantages include, civil service benefits and guaranteed vacation time.

There are a lot of lawyers out there. It's not that easy to be in private practice.

Conversely, the case load is heavy.

Each case takes a litle bit out of you, so you find yourself getting drained. You spend a lot of time in jails and a lot of time listening to problems. There is a great deal of sorrow that you are exposed to, and many times you are in a negative atmosphere. It affects people personally.

As a young law student anxious to defend the public, Joe had thought his job would have a greater impact on people, more of a positive effect on human life.

There are clients that are very appreciative of what I do. There are clients that have been influenced and become better people because I have represented them and spent time with them, and reached a result that came from a lot of effort and concern. But, those are rare cases.

M. ROSS BIGELOW

Superior Court Judge

The judge's chambers. To the spectator, the judge enters the courtroom through a secret doorway and vanishes through the same door at the end of day. Behind that door is an office lined with law books, a house for the judge's oak desk and large swivel chair. It is an office with a bathroom, and a closet where the black robes hang.

The largest trial court of unlimited jurisdiction in the United States is the Los Angeles County Superior Court with an authorization of over 200 judges. The Superior Court is one step below the Court of Appeals which is one step below the state Supreme Court. The number of Superior Court judges in each county is determined by the Legislature as are their salaries. The judge's term is six years, and vacancies are filled by the Governor.

Judge M. Ross Bigelow was originally appointed to the municipal court bench in 1969. He has a Bachelor of Science degree in Mechanical Engineering from The University of Southern California.

When the war was over, I had the GI bill and felt that I should go to graduate school. Engineering wasn't going to be my cup of tea. In my mind, engineering was to qualify me to be a naval officer, so I didn't want to get a master's degree in engineering. Medicine and dentistry didn't sound good. I decided to be a lawyer.

In 1950, M. Ross Bigelow graduated from law school. After his recall in the Korean War, the young attorney hung a shingle out in the new Southern California city of Lakewood and set up a general law practice. To make a name for himself, and gather business for his fledgling law practice, Mr. Bigelow joined civic organizations like the Elks, Rotary, and Junior Chamber of Commerce.

For about the first six months, I did nothing more than pay expenses. Finally, I settled my first personal injury case, and got a real fee. From then on, I took off like a bird as far as earning money.

With another attorney from his law school class, Mr. Bigelow went into partnership. Through the years, he became more involved with Republican politics and was asked to be a candidate for the State Assembly.

My wife and partner said, "Oh, no!" and I turned them down. Two years later, someone by the name of George Deukmejian ran for the same assembly seat. I am very glad that I turned them down and George is where he is today, Governor of California.

When a new judgeship was added to the municipal court, Ross made it known that he was interested. He met all of the qualifications, and was appointed.

Four of us were "down-to-the-wire" candidates. I just had the inside track. That's all there was to it.

After a judge is appointed, he or she must run at the next general election. It may be six months away, it may be a year and a half away. Judge Bigelow has never been opposed in his two elections as Municipal Court judge, and three as Superior Court judge.

Judges must maintain a balanced judicial temperament, and remain reasonably courteous to attorneys and witnesses. Attorneys who work with the judges will know if a judge is not performing up to judicial standards, and it is an attorney who may create opposition in a general election.

The law determines the eligibility requirements for judges. You must be an attorney for a minimum of five years before you are eligible for appointment as a Municipal Court judge. Superior Court judges must have a background of 10 years of practice and/or a combination of 10 years of practice and a seat on the Municipal Court bench. The next step up each state's judicial ladder is the Court of Appeals, then the State Supreme Court. Typically, judges work their way up from the Municipal Court bench.

Many of my colleagues have spent two to four years on the Municipal Court before being elevated to the Superior Court. Some of them come directly out of practice to the Superior Court, but the

Governor has indicated that he wants to see people come up step by step, although he is putting some people into the Superior Court directly from practice.

Judge Bigelow is currently a Superior Court judge in civil court. Civil law is the body of law dealing with the rights of private citizens. Other courts in the Superior Court include, criminal, juvenile, and probate, among others.

Court hours begin at 9:00 a.m. and end at 4:00 p.m. A typical day in Judge Bigelow's Civil Court involves a jury trial. With the jurors, the judge takes testimony from witnesses, documents into evidence, and hears all the facts pertaining to the case. The morning session lasts from 9:00 a.m. to noon, with a 15 minute break. Essentially, the break provides the court reporter an opportunity to rest from the strain of transcribing all of the oral testimony. After an hour and a half for lunch, the process continues.

Another typical day would be like today. We sent our jury out two days ago. By sending them out I mean that we finished taking all the evidence, heard the arguments of the attorneys, and I instructed the jury on the law. I then go into chambers and work on Submitted Matters.

Submitted Matters means that I have tried a case where the jury was waived to me. It's a case under submission. I have to make the decision. I do my own research and write my Announcement on Intended Decision. The Statement of Decision will be based on that, then the Judgement.

Other matters arise and must be taken care of. There are motions for a new trial in a case that was previously heard, motions to tax costs to allow attorney's fees, and motions to set attorney's fees from other civil cases which the court has already handled.

I also get requests for voluntary settlement conferences. I try and sandwich some of those in, meet with the attorneys and claims adjuster, hear both sides, and try to bring about a settlement. I give my opinion as to where each side should give a little bit.

In a jury trial, the judge has limited authority to enter a judgment that is contrary to the jury's decision. The judge's reasoning must be clearly substantiated in the facts of the case.

I would be subject to review in a court of appeal. I can order a new trial on all issues or on a few issues. Or, as I have done if I feel that the jury has awarded too much money, will say that the plaintive will either accept a reduction or I will grant a new trial. Subject to the rules of law that govern me, I have final say.

Most often, the court is dismissed promptly at 4:00, allowing for regular daily hours. However, if a witness should appear to be finishing up when the clock strikes four, the judge will keep court open until the witness has completed the testimony.

At home, Judge Bigelow spends at least an hour and a half each day reading law journals to stay on top of the constant changes in procedures and practices of the law.

Our day doesn't stop when we get home. If it does, your learning has also stopped. That's one of the fascinating things about a field like this. You continue to learn throughout your entire career.

Within the Superior Court of Los Angeles County, judges do not set their own calendars. There is a master calendar, and each judge must notify the judicial secretary when they are open. Upon notification, they are immediately sent another case.

We start picking a jury, and going into a full jury trial. I won't report "open" until I have some of these backed up submitted matters taken care of.

For Judge Bigelow, the process of jury selection is the dullest part of the trial. Once the jury is picked, each case is basically different. The differences prevent the boredom of repetition.

It may be the same type of accident, but each one is slightly different. In civil, the variety of cases is amazing. I don't know whether I am just fortunate, but I don't get a whole string of intersection accident cases.

The challenge of the profession is the primary advantage. It is an interesting career that provides the chance to make decisions that the average practitioner would never get.

An advantage is the concentration of one type of law. As judges, we try cases back to back. Attorneys may work on one case for years. It's not the only case that they are working on, but even the best counsel will only try three or four cases a year.

In a large court, a judge with seniority has the opportunity to change to another court. Judge Bigelow spent nearly six years trying criminal cases and grew weary of the gruesome details day after day. Though he is still academically interested in criminal law, the switch to the Civil Court was a welcome change.

Another advantage to a judgeship are the set hours.

I don't think we put in as many hours as practicing attorneys. On the case I am working on now, more days than not, I send the attorneys home with work to do. They go back to their offices, and I drive home.

Judge's salaries are determined by the legislature, and a disadvantage to sitting on the bench is the diminished chance of making as much money as a practicing attorney. However, there is a positive side to a fixed income.

Superior court judges make about $75,000 a year. But, in addition to our salary, there are a lot of side benefits. The county pays over $300 worth of things like premiums on health insurance, life insurance, and dental insurance. After 20 years, I will be able to retire on 3/4 of my active duty pay, and that will go up with the current pay scale for the rest of my life. I can go back out and do whatever I want, whatever tickles my fancy. A private practitioner would have to be putting away a lot of money to reach that same point.

However, judges are under restrictions of routine. They must be in their courtroom at the specified time. There are no Wednesdays off to play golf, no six month tours of Europe. Instead, a judge is allotted 21 days a year of vacation. There is no limit to sick leave, up to six months. If after six months there is a determination that he or she will not recover in the near future, the judicial council will grant a medical retirement.

Each judge is assigned to a specific court. If the Presiding Judge chose to assign a judge to another court, he or she would be obliged to comply.

After 16 years on the bench, Judge Bigelow has found that certain decisions are tougher to make than he would have imagined as an attorney. The stress level is very high.

You are dealing with people in tense stress. Out there in the courtroom, I sit up on that bench, wear a black robe, and am the center of attention almost all the time. I am conscious that I am running that show. I've got maybe four attorneys and sixteen jurors, and what I say goes until they can get me reversed on appeal.

If you are conscientious, it will certainly cause you to be under stress. It's a matter of handling it, what you do with it.

Governors are appointing increasing numbers of women to judicial positions previously dominated by men. To be a judge, you must first be an attorney. In Judge Bigelow's law school class, five graduates out of 110 were women. Women have currently flooded law schools across the United States, and their numbers will most certainly be reflected in future judicial appointments.

Statistics indicate that, for the most part, a Republican Governor will appoint a majority of Republicans, and vice versa. Involvement in politics is one way to move towards a judicial appointment.

They have appointed some judges right out of the State Senate. I don't think you have to go as far as committing yourself to being a politician. I think you should be active in politics, like party organization, because when an opening occurs, something has to bring you to the attention of the Governor. You won't be the only shining light for him to appoint. You will always have competition, heavy competition, and if you haven't paid your dues, you won't get appointed.

Paying your dues is essential. You have to be very good at what you do. There will always be the political side to judicial appointments. Governors want to appoint judges who have a similar philosophical outlook.

WRITING

She broke her ankle and had to stay in bed so she asked her husband to bring home some paper. "I might start a novel," she said. She ended up spending ten years on the project, writing a story about a young woman named Pansy who lived in Georgia around the time of the Civil War. Later, her publisher changed the name of the heroine to Scarlett O'Hara and the book to *Gone With the Wind*. One of the most successful novels ever published in America, Margaret Mitchell's book is still in print 50 years after its initial publication and has sold over 22 million copies.

That's one side of the writing coin. Less known are the hundreds of other novels written by women and men, many of which never find a publisher willing to print them.

This dilemma makes writing one of the most challenging of all occupational fields. The magnetism of seeing one's work in print attracts many into the field. The sense of creativity which comes from completing a writing project provides, at a minimum, psychic income, and may or may not sell enough to support your life style.

The written word passes knowledge, social customs, and pure entertainment from generation to generation. The impact of writing is everywhere around us today. Think for a minute of how it affects your life:

- TV shows, interspersed with commercials
- Direct mail advertisement for products you want or detest
- Birthday or other anniversary greeting cards
- Magazines of general or specialized interest
- Reference books providing information on career fields
- Short stories in magazines or books
- Billboard and other outdoor advertisements
- Daily and weekly newspapers
- Novels and other general fiction
- Instructions on how to assemble appliances

Talent, technique and instinct play major roles in each writer's work, with a key to success found in the discipline to sit down and clearly commit thoughts and ideas to paper.

The reality for most books is, they throw them out onto the floor of the Coliseum in gladiatorial combat with one another. The books that stand up, bloody, but still stand up on their feet, will get a second printing. And this time, the publisher will take out a quarter page ad in the New York Times.
David Chandler, Novelist

The writing business also involves agents, networks, studios, publishers, publications, and a variety of other influences.

You will find that agents are looking just as hard (for good writers) as you are hoping to get in. If your book is terribly good, meaning from terribly good trash to John Updike, they're looking for you.

The secret is to write a book that is so good that if someone reads two pages, he'll want to read the rest of it. You don't go to an agent and say you are going to write a great book. Write it.

David Chandler

There is an old Chinese proverb that a long journey starts with a single step. Few people can predict what success they may have in a writing career. The best advice from successful writers is to write, write, write. Write as much as you can, whenever you can, for whomever you can. Follow this up by reading and rereading authors whose work you respect and whose style you find appealing. Study how they use language, and ask people to criticize your efforts.

Then, when you're ready to sell your work, the first step is to find out how to best present your writing, whether it be a novel, screenplay, teleplay, or magazine article, in a professional manner. With perserverence, talent and know-how, your work will eventually be seen, and possibly sold.

IRVING WALLACE

Novelist (The Seventh Secret, The Miracle, The Word, The Almighty)

Ronald Reagan was his recruiting officer for the army. As a young man entering World War II, Irving Wallace was placed in a motion picture unit writing for films like, "How to Fly." While in the army, he heard that the Signal Corps propaganda unit needed a writer who had spent some time in Japan. Before Pearl Harbor, Irving had been in Japan writing for magazines. He was the perfect candidate for the position and transferred to the new unit—a unit under the direction of Frank Capra. During those years in the army, Irving worked with Frank Capra and John Houston. He learned a lot about movies, and after completing his tour of army duty, went to work in the film industry. But writing for motion pictures wasn't for him—Irving Wallace wanted to write books.

As an author, I am free and independent. I am the producer, the actor, the director, everything.

Now, several successful books later, Irving Wallace leads a life that he loves. His office, built onto his house, is a huge cathedral of books stretching from the floor to the rafters of the endless ceiling. The scent is leather and rich wood. He sits behind a massive desk beside an ancient black typewriter—the tool of his trade.

Sometime about noon, Irving Wallace rouses and faces the day. He hates mornings, preferring instead to work into the wee hours of the morning.

I hated getting up for early classes when I was going to school. I couldn't wait to graduate from high school so that I could keep my own hours.

The freedom inherent in a writer's life impressed Irving. Writing was one of the few professions where he could maintain independence and be his own boss. He liked that. In 1931, he sold his first story for five dollars. "I was a little kid. I said, 'Wow!' "

During summer vacations from his Wisconsin high school, he wrote, starting non-fiction at 17. They were never published, but he continued writing fiction and non-fiction, and eventually began selling his work to magazines.

My first sale was an article, my second sale was a short story. Very small magazines. It was from books like The Writer's Market, *that I learned that there are magazines that pay money. I didn't know that.*

You start with places that pay $25 and $50, and hope you get up to where you get $1,000 or $3,000. That's one writing field. Inevitably, it should lead into books where there's a chance to really starve or make a lot of money.

As a novelist, there are many phases in Irving's work. A substantial amount of time is spent in thinking about each aspect of the novel before he ever writes a word. Research must be completed and an extensive outline worked out. The outline, he stresses, is the most difficult, yet most important, step in the process of writing a novel.

A lot of writers I know have an idea or a character and they start writing to see where it goes. The fact is, it often goes in the wrong place and they don't get an interesting book.

Irving takes an idea and a character, and thoroughly thinks through each move the character will take—his motivations, and problems that can arise in the course of the plot.

For example, here's a black man who is a Senator and by accident becomes President of the United States for two years. I say to myself, what would happen? There are people who would not want him to be President because he's black. Who are they? One of them feels that the Secretary of State, a pure white easterner, should have been President, but he wasn't in line. Then you have a southern Senator, and you have a good friend of the black man . . . that's how it starts. You think it through.

Never show your work to anyone until it is completed.

Too many writers get their kicks through getting compliments by talking about something that's not written. If you've gotten a reward before you've written it, you're liable not to write it. You can go around saying, 'I'm a writer', but you're not writing.

Self-discipline is the key to a successful novelist. There is no one telling you to write but the bills that appear in your mailbox. There are no guaranteed paychecks.

When I was a kid, I admired F. Scott Fitzgerald. I always saw pictures of him on the Riviera with champagne. I said, 'What a life!'

It's not that way at all. Those people, in order to write the books that they wrote, had to sit by themselves in a room, hour after hour, without champagne, without the Riviera, and without women. They had to sit with that damn typewriter, or that pad and pencil. Beginners don't realize how lonely it is. You must have confidence and discipline.

If you are a person who blocks out easily, or just wants a moment of rare inspiration, forget it. None of the writers, the biggest, depend completely on being struck by the idea of the century. They think, they observe, they hope, and suddenly they get excited about something. You learn writing by reading other writers, first for pleasure, then to try and see why they open up this way, and how they introduce the hero or heroine.

The realities are grim. A handful of novelists make a lot of money while the rest starve.

All the publicity you see is nonsense. There are only 15 books on the bestseller list, and even those don't make much money. Some do, but very few make a living. Just because you see them in the store, it doesn't mean they are selling.

The average advance is $5,000 to $10,000. Bookstores return paperbacks and hardcover books after six months if they haven't sold. Success in selling your work doesn't end with finding a publisher who will put your book in print.

Irving Wallace began with Alfred Knopf, a prestigious publishing house. He was pleased to have it publish three of his books, but found he couldn't live on the money the firm offered. Knopf figured "you could live off the prestige."

His following novel was auctioned off.

An agent will get a book, part of a book, or an outline that he thinks is hot stuff. He'll go to six publishers at once, give it to them at the same time, and ask them to make an offer. Presumably, the agent goes only to the best houses, houses that you could live with.

Simon and Schuster won the auction for The Chapman Report *in 1959. I liked them and they liked me, and I made a lot of money for them, and they made a lot for me.*

An agent is not essential, but a potentially valuable asset to placing your book with the right publisher. There are approximately 40,000 new books a year. Irving believes that the 10 to 15 percent commission is well worth it. The problem, for a new writer, is obtaining an agent who feels strongly about your work and will work toward successful publication. With a non-fiction book, a substantial third of the book will usually be enough to spark an agent's interest. Both must be accompanied by a detailed proposal letter encompassing every aspect of the book to be sold with researched information stating its potential market. The agent needs to know that he or she is taking on a capable and well-informed writer. This is no place for dilettantes. Agents want to deal with professional writers who will make a profit.

If you've never been published, it's hard getting an agent, but it can be done. You do it through recommendation.

Writers shiver a lot. All they want to do is get that book out and they are afraid that if they demand too much, they won't get the book published. An agent is worth the 10 percent.

Most of Irving's stories take place abroad. Travel is great, if you have the time and the money. If you don't, research is the next best thing to being there.

You don't have to go there, but it's better to go. When you get there, you get a lot of ideas, make notes in your hotel room, but you come with an idea.

I have to do basic research because I have to know about the subject. For the book I'm doing now, I have to know a lot about the end of World War II in Berlin, and I have to know about Berlin today.

Once, when I was a kid, one of my favorite writers was James Hilton who wrote Lost Horizons *and* Goodbye Mr. Chips. *He was having a book signing party in downtown Los Angeles, so I took a bus down to L.A., bought a book, and had him sign it. As he was signing it, I said to him, 'You know Shangrila? Did you ever go to Tibet where it takes place?' He said, 'Yeah.* National Geographic Magazine.'

Da Vinci never ate the last supper, but he painted it.

Irving Wallace feels fortunate that he wrote four books before reaching success.

I say fortunately, because I didn't come out from under a rock. I'd been writing books and being published by Knopf, but not making a living. I had to work in movie studios, or write for magazines, and write the books on the side. In other words, you work very hard, you don't loaf around much, because you are burning to get into the book field. I had written one novel that was published, but unsuccessful, but it gave me confidence in the fact that it was published. I made a few thousand dollars, and had the confidence to undertake something that was a little more daring, had a few more characters.

Writers are continuously working in one way or another. It's an obsessive profession of 24-hour days, and to be successful, must remain a guiding obsession in your life.

There is no faucet to turn off. I sit with you and I say wouldn't she be a good character for a story. It goes on automatically.

We writers don't retire, as such. You can't turn it off ever. You may not work as obsessively as when you're young. I do try and imagine that I'm working for some imaginary person. I keep a record of how many pages I write a day. It's a discipline. Otherwise, it's just air and blank pages.

On my desk, you will see the oldest typewriter in history. I was 13 when my parents gave me this rebuilt typewriter, I've been rebuilding it ever since.

ELIZABETH FORSYTHE-HAILEY

Novelist (Joanna's Husband, David's Wife, A Woman of Independent Means, Life Sentences)

ROSEMARY ROGERS

Novelist (The Crowd Pleasers, Lost Love, Last Love, Sweet Savage Love, Surrender to Love)

Though the process of writing a book is basically the same for men and women—maintaining the discipline and dedication to commit words to a page—the experience of combining parenthood with the solitude needed to make it in their professions can be dramatically different. These two women writers have successfully combined motherhood with the mastery of their art form—not an easy task.

Elizabeth Forsythe-Hailey began work on her first novel, *A Woman Of Independent Means*, in the morning hours between 9:00 and 11:30—while her youngest daughter was off at nursery school.

I had to write fast. I never had time for writer's block. By the time she started grade school, I had a first draft.

The plan for her first novel was to experiment with a letter format. "I didn't feel that I knew very much about writing novels, but I knew I could write letters." Her initial idea was to write about her observations of all that was happening around her.

My first idea was going to be a book called Letters From A Runaway Wife. *There were women I knew who were walking out on the whole thing—being mothers and wives. My husband said that runaway wives were a passing thing, and they would come to their senses by the time I had the book written. So he said, if you are going to write a novel, why don't you write about a woman who doesn't have to leave home to be liberated? Why don't you write about a women like your grandmother.*

That's exactly what Elizabeth did. After about three years of following her morning writing ritual, the book was ready to set foot in the publishing world and make it or break it on its own. It made it—and was published as a result of a fluke.

There was an agent showing it in New York, and months would go by and we weren't getting any answers. I showed it to the agent on the west coast who represented my husband for television, just to show him that I could write. I didn't expect him to do anything with it. He got kind of impatient because nothing was happening in New York, and a scout from Viking press came through California, and asked if he knew of any manuscripts. He said, 'Well, this isn't really mine to show, but I'll let you see it, but I need it back in 24 hours.' It was the greatest way to sell anything. It was like contraband. So, she was very excited by it, and took 48 hours, but made an offer.

To her pleasant surprise, the book was a success. Suddenly, Elizabeth was a professional writer in the eyes of the world. There were book signing parties and selling tours—and publishers were eagerly awaiting the next one. She felt a change occur.

In some ways, a second novel is always a hurdle for anybody, I think. You have this terrible feeling that you may just have one good book in you—that it was just luck. With the second one, you really have to know what you are doing. Also, I was determined to get as far from the first one as I could. I wanted to write a contemporary novel, and really write a novel, invent a situation, characters.

Elizabeth deliberately turned down a contract in exchange for the freedom to work at her own pace, without time pressure. Like her first book, the second one took about three years from the first to the final draft. Again, success greeted this now-established novelist. *Life Sentences* took off.

I think for a woman, especially, the only hard part is learning to take yourself seriously. I've been fortunate in that, by having my book published so quickly and having it be a success, the outside world reaffirms the value of what I've been doing. But, I have friends with very good unpublished novels, and I know it's very hard.

To all beginning writers, Elizabeth advices preparing yourself for all kinds of twists and turns in life.

This idea that you should know at 18 or even at 21 what you want to do, and go at a straight line toward your goal, is likely to get you in a lot of trouble. I think it's harder for young women today. The pressure to have it all is enormous—to try and work toward your professional goals and at the same time to have a personal life and get married and have children, and do it all at the same time. You can do it all, but you don't necessarily have to do it all at once. I'm glad that I was able to be a full-fledged mother to my children.

When I was working on the second novel, I was thinking that I just didn't have the technique that I needed, I don't have the skill. Here I am, 45, almost 45, and I am a beginner. I needed more time for trial and error, more time to make mistakes. I felt an enormous pressure to be good at it, because I was so late in starting. But now that I have the second book finished, I'm OK. But, I think that there is a time for everything, and I had so much more to write about at 40 than I did at 20. I think that being a writer is one of the few professions in this very youth-oriented country that really considers age and experience an asset. It is something that you can continue to do.

I was an enormous fan of Rebecca West, who died last year at 80, having just sent in her new manuscript to the publisher. Boy, that's the way I want to go, leaving my work behind me, and being in the thick of it right to the end.

Write for yourself. Use your own instincts as a gauge. Most likely, you will find that the world of readers is full of people who feel the way you do, and have an interest in what you have to say.

It's been an exciting feeling. You tend to think that nobody else is feeling all these emotions. It's wonderful to write about something that you feel is very personal and discover that a lot of people share your feelings.

You can't really write fiction without sounding it against yourself. You just hope that you're not alone. Someone once said that a very good rule for writers is to write what you want to read, and that's what I do. I write about things that nobody seems to be writing about, maybe because they think it's too ordinary. I find great drama in how very decent, well-meaning people get through their lives, especially today. There are so many options and conflicts. The outside world is in such chaos. You shoot for the moon, and if you fall short, you just start over.

* * *

A rumor passed through a bookstore behind a Rosemary Roger's display. The people spoke in hushed tones, a bit of envy. "Did you know that she travels around the world, lives her stories, then writes about them?" Oh, what a fascinating and clandestine life!

Rosemary Rogers laughs when she hears this—in reality, she lives in a New York apartment and rarely sees the light of day when she is writing. Her family comes first. She cooks for them, and drops her pen at the first sign that they might need her. She's a mom and her world remains with her family—and within the confines of her imagination. "Most of my novel ideas come from my dreams."

Rosemary has been writing since she was eight years old, inventing stories as a child to tell to her brothers and sisters. She was first published in 1974.

Writing was my escape, really. It was an out for me when the kids were asleep, and I'd done the dishes and the cooking. Everything was done, and I hate the TV, so I would just write. That's the way it still is.

Rosemary does not call herself a romance writer, but a novelist who writes about romance, action, adventure and the development of characters. Her typical day is to start writing at 12 or 1:00 in the morning, and write until about 1:00 in the afternoon. Then she sleeps. The first thing she does when she wakes up is cook. "I am a cook. I love to cook."

A perfectionist, Rosemary is anxious to get her manuscripts back from publishers to reread, and carefully take care of the "picky little stuff". Her nighttime writing environment is filled with soft music, solitude, and the stillness in which she can relax and let inspiration flow from the top of her head. Her routine continues nightly, but she doesn't push it, fearful of stiffling the natural creative process.

Rosemary Rogers sold her first novel "over the transom", meaning she sent a copy of the manuscript directly to a publisher who accepted it. An extremely rare occurrence. Since then, each book she has written has been under contract, and she generally completes them six months to a year before the contract date is up.

And then, they would deliberately hold it back, which used to really upset me. I had a lot of writing packed away in closets. I just wrote for my own release, my own therapy. When you're bringing up four kids, it's not easy.

At the beginning, as an innocent in the publishing world, Rosemary found that she was being taken advantage of.

I did about seven or eight books without knowing any better. Of course, I didn't have an agent. Very few agents take a brand new author.

However, the lengthy, and at times unrewarding task of finding an agent for your work pays off. Publishing royalties don't stop with bookstore sales. There are movie rights, European sales, and other avenues that most writers don't know about. Rosemary learned the hard way.

In the evenings, preparing to write, Rosemary plays what she calls the "what if" game to invent characters and different situations. It is an important step in allowing her imagination to flow freely and allow her to get to know characters intimately.

I even have the background music when I am thinking of the plot. Then, the plots change. All of a sudden, the characters become like living people.

I work from my head and my feelings. I'm an emotional writer.

Her advice: write, stay away a week, then look at your work and be ruthless.

Cut your own book to pieces and rewrite. I have thrown 450 pages away because I was going in the wrong direction.

I have faith. I believe in reading, and I believe in rewriting and polishing.

Know what you want before you get into it. Prepare yourself for a life of solitude. Enjoy being alone. And be prepared for the realities of promotion and publicity.

I want to make up for the things that my children missed out on. It's hard as a mother, trying to make your kids understand, that if I have to go on a tour, for example, I would rather stay home, but you have to explain, and hope and pray that your kids will understand. I want to make up to them for what they've missed.

I don't want the celebrity. I would like to go out and get in a cottage somewhere, and go barefoot, back to the earth. And cook on a wood-burning stove, and have all that I am supposed to have. I don't have to have material possessions any more. I have found now that the most important thing is the truth. I have had people steal money from me. I would have given it to them if they'd asked me. Tell the truth. That's what is really important.

RICHARD A. STEEL

Playwright, Screen and Television Writer (California Crazy, The Stud, The Love Connection)

He lives in a powder-blue victorian house with a Doberman watchdog that is as sweet as a puppy, and a broken answering machine that is missing a vital cord. He is a funny man. A storyteller. The ups and downs of his life provide endless material. No one, not even his mother, knows how old he is, since he has denied even to her the actual facts of his birth.

He is a New Yorker. He had imagined people throwing money at him as he exited the plane in Los Angeles. He doesn't drive. He never quite got used to wearing light colors and wouldn't be caught dead in a tennis outfit.

He misses the late nights and the pastrami sandwiches of Manhattan. He swears that even the coffee is different out here. He wants to go back, but rarely does. It's a "grass is always greener" syndrome. You can take the man out of New York. . . .

Richard has been writing professionally for the past ten years. Even while working as a director of small theater in New York, he never lost his desire to write for the stage.

The theater is more exciting, for me, than movies. Now, I do mostly television. My partner and I write screenplays also, but that is constantly being interrupted by going to pitch television ideas.

At 7:30 each morning, Richard is out of bed, dressed, and sipping a cup of California coffee at his typewriter. He warms-up by writing letters, ideas, or anything that might enter his head. It is a time for thoughts to flow freely. A time to get the creative juices in gear. Afterwards, he is ready to bicycle the two-mile stretch to his partner's house to begin work.

We usually schmooze for a while. The most difficult thing is getting started. It's easier with a partner, because the partner feeds into getting going. Well, it could be the opposite way also, because the partner could say, 'I'm tired', and that's all you need, someone else to blame for not working. Immediately you go into, 'Let's have some breakfast. Let's go have pancakes.'

The first step is the daily scan through the newspaper for story ideas.

Every television writer, and every screen writer in Hollywood is doing exactly what we're doing, going through the paper with a fine-tooth comb to find one thing that will spark a story to sell for television. I think this is how the newspaper survives.

Currently, Richard, and his partner, Arlene, are writing a screenplay based on an actual event found in the newspaper.

A man and his wife tried to defraud an insurance company by faking his death in a rowboat. He and his friends went out fishing, and they came back and claimed that he had drowned. They were all soaking wet, and it all looked incredibly legitimate. He had heavily insured himself before this. Three of the insurance companies started payment immediately. The others held back because they claimed it wasn't an accident. One of them, responsible for most of the insurance money, smelled a rat. They investigated it for over a year and tracked the guy down in England.

So, when we read this, we knew there would be a lot of people writing this up with all the dramatic intrigue. But, we found it hysterically funny. What if the guy was John Candy? He plots this mad idea, and his wife, once he is supposedly dead, starts getting all this money. She begins to really enjoy it. She has a Mercedes, she has furs, she starts dating other guys, and she doesn't want this fat man back. He has no way of coming back. If he did, he'd go to jail.

On the average, the partners work four to five hours each day. In the morning, they decide on a goal of completed pages or completed hours, and stick rigidly to their objective.

A treatment for television is the synopsis of ideas in a narrative form. It is a brief, yet descriptive capsule of your ideas for a television pilot, series, or episode. A part of any television writer's work will be the writing and presenting of a treatment.

There are a lot of adjectives used to describe how funny, and wild, and zany it is, and how marvelously entertaining and fun-packed it is. Sometimes we will put in dialogue, but we will always make it funny, so the person reading it will laugh.

Generally the process is as follows: Richard and Arlene will call a producer, tell him that they have a great idea, and set up an appointment to pitch the idea to him. If the producer responds positively, he will ask them to write a proposal or treatment and bring it to him.

After the producer sees it, he'll either say, 'I like it, I'm going to try and get us an appointment with the network', or he'll say, 'Thank you, but I don't think this quite works. If you ever have anything else, bring it in'.

Unless you already know someone who can give you a "leg up", it's next to impossible to get a foot through a major producer's door.

Although, when I first got to Los Angeles, I never had a problem. I always managed to get in even without an agent. I think I was just gutsy then. I would say, 'Hey, I'm in from New York, I've got two minutes, I want to see you, I've got some great ideas'. They would see me all the time.

Now it's different. I think there's more paranoia around with people getting sued all the time. People are a little crazier now.

One of the secrets to success in scriptwriting is cultivating the art of making contacts, and the finer art of maintaining the preparation required to take advantage of opportunity when it does arise. When you do get an appointment with a producer, you'd better have something terrific to show him.

Once the producer has set up an appointment with the network, he will accompany the writers to the meeting. The network meeting is a time to pitch. The ability to effectively pitch an idea is generally considered the most difficult, yet most necessary aspects to writing for television and motion pictures. It is a process of salesmanship. You are not selling your well-practiced ability to write—you're selling your idea to network executives.

It's a very weird procedure. Arlene and I rehearse it. It's a major thing. We figure out who is going to say what. If it's comedy, I would dress funny. I would even dress light.

It's always a very tense situation, even though there's always an air of real friendliness involved.

The first time I ever pitched anything to anyone, was to Universal. To this day, I don't know how I got this appointment. I went up to pitch three series ideas to them. At the time I didn't even know what pitch meant. I went to the black tower (at Universal), and all these executives were sitting in front of me. They said, 'O.K., pitch'. I didn't even know what they meant. I had three proposals in my mind, all nicely typed, bound, and I thought, I've written it, go ahead and read it and tell me whether you like it or not. They didn't want to read it, They said, 'Tell us about it'.

In the network meeting room, there are several people sitting on a couch ready to be entertained and sold on your idea.

You do about three minutes of insane kibbutzing. You say, 'Oh, I love the color of the walls. Gee, your view is fabulous'. It's that kind of nightmare where you are trying to find things to talk about to ease into this thing that is about to come up. It's totally insane. Arlene and I just laugh and joke with each other for a while, and hopefully something is going to happen.

Everybody's tense. The producer is sweating because he stands the most to lose in the project. And then we have to sell it, just one idea. You are trying to be as funny as you can. It's so hard. If there's no reaction, automatically Arlene and I start skipping less important characters.

It has nothing to do with writing. You're selling. It's always the writer who has to do this. The producer sits back and watches this spectacle unfold, occasionally commenting on it. If we may have said one thing that goes just the wrong way, too defined, he'll come in and say, 'But we could go this way, too. It's not too right, we could go left with it too, it's sort of a left-right character'.

The process of pitching is contrary to Richard's belief in what the true art of writing is all about.

Writers are not known to be particularly aggressive in that area, that's why they became writers in the first place, so they could sit at their typewriters and not have to deal with people. In Hollywood, you have to be a salesman.

Some fine writers, dramatic and comedy, are really not particularly articulate when it comes to their own work. You have to go in and say, 'Look what's happening in the world today! It's this, it's that! It's Name of the Game and Wild World of Sports! It's Barney Miller and Cheers! It's the perfect vehicle for . . .'. You really have to get them at every angle. It's so hard to do.

During the pitch, the network people take notes. They rarely take the proposal you have so carefully written. Notes in hand, they approach their supervisors, the men and women holding the power to make the decisions. In that meeting, they discuss the idea that the writers and producer presented. "Then you wait. Usually it's immediate, although in both cases I've been to the network, the decision took a long time."

At the end of the process, one of the network's options is to take the idea, but get another writer to write the pilot.

They can buy the show, and you get X amount of money, which is not a lot of money, and a percentage, which is minimal. However, if you write the pilot, you get a nice amount of money for writing it, plus a big chunk of the show. There are a lot of writers who don't come up with any ideas, but who write pilots based on other people's stories.

The writer then has the option of refusing to sell the idea unless he or she writes the pilot.

But, basically, you only have three places to go. CBS, NBC, and ABC. Sometimes they'll go with you. Sometimes they'll want you to write it in collaboration with another writer who has done a lot of sit com pilots. I can understand that. They have to protect themselves.

Richard sees the advantages and disadvantages to the writing profession in terms of comparisons between writing in New York for theater, and writing in Los Angeles for movies and television.

In New York, as a writer, as a playwright, no matter what the company, whether it's Broadway, or a tiny company, when the writer comes to rehearsal, there's a hush. There's awe. There's coffee poured. People say, 'I hope you don't mind, but I'd like to change a dot to a dash'. Or, 'I'm having trouble here. Do you think maybe we could cut this word?' There's this incredible respect for the word, and for the writer. Actors and directors will be hovering around your every golden word. And at the end of the week, you get $2.50 for all this respect.

You come to Hollywood, and you walk into an office, and the secretary says, 'Oh, the writers are here. It's down the hall, right next to the closet. You know your office, it's the one with no windows'. You are thrown into that room, and chained to a desk for twenty hours a day. Everyone from the producer to the janitor has rewrites for you, and is telling you what's wrong with this thing, and is keeping you there demanding rewrites. You are thrown old bagels that the secretary no longer wants. No respect what-so-ever. And at the end of the week, you get a check for $25,000.

To me, that sums it up.

BERNARD SLADE

Playwright (Same Time Next Year, Romantic Comedy, Tribute)

A small cabin in Mendocino, perched on a bluff overlooking the ocean, is the setting for the filmed version of Bernard Slade's play, *Same Time Next Year*. The Broadway production was a smashing success—years later, it's still produced all over the world. *Tribute. Romantic Comedy*. Bernard Slade has a string of successes.

Endora popped in to cause problems for Samantha and Darrin. Sister Bertrille flew over the convent holding onto her aerodynamic habit. The Partridge Family rehearsed in their garage. *Bewitched*, *The Flying Nun*, *The Partridge Family*—more Slade success stories.

Bernard Slade, playwright with three Broadway hits to his credit, created television shows, has written screen adaptations of his plays, and his plays continue to draw large audiences all over the world. He is a talented, successful writer who has worked hard to obtain and maintain his success.

The Malibu home, with its sliding glass doors open to the sounds of the ocean, provides the perfect environment for writing. Bernard, fiber point pen in hand, sits alone in his home and creates.

Bernard Slade began his career as an actor. He was acting in a play when he decided to write a television part for himself. The hour television play was sold, but he wasn't hired to play the part.

I think it helps writers if they can be actors. They don't have to be good actors, they can be terrible actors. Some writers are not equipped to be actors at all. Tennessee Williams was never an actor, or Arthur Miller. But, I think that you do pick up a lot by osmosis, and by seeing everything that you possibly can. I was fortunate that I made a living for ten years as an actor, working constantly. I was in front of an audience practically every night.

It's especially important when you are writing comedy. Even if you are just starting, get involved in amateur productions so you can see how a play is put together work from a practical basis.

Bernard Slade was born in Canada and educated in England during World War II. His family moved several times during his youth, and consequently, he attended about 15 different schools.

At the time, I didn't like it. Looking back on it, it was probably an advantage in a sense because it gave me exposure to all sorts of places and people.

He isn't convinced that a college education is essential to being a good writer. If you can afford the time and expense of college, it is an opportunity to absorb a variety of information and experience. English literature courses provide a valuable literary background, but the most important thing is to write.

Most writers are readers on their own anyway. They are self-educated. Many great writers had no college degree.

There is a famous writer, I think it was Sinclair Lewis, who was lecturing and he asked, 'How many here want to be writers?' About 90% raised their hands, and he said, 'Then why aren't you at home writing?'

Bernard Slade holds the belief that writing talent will show up early in a young person's life. It isn't something that someone can merely decide to do.

It's always rather offensive to me when someone, say 40 years old, says, 'Oh I think I'll write'. If no spark of talent has ever shown up, they might as well say, 'I think I'll become a concert violinist, or do brain surgery next week.'

Writers are avid, avid readers. There is a fascination with fantasy and the printed word. I don't think it is something you choose to do, I think it's something that chooses you. It's very difficult, and there is enough rejection and pain that you better have this tremendous desire to do it.

There is a vast difference between writing plays and writing television. In the late 1950's, finding a greater market in television than in theater, Bernard wrote what were then essentially one hour television plays.

So, if I was going to do a pilot, like I did for The Flying Nun, *my attitude was, 'If I have to do this, it's going to be the best possible* Flying Nun *that there will ever be'. You can't go in with the idea that this is junk and write down to your audience. It's like people who think they can turn out a bestselling novel. They think that it is beneath them, but they could turn out a Harold Robbin's novel, whatever. It's not that easy. The point is, when Harold Robbins writes, he believes in it.*

Currently, most television half hour comedies are three camera shows on tape or film. They are staff written. A writer completes a script, and during the rehearsal process, the staff writers revise continuously until the show is shot.

I would find that very difficult to do because I have a great sense of pride about my work. As a matter of fact, when I first came down here, somebody changed two words and I screamed bloody murder. I felt that if things had to be changed, as they often do because of the practicalities of the business, I wanted to be the one to change them.

For Bernard, one of the main problems of writing television is the fact that you are a "literary mimic". The characters have already been created, and the writer must try to copy them.

It defeats the purpose of what a writer really should strive for, or find, which is his own voice. That can only come out if you have the freedom to create on your own. It isn't something you sit down and analyze, but every good writer will develop one over the years. It often has to do with one's background, a style, a reflection of one's tastes.

In television, the problem is, that if you are commissioned to write something, you give up the freedom of what to write. It's a little like being a tailor. You want the pants a little shorter? You have to know the rules and do the best possible work within those rules.

In the theater, the playwright has enormous control. He or she has approval of the casting, the director, and is intimately involved in the physical production of the play.

The fact of the matter is, if you are going to be a writer, you have to consider the fact that you must go into a room and be alone. I am naturally gregarious. One of the things that attracted me to the theater, and one of the reasons I write today, is that I write to go into rehearsal to meet new people where there is a social activity.

Bernard Slade's typical day varies with the point at which he is involved in a play. "There is thinking time and writing time, and often I will think about an idea for a year."
When he is writing, he writes every day for about five hours with a fiber point pen and a pad of yellow paper.

I don't use a typewriter. I write long hand, so I can write sitting anywhere. I used a typewriter until I came from Toronto to Los Angeles. I was so anxious to get into the sun that I started working with a pad outside and have never gone back.

I find that I edit less when I write with a pen. Writers get caught up in certain kinds of fetishes. I buy fiber point pens. I like physically seeing something on paper. Other writers get hooked up with technology and get into the latest typewriters and word processors. It's got nothing to do with writing.

It's not the first draft, but the 14th draft that separates a professional from an amateur.

With the first draft, your internal editor should not be at work too much, you should just let it all come. Slowly, you start to look at the material and your editor starts to work—you refine it. Sometimes the chemistry and the dynamics of the characters don't quite come off, and so you are refining and trying to capture the essence of those people. Sometimes it happens very quickly and very easily.

With Same Time Next Year, *I wrote it in six weeks, and it was pretty much the version that was performed. One of the characters in my next play,* Tribute, *the one that Jack Lemmon played, was based on someone I know so it wrote very easily. The boy, however, (in* Tribute*) who was 22 and sort of unformed, was very hard. I did a lot of drafts of that play.*

A mistake that many writers make is to think in terms of plot rather than character. Bernard emphasizes that the characters are the most important aspect of good writing. They must be real, interesting, and unforgettable.

Often a very good actor works the same way a very good writer works, they write in character. A first class actor is very specific in his sense memory. When he is portraying someone, he is using part of his life, and it is a specific image that he is carrying in his mind. With a writer, it is the same thing. You have to get inside that character. Something mystical happens.

If you look at great plays, they have wonderful characters in them. In A Street Car Named Desire, *you think of Blanche DuBois or Stanley. There's Willy Loman, Hamlet, whatever, it's the characters that made it, not the plot. Narrative is important in that you should constantly surprise the audience, in a way that is believable, but you generally start with a character.*

If a writer is male, then people think when they read his work that the male character is him. They never think that he wrote the female characters, too. Quite often, the women I write about are much more like me than the men are. Most writers, if they are any good, are adrogenous to a certain extent.

A negative aspect of a writer's life is the fact that he or she can easily miss out on life itself. You must stand outside of life and observe. "Even when you are going through an emotional experience, there is a part of you saying, 'I must remember this, this is how I felt'." The cliches about a solitary life are true. A great deal of time is required to sit alone and daydream.

Essentially writing is daydreaming. You are fortunate if you get married and have someone who will create a world where you are left alone. It becomes obsessive. It has to be to be good. Often, you become much more involved with the characters you are writing than sometimes with your own children. There were whole years when I was young and writing all the time, that are a blur to me. I can remember shows I was writing.

The amount of stress carried by the playwright can be enormous.

There is nothing I would think more stressful in writing than having a show open on Broadway. Everything is rolling on one night. You have put a lot of work into it.

Someone once asked a writer how long it takes to do a Broadway show. He said, 'Four years. One to write it, one to get it on, and two to get over it.'

On opening night, Bernard is rarely in the audience. "Often, I am somewhere throwing up." It is a night to face the critics. If they don't like the play, it won't run.

Theater reviewers are more vicious than any other sort of reviewer. They generally write about the writer. They treat you as if you have committed an ax murder sometimes. For a young writer, it can be really devastating.

Bernard Slade has three Broadway hits to his credit, and a play that closed in one night.

It does damage you. When the play closed, I really thought I was going to get through it unscathed. I thought, 'I am due for a flop'. The percentages of hits are very rare. I thought that I went through it fairly well until I started to write again four months later. I got a panicked feeling that I was sitting down to write for a year to see if one critic from the New York Times *likes it. It blocked me.*

To stand in the back of a theater and witness a thousand people laughing or crying with your characters, however, is a playwright's delight, and the reward for the long hours of work.

There is nothing like it in the world. There is a tremendous elation when something does work. Writing is the celebration of the human condition. It doesn't mean that everything has to have a happy ending, but if you are writing about life, you are celebrating life. It puts people back in touch with what is good about themselves. There are tremendous rewards. You really have to want to communicate, it's not necessarily that you have something to say, it's that you want to say it.

A successful Broadway play can insure financial stability for the rest of your life. The play may lead to a movie sale or be produced all over the world with the resulting royalties. "Even if the play is not adaptable to the screen, if it's successful, it's like the stamp of approval."

People always ask what you learn from more, success or failure. People always say failure. Well, it's untrue. Success can teach you a great deal. What success does is give you the encouragement to go on and fail, to take chances, risks. Failure tends to make you draw in and start to pull back to the tricks that you know have worked before. That can be death as a writer.

Experience teaches you a certain amount of technique and allows room for the confidence to write more. Writers tend to write about people of their own age group, so a young writer with minimal experience can capture the essence of youth. However, one success doesn't insure another. Each attempt speaks for itself.

Each time you go back and sit in front of that piece of paper, you are starting from square one. Of course, you have a certain knowledge, but the world is littered with people who have had one great novel or one great play.

You are going to get rejections. It doesn't matter who you are. If you are successful, they will want to read it, but that doesn't mean they will want to do it. It's very difficult to know who you should listen to. There is an old saying that if 15 people tell you that you're drunk, you'd better lie down. If you are getting the same reaction from that many people, maybe you should listen. But in the past, I've had rejections where I have been stubborn about something, and I was right.

Part of the talent of writing is observation. It is essential to observe people in a variety of environments and experiences. A good way to observe is through a variety of different jobs. Learn about different professions. Put yourself in situations where you will come in contact with people you might otherwise never meet.

The danger of writing is that you get too reclusive and cut off from the world, and are essentially writing about the world from memory.

Read everything you possibly can, and see as much theater as you possibly can. With that background, write, write, and write some more. The technique of writing improves with execution.

You are going to fail if you think that you can just sit down occasionally and dash something off.

LAWRENCE J. COHEN AND FRED FREEMAN

Television and Motion Picture Comedy Writers
(Start the Revolution Without Me, Empire, The Big Bus)

The small campus theater was filled with students. It was the week of finals. Guilt descended—they should be studying. As an enticement, or tension relief, the campus advertised a rest from the weariness of exams. *Start The Revolution Without Me*, 7:00 Tonight! A funny, wacky, departure from reality.

Lawrence J. Cohen and Fred Freeman were the brains and wit behind the movie. As they wrote each scene, behind the closed door of an office suite, they knew little of the effect they would have on future graduates. They would have been proud to have heard the laughter resounding through the aisles on that tense day so many years later.

Larry Cohen always wanted to be a writer, a comedy writer. He wrote for a year and a half before joining forces with Fred Freeman and they have been a successful writing team for the past 20 years.

Fred Freeman began writing in his sophomore year at Northwestern with a college buddy, Gary Marshall. They combined their talents in school, then met again a few years later and wrote together for five years. They worked daytime jobs and wrote comedy at night before landing a job as writers for Joey Bishop.

It was a difficult experience because Joey was a difficult man, but it was training, and I don't think there's any better training today. We really had to work hard to develop stories and characters.

Larry and I were more attuned in terms of point of view, our work was more satirical, so we just got along together.

Larry and Fred currently work for MGM Studios developing ideas for television and feature films.

In our biography we say that we met at a dance, but actually, we met during the Army reserve. We talked about doing something together. It was at one of those Monday night meetings where you put your uniform on over your civilian clothes.

The studio provides a guaranteed salary, a suite of offices, a secretary, and general overhead in exchange for their exclusive services. The two adjoining offices provide a place to work together, and a smaller office for privacy and the opportunity to take care of ongoing business.

Their working day varies with the stage of productivity. A lot of time is spent in coming up with ideas.

Over the years, you learn that you shouldn't really be pressing to get the ideas, but you still do it. You know from experience that the ideas will come, and something will happen.

It's nice to have an idea that you want to write, in contrast to coming in and trying to think of something to write. It's easier doing the actual writing than it is just sitting in a room with someone for 6 to 8 hours trying to come up with something.

Fred does the typing.

In the idea stage, we are bantering ideas around. Sometimes I feel that a better way to write is when you have an idea, if you have the energy and the discipline, sit down and start writing it to see where it goes. You may end up with two pages, and just throw it away, but having something on paper is much better than not having something on paper.

When the actual writing commences, the days are long and intensive.

When we're really working, and are very busy, it is all day long, and I would say at least two or three nights a week, and very often Saturday. The hours are very, very long, the work is very, very intense. It's very exhausting.

Basically, their working style is to talk through an idea, work up some dialogue, then get it down on paper. Occasionally they split pages or scenes, or take a body of the script to work on separately. If one partner is stuck, the other partner will work on it. A team effort in the truest sense of the word.

> *The difficult part is when neither one of you has an idea. As a matter of fact, we have just gone through a three month period, a very difficult period, one of the most difficult that I can recall, in which we were both really dry. Nothing was happening, there was nothing that we were interested in doing. It was very frustrating, we were sleeping a lot. This came off of producing the 6 shows of* Empire.

Empire, created and written by the Cohen/Freeman writing team, was a comedy show that aired for six episodes before the network cancelled it.

> Empire *was a show that (the network) knew was a high-risk show. The kind of material that Fred and I are attracted to is very often unusual and offbeat. We seem to do things that other people don't do. We don't do conventional situation comedy.*

> Empire *was a dark comedy, it was a look at the corporate world which no one had explored that way on television before. It's one of the few things that we thought turned out reasonably close to what we wanted. It was one of the best realized things we've done.*

> *The network was very uncertain about it. Our sample and our trial on the air was so short, and the 8:30 time slot, that we thought was too early, was against some very difficult competition. After the third episode, the show was not doing the numbers and the network was not going to stay with it any longer.*

> *The networks are having a lot of doubts about the half-hour format. They are going more into hour comedy-adventure, and less and less into the straight half-hour.*

The ratings will affect, to a certain extent, what you write if you want to get your show on the air. "The danger is when you move too far away from what you do best."

> *Things have gotten a little bit worse, I think, in the last couple of years. Even if you get something on the air, you have about three weeks, and if the ratings aren't there, the show is over. Unless someone at the network, obviously the president of the network, or someone like that, loves the show and is going to stay with it.*

Write where your talent lies. Do what you do best, and try to work it into a marketable script.

> *Our talent is of a satiric side although satire is not very popular, so we try and get a little bit away from satire, and do stuff that has a broader appeal, but we can still throw in a little.*

The major misconception that Larry sees beginning writers carry is the assumption that if you sell something, it is going to be seen on television or in the movie theater.

> *There is a great deal more development than there is production. For each series that winds up on the air, the one or two that get on the air are the result of maybe 500 ideas that started at the beginning of the season. The chances of something being produced are rather slim. A person can be very busy, and very productive, and considered very successful, and someone will say, 'Gee, when can I look for something', and you have to say, well, I don't know. My last picture actually produced was eight years ago, but Fred and I have been busy all the time.*

Fred believes that beginning writers mistakenly feel that it's going to be easy.

> *Once you get into the form, the realities of television, the problems that are presented, the time frame, you have such a short time to write it, a short time to write and produce, it's harder than you think.*

There tend to be more partners in comedy writing than in dramatic. You have an in-house sounding board. In difficult times, the loneliness of a writer's solitude is eased by another person who is experiencing the same frustrations.

Additionally, a partner provides a built-in discipline. Each partner encourages the other. Conversely, the inherent nature of a partnership requires compromise.

Sometimes you have to compromise, or accommodate something that you may not be totally supportive of. You have to allow for the other person, so you can't do everything that you would want to do if you were working alone.

A certain amount of dependence builds within a partnership that can stifle the creative process.

It's more a psychological, emotional thing. You're not doing the work on your own. I feel that it's important for each of us to work on our own, maybe more so than we do. It's like, when you have an idea for something and you immediately bounce it off someone, it can help, but very often what happens is, it will dissipate because you haven't thought it through enough, and you aren't steeped in it enough. I think that you have to be a little more involved in it yourself, then you can bounce it off someone.

The biggest advantage to working for a studio is financial. There is guaranteed income. You are paid in an overall development deal, a basic fee, then credits are applied against that fee for work that you do. For example, if you write a pilot script, a certain amount of dollars will be added to that amount.

There is hardly any freelance business left, and you'd probably not make the money in television unless you wanted to just write anything, take any show. Most television writers will have studio deals, or be on the staff of a show. They have a certain guaranteed income also, and sometimes they have to deal with a studio, and sometimes not, depending on their status or how well-established they are.

Fulfilling and prolific partnerships rely on the personalities of the partners. There must be a basic trust in one another. "It's like a marriage. Over these last years, I have probably seen more of Fred than I have of my own family."

Hold onto your own ideas, and take care to listen carefully. Effective handling of both egos will insure a positive working environment.

We've been on both sides of having something dismissed. I think it's harmful to do that. It stifles the creative process. You have to allow something to live and to blossom, and then you can look at it and say, 'Naw, I don't think that will work.'

I think that there are always going to be ego problems, but you just have to learn to live with them, and deal with them in such a way that it is not destructive. If something is a good idea, and it isn't yours, you have to allow it.

In television, a successful show is a ticket to freedom.

If you have a successful TV show, you're going to be making money, and you're going to be in demand. Whether the show is quality or not, if it's successful, you're going to be doing well.

When you become a professional writer for television, let's say, you're not like a good novelist who writes to express themselves. You do get certain chances. The price you pay is that it's not in the mainstream, and if it's not in the mainstream, you're not always going to be commercially successful.

The most effective way for a beginning writer to bypass amateur status and write a professional script is to carefully read scripts that have been sold and/or produced. Learn the form. Realize the limitations of the hour or half hour format. Scripts are available through the library of The Academy of Motion Picture Arts and Sciences.

Most people look at TV and say, 'I could write that.' Occasionally, you'll find someone who can. But, there is a certain amount of professional quality required. One of the ways to get that professional quality is talent, and the other way is knowing the form.

Even after writing successfully for 20 years, Fred and Larry still feel the insecurities of the business. It comes with the territory. Contracts expire, shows are cancelled, and success comes and goes with the changing market.

I remember once going to New York, and I had an "in" to meet the head writer of the Sgt. Bilko Show *which was a hit at the time, I was about 19. He said, 'You've got to be prepared to sit in a roomful of writers, throw out an idea, and everyone will just stare at you like you're crazy and say that's the worst idea they've ever heard.'*

When you have a lot of egos involved, you're going to have a lot of people that say, 'Oh, that stinks.' They are going to have their idea. You have to believe in yourself. Somehow, you have to find a way to really believe in something, and feel strongly about it.

TONY PEYSER

Freelance Writer, Playwright
(Danny Irvine Always Has a Good Time, What I Did in the Seventies)

His office is tiny, clean and white. A particle board desk supports neatly stacked files indicating pending jobs. It is a warm place with every available space utilized. Newspaper articles clutter the bulletin board. A revolving paperback library stands by the door. "Kathy loves Sluggo" is punched out on shiny black tape from a lettering device. He thinks of his new bride every time he looks at it.

Each item is a special memento, each piece of paper makes him smile in recollection. They keep his mind fertile with new ideas relating to past subjects. He is always thinking. Scheming and scamming. He knows what it takes to do what he wants with his life, and he does it.

Tony writes all kinds of things for all kinds of reasons. He has supported himself since 1975 as a professional writer.

I've written plays, screenplays, television, advertising copy, cartoon strips, radio ad copy, print advertising, trade articles, freelance journalism, and ad copy for trailers.

At 8:00 in the morning, Tony is up with his wife having breakfast in their apartment. By 9:30, he's seated in his office, behind his desk, ready to begin the day.

At that point, I have usually read the Los Angeles Times, The Herald Examiner, *and* Variety, *and then I am ready to start working. If I have an assignment, I will continue working on that. I will always try to make some other contact with people.*

In a way it's harder than having a regular job because with a regular job, you go home at 5 o'clock. Sometimes I work here at the office. Sometimes I work out of my apartment. I don't really have the sense of going home even when I do go home. You know that you can always be working harder, you can always be writing.

As a freelance writer, there are short term and long term projects. Tony does not let a day go by without getting on the phone, talking to people, trying to get jobs. The largest portion of his current income comes from writing motion picture trailers (previews), and advertising copy for radio and print.

Trailers are the coming attractions. When you go to a movie theater, you usually see two or three trailers before the feature film. It's whole industry, because if you can create some sort of excitement off of a trailer, it can be a huge factor in determining the success or failure of the movie.

There are about 20 trailer companies in Los Angeles and a few in New York. In most cases, the producer of the movie will not produce the trailer, but the studio will hire a trailer company to take clips from the film and put it together with appropriate copy.

Sometimes, this is a rare case, I have written trailers when I haven't even seen the film, I have just read plot descriptions. In some cases, the films weren't even shot and the trailers were being made, for film festivals, for example.

You are writing the narration. An example of the process goes like this: This morning, I got a call from someone I had been recommended to. I went to meet with him, we agreed on a price, and he said, 'O.K., I have a project for you. It is a Michael Keaton movie called Johnny Dangerously.

As it turns out, I already worked on the print campaign for this movie, and as it turns out, he had copies of some of the print ads that had been done in test markets, some of which I wrote. That was nice. He wants me to write the trailer for this movie, so he gave me the script, I'm going to see him on Friday, look at what they have of the movie, then we will sit down, and he will tell me what their approach is, how they want to position the movie in the audience's mind. I will then go home and start writing.

Trailer scripts are normally about one page long, and the writer does about 10 scripts per assignment. The shorter the better. It is a fast-paced process. It's not good enough to be good. Everybody wants everything yesterday.

The people who produced the movie spent all that money to get it down to two hours. I have to now get it down to two minutes.

This type of writing is specific, paring the words down to the essence of the motion picture.

You can't just tell the plot, because if you just tell the plot, in a very straight forward fashion, who's going to go? You have to make it exciting.

Another professional hat that Tony wears is that of playwright. In a small theater in Los Angeles, he produced his original play, *Danny Irvine Always Has a Good Time*. Tony remembers the experience as one of the best of his professional life.

I came up for an idea of a play, and wrote a first draft in basically one night. That was really half the play as it evolved, but I showed that to people and got their involvement.

I'd been going to plays every day for six months, and I didn't see anything that wasn't within my realm of doing. You can learn from the good as well as the bad because there were certain choices that were made. I've probably learned more about writing plays from seeing bad plays than good plays.

A friend co-produced the play with him, and acted in it. They hired a director, and needed to fill the cast.

There were four roles in the play. The pivotal role was Danny Irvine, because we needed someone who was 12 years old. As it turned out, I had seen a good young actor in another play and we went to him. He agreed to do it.

Next, Tony and his co-producer placed an ad in *Drama-Logue* announcing auditions. They held auditions in their office and saw 40 or 50 different people, before making a decision.

We did it as cheaply as it is possible on earth. We had to rent the theater.

One theater charged a flat rate. I mean, we're not talking about a huge theater, 22-28 seats only, so we are not talking about a great deal of money. With the other theater, there was a basic rate, plus they got a percentage.

The producers coordinated all the advertising and contacted the newspapers. The play ran for about three months, two months in one theater, and one in another. The total cost was approximately $2,000, and they broke even.

If you really believe in something, those first things that you do, you have to do it yourself, because nobody is going to have your enthusiasm.

As a freelance writer, you are always looking for some kind of calling card. A calling card is something that shows a certain mastery in anything. Now, I have a terrific one act play, with reviews, that I can show to people. That's something that I didn't really have before, not only a good piece of work, but some validation to it.

There is a certain quality of salesmanship required to be a freelance writer.

I remember years ago, I met a couple of guys who were friends of a friend. They were a writing team, and I remember saying to my friend, 'Gee, you know, one of those guys is really funny, but the other one isn't'. So my friend says, 'Yeah, the one is real funny, but the other is the salesman'.

I was thinking about "Death of a Salesman". The whole Willy Loman notion really depresses me, out there selling yourself, going out on the road. I could never do that. Then I realized, that's what I do. I just do it over the phone.

Tony feels that the worst aspect of freelance writing is the fact that you can write an article for someone who appears to love it, but they still retain the option of turning it down and not paying you. In advertising, the pay scale is better, and they pay you whether they like your work or not.

A big plus is that your time is your own. At one point, Tony made the decision that he needed a raise, and gave himself one. His price went up.

I used to hate the part of having to be here by myself, for hours, days, weeks, months at a time. But, at this point, I'm much more organized than I used to be. You have to be really committed to it.

In freelance writing, it is important to find a way to make a living while you are compiling pieces that will bring more work your way. There are trade publications on a variety of subjects. Flowers. Cars. Computers. It isn't necessary to know all about the subject, you can ask questions and inform yourself as you go along. The important thing is to gather published work.

People want some kind of assurance that somehow this has already been approved or sanctioned or legitimized in some way. If you know someone, they say, 'Yeah, I know his work, it's good'. If you've been published, they say, 'Well, that thing ran in the Times. *The* Times *isn't going to run garbage. O.K. we'll give you a shot'.*

The *Writer's Market* provides a wide range of publications to choose from. Updated yearly, *Writer's Market* is a source book for writers with the names and addresses of everything from religious magazines to gag writing opportunities. Persistence will get you published.

You have to write something on spec which is a nice way of saying, no money. You're going to have to write it up yourself, and try and get it sold, cold, unless you know someone.

Most publications have guest columns. There are places where you can absolutely get things published.

In almost every newspaper in America, there's an opinion editorial page. In the Los Angeles Times *it's called the "Op Ed" page, and they will run guest editorials, short pieces, maybe 1,000 words, by readers. They are very often personal. It may have to do with a death of a loved one. A friend of mine wrote one about driving back to the home town where he grew up. They are personal stories by readers. They don't pay much money, but, the person who edits them, only reads things by people who are unknown. You are competing with people basically on your same level of experience.*

If you've been published, it's like gold, because then you go to the best copy place in town, make nice pretty copies, and send them out.

Make your life happen. Commitment and determination are the keys to success in the freelance market.

The world is not a casual place these days. You can't have a casual career, or one by accident. You have to absolutely make things happen.

* * *

A resounding bit of advice shines through all of the writer's experiences. Get published. You don't have to hold out for Simon and Schuster. Send material to local magazines, and other publications, increasing your chance of getting your work read by someone who reads beginning writers consistently.

Writing and selling your work can be a frustrating and lonely experience.

There is a whole new phenomenon called the mid-list, and the big publishers always want winners. They say this guy has been published for 25 years, and he's been all over, but he has never busted out. We can't afford to pay him his advance, we'll have to pass on that book. William Kennedy, who just won the pulitzer prize, was turned down by 13 houses.

David Chandler

ACTING

Scores of young men and women daily dream of entering the competitive field of acting. They see fame and fortune, worry over the odds against success, crave their moment upon the stage.

Divine appointment. A golden ray of light breaking through the clouds. A tiny, yet insistent, voice beckoning from the footlights. The calling cards of the profession?

In reality, most actors had a positive early performing experience, a glimpse of the profession through friends or family, or a desire to break from a traditional working situation and enjoy the experience of creating other lives. They feel most alive when performing.

This year, thousands of high schools, colleges and community groups will produce plays offering the opportunity for a beginning actor to test the waters and develop his or her craft.

The acting profession is unionized. The Screen Actors Guild, for example, has around 63,000 members today while the American Federation of Television and Radio Artists (AFTRA) reports 80,000. These numbers, however, reflect some overlap of statistics as many actors belong to both unions. Membership eligibility requirements are available by contacting the union offices.

In the working world, many actors are forced to earn income from other professions while they pursue their dream. Few earn adequate livings in the early years of their careers. A study made by the Actors Equity Association reported that of its 35,000 members, only 15,000 earned any money from acting in 1983. Of these, 4,700 made less than $2,500 while 6,000 earned between $2,500 and $35,000. Of the total of 35,000 members, only 650 (or less than two percent) earned $35,000 or more during the year. A similar report came from the Screen Actors Guild which said that only six percent of its members earned $25,000 or more from acting in 1983.

The prestigious Royal Academy of Dramatic Arts in London, its graduates including Peter O'Toole, Sir John Gielgud, Trevor Howard and Glenda Jackson, receives about 1,000 applications each year and admits only 20.

Despite the odds, many people do break into the field each year. They feel the excitement of opening night, the thrill of audience applause, the love of their art and the chance for creative self-expression.

Like any other competitive business, the best preparation for a career in acting is talent and knowledge of the field. With accurate information and expectations, you can give yourself a contender's edge.

BERNIE KOPELL

Actor (The Love Boat, Get Smart, That Girl)

Looking back through years of memory, he thinks about his first paid acting job. It was a miracle. Pay for work that he loved. Now, after eight years of driving to the same television sound stage, he still feels the same way.

In a business where the overwhelming percentage of actors don't work and have difficulty making a living, happiness is tomorrow's call sheet with your name on it.

Bernie Kopell. He's a talented and successful actor with his feet firmly on the ground. He has cultivated the ability to extract life's positive elements and flatly refuses to dwell on the negative. In 1958, he began acting professionally. But before that memorable year, he studied, and was strictly trained, at New York University.

People talk about carrying a spear in Shakespeare. I held a spear for two years before I was permitted to say anything. It was extraordinarily formal by today's standards. It was 'Keep your mouth shut and watch the actors that we deem are fit and qualified to say Shakespeare's lines.'

One of the results of this type of formal training was a proficiency in technical ability, but a lack of experience in performance.

I was very speechified. I was aware of having come from Brooklyn. I was aware of the horrendous speech patterns that were all around me. I didn't want to sound like that. I felt that I would be holding myself down, so I worked on trying to sound like people from other areas.

Landing in California to launch his career, Bernie came face-to-face with the realities of the business of acting.

I didn't know what I was selling. That is a big, big factor. What are you marketing? Let's be realistic and call this a market. It is show business. It doesn't go if there is no business.

I was told by casting people, 'You're not ugly enough to be a heavy. You're not handsome enough to be a leading man. What can we do with you?' It was a very valid question that I didn't have any answers to.

I found myself sitting for a very long time asking myself, 'What am I selling?' Then, by accident, I discovered that I could do accents.

After hanging around a theater group watching, learning, hoping to be hired, he was offered a non-paying role playing a 55 year old dentist from Oklahoma in a six-month run of a play.

Some people think at a certain time that it's an advantage to use you because they don't have to pay for you. It's before you get into the union.

It's not a terrible thing in the beginning to do things for free. It's a great opportunity. How you live is perhaps less important than doing something to advance you toward your goal.

Everyone else in the cast was getting paid, so I had to swallow my pride, but I was in a professional company, and going through the routine and beginning to understand what it was to get a laugh.

The experience proved invaluable. Each night's performance provided new insights into Bernie, the working actor—a new role for him. Soon, an evolution occurred. He was 27 years old, with pancake make-up, a fake moustache, and grayed hair. It worked. The package he presented to the audience and cast worked—he was able to show his marketability.

I showed these people that I was reliable, sincere, capable, professional. I could deliver.

The next thing that came up in the theater, they moved me in after somebody else opened the play. I got paid that time. I remember looking with awe at this check for $33.35 in big stamped numbers. I said, 'My God! I am a professional actor.' I still get excited thinking about it.

Financial success came later. To support himself, Bernie drove a taxi, was a stock boy at a Blue Chip store, and sold Kirby vacuum cleaners.

I was always determined that acting would be my area. I really didn't want to do other things with the exception of jobs to sustain my life.

Some actors advise planning a back-up career as a safety net. Others suggest jumping right in. But, sometimes when you have a net, you'll use it when you feel you're too close to hitting bottom.

There are many roads to Rome. There are many roads to ruin as well. Everyone has their own approach to things. After all of these years of experience, I would never say that A is right and B is wrong. Go with your own individual voices.

I can remember from my days of therapy, the doctor said, 'Consistently and persistently pursue your goal.' I remember being so frustrated. I had gone out on 60 or 70 commercial interviews, and nothing was happening. I was ranting and raving in his office and he said, 'Are you finished?' After I had exhausted myself, I said, 'Yes, I am finished.' He said, 'Keep on going out.'

If you understand what your goal is, you will have unsuccessful attempts. In studying biographies of anyone who has done anything, the thing you notice is that they fell on their face again and again and again. The point is, you get up and get back in the race.

Developing patience is essential. There is a certain continuity and consistency to careers. One milestone will trigger something else. Often, it will seem that nothing is triggered for a long while, but everything you do is important.

There is a very powerful philosophy that I just happened to stumble on when I was selling vacuum cleaners in 1959. Someone had a record playing in the back (of the store) and a voice was saying, 'Your mind is as the earth. Whatever you plant in your mind will grow. If you plant onions, you get onions. If you plant potatoes, you get potatoes. If you plant negativity, you get negativity. If you plant positivity, you get that.'

Rather than accept tons and tons of negative that has been passed on from generation to generation, unquestioned, let these things dissolve and chose the things that you want. This has been a great sustaining, working philosophy in my life.

Bernie Kopell currently plays the character "Doc" in the long-running series, *The Love Boat*. The lifestyle of an actor in a television series is perhaps the most even of any other acting job. It's a five day a week job. It takes six working days to produce one hour-long episode.

Most often, Bernie's call to the set is at 7:15 in the morning. Occasionally he is called in earlier and can leave early, and on rare days, he is not called in at all. Generally, however, he puts in a full day, arriving home from work at about 7:00 in the evening.

I get up at 5:30 in the morning, very grateful, very pleased to be getting up at that strange hour. If I'm working all day long, then I don't have to bother about occupying myself. But, there might be a day when I'm in the first and the last shot. This means that I'll have a lot of time. So I say, 'This is your life. What are you going to do with those hours?'

I learned Spanish. I brought in Berlitz cassettes and learned a fairly good working Spanish. I've read some wonderful books. I've co-written eight of the shows.

Generally, there's ample time to study lines during the day.

That was another hang-up I had at the beginning. Years ago I was going with a girl who said, 'Oh, you'll never guess what happened! I was on The Donna Reed Show *and just before shooting, they came over with these big script changes and I had these long speeches and I had to change everything.'*

When I heard that, my heart turned over in my body and I thought, 'Maybe I'll stay out of the business another few years until I am ready to deal with this'.

Early in my life, I was told by an authority figure that I had no memory. So, that became my law. I believed I had no memory. But, I do have a memory. I am now the authority in my life. Now I'm "ring-wise" and know what I can and cannot do.

Although Bernie has the experience and the confidence to know that he has enough time to learn and deliver his lines with assurance, he does study his scripts at home each evening.

Sometimes in television, there is a glib approach of 'Why bother really studying this?' But, I like to study the script as much as I can to give myself the benefit of the doubt. I like to relieve as much pressure as possible on that magic moment of truth when I'm in front of the camera and 75 people are back there expecting a professional job.

Never minimize that. There is always someone as good or better than you waiting to come in. Before your body hits the ground they will recast. There is no time for indulgent nonsense.

After eight years as one character, Bernie sees it as an advantage to have character recognition. It's the greatest opportunity he's had as an actor at this stage in his career. Now, he's in a position where he can spread his wings and put together a summer package to do a play when the show is on hiatus. Life comes full circle, and the taste of success is sweet.

I look at my life and I say, 'Gee whiz, look at all the things that can happen if you just hang in there!'

BUCK HENRY

Actor, Comedian (Saturday Night Live, Heaven Can Wait)

He is a funny man. Period. He is a talented man. Exclamation point. Since Buck Henry began working in 1961, he has never been out of work. "But it took me a while to start . . .".
In his varied career, people have come to know of Buck Henry for a variety of reasons.

Saturday Night Live, of course, has enormous notoriety, but I was doing that stuff on The Steve Allen Show, *and in 1965 on* That Was The Week That Was. *Then, I stopped for a long time to write, mostly.*

Coming out of a fairly traditional educational background, Buck attended several schools in the east and the west, ending with a bachelor of arts degree in English at Dartmouth College. A few years before Dartmouth, he had worked in a theater as a professional actor.
What made him decide to act?
"Somebody asked me if I wanted to be in a play. I said, 'Sure.' "
Now, when asked how many years he has been acting professionally, Buck responds, "38, I think". Though he has not been on the stage in many years, with the exception of variety shows, he views stage acting as a much riskier business than film or television.

To be there night after night, having to find a way to get back to a level of performance that is not only acceptable, but one hopes inspiring, with a new audience every time, and each performance a new experience, does seem like a more substantial way to earn acclaim.

Of course, there are many really good stage actors that don't make it particularly well on screen, and vice versa. Mostly stage to screen difficulties have to do with physical appearance, looks, voice, things that are given or not given to an actor. In the other direction, it is usually film actors that don't make it on stage because they lack training or passion.

If he were offered a great stage role, he would grab it in a moment.

I am not sure I could do a great part. I won't pretend to think that I am qualified to do something really difficult, probably I'm not. But I would sure take a shot at it.

Buck's is not a typical career. He had always intended to write, but enjoyed his acting experiences along the way. For the last 15 or 20 years, Buck acts most often in things he has written.

I have never written a part for myself. I do them accidentally. I would be reading with the cast or the director and I sort of get stuck in a role.

A typical day in Buck's atypical acting career begins with a 7:00 or 7:30 call to the set.

The hardest part of being an actor is getting up early. Getting made-up is the second hardest part because it is really boring and uncomfortable. Then, it is very much like being in the army. There are enormous momentary highs between which you wait.

The length of my day depends on what I am required to do. It could be two hours, it could be 14 hours.

From his point of view, Buck sees the biggest pluses to acting as a profession in that, if you are successful, you can make an enormous amount of money, have a lot of fun, and travel widely.

A disadvantage is a kind of paranoia that all actors have about having worked for the last time, each time they do a job. Particularly with television, it's a paranoia of being used up and having a very short life as an actor, of doing material that is second, third and fourth rate.

Also, there is a peculiar disadvantage, more to actors than actresses, that I have heard voiced by some very fine and very successful actors about it being sort of a trivial way for a man to make a living.

I think there are some built-in problems with a life of only being an actor. That's why many successful actors try and branch out and do something else.

Specifically with acting in a piece that he has written, Buck sees it as a vacation.

The writing is the hard part, the acting in it is like a bonus gift. It gives me an excuse to hang around. It keeps my insurance paid. I think that Screen Actors Guild insurance is one of the best plans there is, but I'm not sure. I belong to so many guilds. I think there are five of them and so I am covered for anything that might happen, including a headache.

Buck's success has been a product of the successful combination of luck and hard work.

There is no question that I have worked really hard. I have no love for hard work, but it is the only way that I can get to do what I do, and live the way I live. But, it is also luck. It's luck that comes out of some sort of application. Even if it is just showing up in a lot of places and knowing a lot of people.

It's odd. One doesn't know what one would have done lacking the vagaries of life. If I hadn't been in a certain bar in New York on a certain evening, a friend of mine wouldn't have said, 'They are looking for someone to take the place of somebody at The Premise,' an improvisational theater in New York in the early sixties. I wouldn't have happened to go down and get the job.

When I was writing "Get Smart", had I not been a friend of George Segal's, with whom I had been in The Premise, I wouldn't have been hanging around when he did Virginia Wolf *with Mike Nichols, and Nichols wouldn't have thought, 'Say, why don't we take a crack at* The Graduate.' *So, those are the fortuitous accidents that happen, although other more or less fortuitous accidents might also have taken place.*

Ultimately talent and ability will show up.

There aren't really any great actors or great writers hidden in the woods. Sometimes it takes a long time, and it does take those accidents.

Buck's advice to anyone thinking of acting as a profession: "Learn about computers. Think about chemical engineering."
It is a very difficult life, both socially and psychologically.

I think you have to know fairly early on that it is a governing passion and that the passion is more important than anything else. You must have a real conviction about your ability, about some kind of talent or skill. I was around theater people all my life, as a kid. I had a sense of it before I ever started. Television has given everyone a chance to be famous for a minute or two, but the turnover is real fast.

Has Buck Henry had a good life?

Considering the alternative, yes.

BRIDGET HANLEY

Actress (Chattanooga Choo Choo, Ohara, Here Come the Brides)

The life of an actress is exactly that: life. Life and the art of living it between the lines. Babies are born. Dinner is made. Rehearsals are scheduled. Many actresses feel the pressures and pleasures of juggling their careers with two of the most challenging roles they will ever play: wife and mother.

Rearrange the carpool schedule. Mommy got a series.

In 1964, after graduating from The University of Washington as a theater arts major, she packed her bags and set off to take New York by storm. En route, she stopped in San Francisco to visit a girlfriend who was an actress performing in a production of *Private Lives*. From the darkness of her orchestra seat, Bridget Hanley watched her friend perform, she watched the scenes change, watched the final bow. After the final curtain descended, she marched up to the director and announced, "I would like to audition for you."

> *At 2:30 the next morning, the phone rang. The girl that was playing the bronchial French maid in the production had become very ill and they needed someone to go on for her. So, I practiced my bronchial cough and my French and I went on that night.*

It began as a temporary job and grew until she set her bags down and decided to stay a while. Each time Bridget thought about continuing onward to try her luck in New York, she would switch to another part of *Private Lives*.

> *Then, I went into the lead in* Under the Yum Yum Tree, *got my equity card and started getting a little money. I got a tacky little apartment on Bush Street in San Francisco. I guess I've been a professional actress since then.*

Bridget Hanley was no stranger to San Francisco. She spent her first two years of college at San Francisco College for Women. "Then, I got into a fight with the only drama teacher because I only got to play men's roles." She returned to her hometown of Seattle to obtain her degree. Prerequisites completed, Bridget took one oceanography class and the rest drama for her last two years in college.

> *It was like two years of summer stock. They had three theaters that ran simultaneously all year long. I could be rehearsing and playing in some show constantly.*

> *For anyone who wants to go into the field but is still a little quaky in their boots to set off and take the world by storm, it is a wonderful launching pad.*

Currently, Bridget is an actress, a mother, and a wife. Three demanding careers. The ups and downs of her professional life have ridden alongside her family. The dreams of the actress have successfully merged with the demands of motherhood like tributaries flowing into a lake. The whole would not be complete without the contribution of each component.

> *I think that everyone in my time, and even now, really sets out to be artists. To most people, that means the theater. We all still have a great drive and love and desire to do that, but something rears it's ugly head called 'the need to support yourself.'*

> *A lot of women feel that when they work in the theater, they have the daytime to be with their children. It is really quite lovely. On the other hand, you have absolutely no life with your husband. It's like a double edged sword.*

> *Still, I would love to go to New York. The one time when it looked like I could go, the writer of* Under The Yum Yum Tree *wrote another play and called my agent to see if I was available, I was pregnant. My big chance to go to New York. I was so fat I couldn't even walk.*

Hollywood. Movies. Television. The market changes. Youth is more of a factor in Hollywood than it is in New York. Many scripts revolve around young characters. An actress at 40 reaches a difficult time in her professional life. Too young and too pretty to play mothers, too old to play girlfriends. There is simply a dearth of parts for women in that age group.

There are so many of us in this age range, with a name or not, that everyone is tearing after the few jobs that are available. It's really hard. It's a time of being out of work a lot.

Sometimes I wonder if it's age, or just that belief when you are younger that everything is possible. I look back and I see that my chutzpah was amazing. It was wonderful to have the blind belief of 'Why not me?' Now, there are so many numbers involved. I do know, however, that I will make enough to survive, and that's nice.

Artistic survival as well as financial survival is the name of the game.

I belong to Theater West (an association of actors, writers and directors) and it has saved my life. I can go there and work out emotionally and mentally. Usually during the school year, I spend the day rehearsing at Theater West. I pick something that I would really like to work on. If I have a particular acting problem, like crying, for example, I can technically figure the problem out.

Each morning Bridget is up at 7:00 putting out dog food, fish food, and people food. With her two school-aged daughters, the day varies with the school schedule. During pilot season when new shows are being cast and shot, Bridget lives off of calendars and lists, and tries to stay flexible.

It can be a last minute thing. They want you available to them at all times. Agents don't want to know family. They think you must have that all figured out. You have to roll with the punches.

I spend my life getting ready. You get ready for the job, get ready for the trip to the job, get ready for the interview.

During the busy season, she can go out on four or five interviews a day, including theatrical as well as commercial interviews. You can be changing your clothes in rest rooms and the back seat of your car.

My daughter went to a play at a local high school. Her friend's uncle was in it and he took Bronwyn and all the little girls back stage afterwards. He asked them, 'How many of you want to be an actress?' All the little girls raised their hands except Bronwyn. She said, 'No way. You have to go on too many interviews!' She had a realistic picture of it.

Bridget feels that the biggest thrill in her profession is the incredible outlet for all of the little people who live within her.

I have a good excuse, and get paid to use the theater for therapy many times. It's wonderful to be liked when you're liked. There are those moments when you really feel full and you have made that completion. It's the most fabulous feeling in the world.

This business is so joyous when it's joyous, and it's lousy when it's lousy, but it's never mediocre. It's never boring.

You never really grow up. For better or for worse, many actors stay in close contact with the child inside of them. They work at playing, pretending, and feeling emotions without the screens and censors of adult reality. Bridget sees part of the fun of life in avoiding becoming too set in her ways or overly concerned with how she should be at various stages in her life.

The life of an actor is a very risky one at best. You don't know from one day to the next how long you have whether it's financially or physically.

At times it's worse than having a temporary job, and at times it's worse than having double shifts.

One of Bridget's misconceptions regarding acting was the discovery that it's not always fun. She knew she felt most alive on stage. She knew it was where she wanted to be, but it is a lot of work. You've got to keep at it and open up even when it's painful.

One thing I learned, and would love to pass on, was that everybody always talked about the casting couch. I am here to tell you that never once in twenty years did anything in bad taste or extraordinary in that area ever happen. I really think that it's a two-way street. If you are big enough to take care of yourself, you can get through unscathed in that area.

A show biz adage whispered in all young actor's ears is that people hire their friends. It's who you know that will further your career. Bridget cautions that it can work against you, too.

We have an awful lot of friends in the business who think of me as Bridget, mother of Bronwyn and Megan. They ask me, 'Are you still acting?' But, because friendships are so valuable, I would rather have the friend than the boss. Knowing someone too well can go against you, also.

There is always someone who is not going to get the job, and there are always going to be a million different reasons why. Sometimes actors need reasons why they didn't get picked and it's easy to say, 'Well, they got hired because they are a friend.'

Her best advice: Get a suit of armor, a sword, a big heart, and hire a big black dog to be with you at all times. More than anything, you've got to have a suit of armor for your emotions, but one with a lot of trap doors so you can let them out.

Learn how to be alone. Learn how to be happy with yourself when you are by yourself. Be prepared at all times for everything. Study. Go off and do repertory theater until you are ready to take Hollywood by storm. It will hold you in good stead for the rest of your life.

You can come and take this town by storm physically, but if you don't have anything to back it up you are going to be in big trouble. It's harder to start back the second time. Back up your face with your craft.

CAL GIBSON

Actor (Stay Hungry, Night Court)

She robbed me of my virginity when I was of tender age.
She makes me happier, yet sadder than most anything or anyone I've ever known.
She at times makes me look shiftless and trifling in the eyes of others.
She shares with me the greatness of kings, and the company of thieves.
She destroys my relationships with other women.
She is a bitch,
She is a lady,
She is . . . theater.

Cal Gibson

1964. Irish Hills, Michigan. While still in college, he performed for the first time as a professional actor. It was a summer stock production, but still, he was an actor.

Shortly afterward, Cal Gibson was drafted.

I used to do shows while I was in the service. I would entertain at different clubs. Sometimes on the weekends, they would fly me to another base and I would perform in the officers club the first night, the NCO club on the next night, and the EM club on Sunday night, then they'd fly me back to my base in Anchorage. They paid me 100 bucks a night. It was pretty good for a private in the army.

After completing his tour of duty, Cal teamed up with a partner to form a black and white comedy team. They lived in Alaska, and performed in clubs around the state. One evening, a man sat in the audience. He loved their act—and he changes their lives. Waylon Jennings asked Cal and his partner to tour the country with him as his opening act. They agreed, with the ultimate goal of working their way out to California.

In the black and white comedy team, people expected to see something racial. We would usually do our racial material up front, get it out of the way, then go on with just being funny.

They made it to California and decisions had to be made. Then, tragedy struck. Cal's partner died. His mourning period was a time to step back, take a hard look at his life, and organize his priorities. Life was simply too short and too precious to waste.

Cal wanted to act. He had been trained as an actor. He was good. That's what he would do. The next step was obvious. He got himself an agent, a nighttime job, and proceeded to go out on theatrical auditions and commercial calls.

You never know when the auditions are going to come. I go out once a week on the average. There are some weeks, however, where I may have three or four.

Cal chose to seek the additional guidance of a personal manager to work with his agent.

Sometimes the agent is working to get you in the front door, and the manager may be attacking from the back door. Hopefully, they are able to get you in one so you can be seen.

It's the personal manager's job to see that you get with an agent who is going to promote your career, and one with whom he can work well.

The audition. The interview. Managing pre-audition stress is a giant step toward success as a professional actor. The more relaxed and confident you are, the better you will perform once you step through the door.

Cal arrives at every audition approximately one half hour before his scheduled time slot. Generally, his agent or manager has given him a brief description of the character for which he will be reading so he's had the opportunity to dress like the character and to enter the room carrying himself as the character would. He picks up the scene that he will audition. A half hour is usually ample time to prepare.

The environment inside an audition room varies with each situation. Tension levels can be high or low. There may be three to four people, or six to eight people smiling or sitting stoned-faced. They may appear eager to watch you perform, or tired and anxious to go home. Most often, the actor will walk into the room and meet the casting director, producer, and director of the project. For larger roles, one or more of the other actors might be present. For commercials, people from the advertising agency might join the group.

When I get in the room, I always like to ask them exactly what they had in mind. I like to ask, 'If you could describe this character in one word, how would you describe him?' That usually gives me something to grab hold of, and then I can come as close as possible to what they are looking for.

Some directors and producers are receptive to a question regarding the character, some are not. If the actor allows it, the situation can be very intimidating.

I find that, if I can put them at ease, I can also put myself at ease. These people are staring at you, so if you can take it away from them, and put yourself in control of the situation, it makes it easier for you.

After participating in the Harvey Lembeck Comedy Workshop, with some of the things that we go through, I can't really be intimidated by a lot of people in this town. It's a good thing to feel.

Most of the time, the people who are watching and judging you are interested in putting you at ease. They are concerned with their product and of hiring the best person to promote it.

There are a few who like to intimidate. Maybe they don't realize it, but I think some of them enjoy it. Some actors intimidate themselves before they even get into the room.

Casting in the first place, is a very subjective thing. You have to look at it that way and never take it personally.

The decisions that are made after every actor has auditioned are based on a multitude of things. If you don't get the part, don't try and figure out the reason. Instead, work toward building the security of knowing that each time you go into an audition, you do your best work. Look forward to the next, don't look back to the last.

The amount of time that elapses before a casting decision is made also varies. The phone may be ringing by the time you get home. You may not hear for a couple of weeks. Generally, however, producers and directors are interested in casting their projects as soon as possible.

As a black actor, I run into different problems than some white actors run into. There are unfortunately not as many roles available to me as there are to some other actors. Black actors tend to get called on cattle calls where they need black actors. I want to be considered on the basis of my talents and to have the opportunity to audition for anything and everything.

There are not a lot of black people in control in this particular industry. Until blacks are able to get into the areas of control, it's going to be a slow process.

Cal Gibson has appeared on television in shows that include: "The Dukes of Hazzard", "The Jeffersons", and "Barney Miller", as well as parts in two feature films, "Stay Hungry" and "The Seventh Dwarf". The biggest misconception he had about his profession was the belief that he would be offered more roles.

I did a television series, "Park Place." I have done any number of shows. There are a lot of people who come out here and never get a job. So, in a sense, I have been successful, but not as successful as I want to be.

One of the ingredients for success and longevity in the acting business is to surround yourself with honest and genuine people. Protect yourself. It is easy to fall into the wrong hands if you're not careful and selective. Check credentials. Go with recommendations from people you trust.

Involve yourself in a good equity waiver theater where you'll get good people around you who can give you the proper guidance. There are a lot of traps. They can help you avoid them.

This town is very social, and many times it really is who you know. But being social isn't enough. Back it up with your talent.

Cal offers one word of wisdom to anyone thinking of entering the acting profession: "Don't."
What makes you think you are good enough to do it? Why will you succeed where many others have failed? What are you prepared to do if you don't make it as an actor?

Then, if you are discouraged, you shouldn't have wanted to be an actor in the first place. If you aren't discouraged, prepare yourself by taking advantage of everything your school has to offer. Go as far in school as you can to prepare yourself to make a living while you pursue your career as an actor.

I just turned 40 yesterday. No one believes that I'm 40. It's been just recently that they have allowed me to play fathers. I'm just getting out of the 'kid' stage more or less. That's why you need other areas to devote your time to.

The day the phone rang and his agent said, "You got the part, they want you for the series," one of Cal's dreams came true. He was making more money than he had ever made before as an actor. The cast believed that they were doing a show that would go on for years. For one reason or another, it didn't make it past four shows.

So, I had some money that I had put away to live on. The question was for how long. Pretty soon, you have to make a decision. 'Am I going to be an out-of-work destitute actor, or am I going to continue to take care of myself and still pursue my goal?' I went back to work in a (regular) job.

Some actors get so caught up in it that they delude themselves. Acting is a wonderful profession, but it is just a job, and we have to be prepared to think of it as that. If you start believing everything the public says, I think that is where you get into trouble. It's a fun job, it's a job that I love, but it's only a job. It takes going through it to be able to put things in perspective.

LESLIE NORRIS

Actress, Comedian (The Boyfriend, Grease)

Standing five feet 4, and 106 pounds, she resembles a petite Ann Margaret. Long auburn hair and hazel eyes. Her voice is unique. High and soft. But, in a business known for stereotypic assumption, Leslie Norris is in a class by herself. She does stand up comedy and can outsmart most anyone. There are some lucky people out there, people who get discovered. But, are you going to sit around and wait for that to happen? No, she most definitely is not.

Leslie goes up for nearly every part that's possibly right for her. She goes to stage interviews, industrial shows, equity calls.

I find most of them out for myself. I read the trades, I mark down auditions, names I should send letters to. I talk to other actresses, talk to people. I do an improvisation class every Monday. I am there with other actors who are working, or have worked. You hear about things. I invite people to come and see me perform.

You really have to make yourself do it because it's easy for an actor to get lazy.

An actress? A comedienne? Leslie describes herself as an actress who does comedy. Each weekend, you will find her performing her stand-up routines at various comedy clubs. She can't think of a better chance for exposure or a better way to showcase her talents.

I'm doing 10-20 minutes of material that is just for me. What better audition could I have? You can't just depend on an interview. There are hundreds of women who can read the lines they give you. You don't get a chance to show what you can do best.

In terms of preparation for the realities of an acting career, one experience stands out as the least helpful. College.

I went to college thinking that you needed to do that before you got anyplace, before you hit New York. Now I think, the younger the better. The biggest shock was realizing where I should have been. I should have been in Hollywood by the time I finished high school. If I had been here earlier, it would have been much easier.

If you really want to have it, have it. Go to New York. Take classes.

Another eye-opening experience was Leslie's perception that men run the business.

They don't want you to be smarter than they are. They don't want you to be funnier than they are. If you're pretty, they want you to be dumb. In an interview, I don't feel that I can really be as honest and intelligent as I am. The older women are getting the chance to be smarter, the younger ones aren't.

If you are really very unique, it's going to be a lot tougher. Nowadays, the network wants you to fit a certain slot. They want you to be exactly like somebody was before you.

Though she has yet to achieve the success and recognition that she knows she will eventually capture, Leslie already has some acting credits to call her own. She is a fighter. 10 years in the business have not dimmed her hopes. She is certain that time and talent are on her side. Her job is to perfect her craft and stay open to all the upsets and victories that the future is sure to hold.

I lost both of my parents very early in my life. I feel that that is the worst life can be. Losing a part can't be as bad as that. It puts things in perspective for me.

People haven't a clue how to deal with failure. You have to say, 'I made it. I survived. Nothing will stop me. No one will discourage me. I belong in show business.'

STEVE TRACY

Actor (Little House on the Prairie, West Side Story)

His hair is curly and rests a comfortable shade between brown and blond. Each day he works out at the gym for two hours, fine-tuning his instrument. His decision to act came quite unexpectedly.

In elementary school, I was a problem child. I was hyperactive, wouldn't sit still, always entertaining the class. I finally got into the fourth grade, and my teacher took me down to The Community Children's Theater Program to audition for Rumplestilsken. *I got the part. I was about two feet tall, this six-year old midget, with the lead role. I had no idea what I was doing.*

Then, on stage in front of 500 people, I forgot a line. I didn't know what to say so I just turned to the audience and made some smart remark that had nothing to do with the play. I got a huge laugh. I just stood there, beaming. I can still remember thinking, 'Boy am I smart!'

From that point on, there was no doubt in my mind that acting was what I wanted to do. I never really considered anything else.

Steve Tracy is now 30 years old and 5 feet 4 inches tall. "It leaves me in a very awkward, hard to cast position." When he was younger and looked younger, he was often cast in teenage character roles, and young adult roles. At 30, he is too old for teenage parts, but not quite old enough to play doctors, lawyers, husbands, and fathers. He finds himself stuck in an actor's limbo.

In 1979, Steve landed a part as a regular on the hit series, "Little House on the Prairie". He was with the show until 1981.

The schedule was very regimented. Because there were so many children on the show, it was necessary to schedule the shooting in such a way that they would work half a day, and go to school for half a day. I never worked an entire day because the adults are in the scenes with the kids.

Generally, I would get up at 6:00 in the morning, get to the studio by 7:00, have breakfast, get made-up, and work until 12:00 or 1:00 in the afternoon. Or, I would go in at 11:00 or 12:00 in the afternoon, and work until 6:00 or 7:00 in the evening. It was a nice deal.

Conversely, while working on location for a film, Steve found himself involved in a day and night commitment.

I did a film in San Francisco. We were up there for nine weeks, and out of those nine weeks, I would occasionally have an evening free to go out and do something in San Francisco. Most often, I was up at 6:00 in the morning, into make-up, shooting all day, and studying and preparing all evening and going to bed early.

Now, Steve's days are divided in two: days when he is working and days when he is not. The days when he is not working far outnumber those when he is.

I got my SAG (Screen Actors Guild) card in 1976. In 1977, I made about $3,000 as an actor. In 1978, about $8,000. In 1979, about $15,000. In 1980, about $40,000. In 1981, about $30,000. In 1982, about $20,000, and in 1983, about $12,000. I had a swell going for a while, then the age hit.

He believes, however, that the days when he is not working are the most interesting. After his morning work-out at the gym, Steve tries to find a situation where he has the chance to watch people. He gets on a bus, goes to the movies, looks for all types of human exposure.

To supplement his income, Steve works part-time as a waiter on the evening shift.

A lot of actors don't recognize the value of work experiences where you are dealing with the public and learning about human nature. That is what an actor does, he interprets human behavior. It's an opportunity to do those kinds of things.

Commercials can be a main source of income for an actor. Consequently, Steve goes out on as many commercial auditions as possible. In the winter and early spring, a lot of commercials are being produced in Los Angeles. In summer and late fall, many of them are done in New York to take advantage of the weather.

For television, July through February is the busiest time of the year because all the television series are shooting. The actor must be prepared for the seasonal lulls of the business.

Relying solely on your agent to call you for auditions can be a lonely and frustrating experience. The more you are involved in your own career advancement, the easier it will be to handle the stretches of unemployment.

I read the trades and talk to friends in the business and hear about things that are going on. I often read that book rights have been bought. Many times they are books that I have read, so when I know that they are planning to make a movie out of it, I mention it (to my agent).

I try and keep my ear to the ground, but I don't go out there and pound the streets the way I used to when I first started.

What does he mean by "pounding the streets?"

Make your face known everywhere. Really try and initiate work for yourself. Go to every party, get into every screening that you can, and get familiar and friendly with every person, even if you don't like them, because they may help your career.

It did help me. It exposed me a lot. I made a point to stay in contact and friendly with everyone with whom I've studied, everyone I did a play with, and everyone I worked with on a film. Even when I was starting out and just doing day work, I would try and build relationships. You need talent, but you have to have a gregarious social repartee.

Now, when Steve comes across a part he'd like to play, he approaches the situation differently.

I am tired of playing bookworms, or the little buddy of the handsome leading man who is supposed to be a coward and turns out to be a hero. I want to play a psychotic. I want to play bizarre characters. I want to play some romantic roles.

There is a movie being written about a marginally retarded man who is almost smart, but not quite. They want someone who could realistically portray his mannerisms. I've studied special education and worked with the special Olympics, and am familiar with Down's Syndrome and the differences between Down's Syndrome and other mental illnesses.

I pursued it very actively. I kept writing these people, and writing and writing, and had my agent call and call. Finally they decided that physically I'm just not right for the part. I wouldn't let up on them until basically they slammed the door in my face and told me to leave them alone.

Get into a good acting class. An academic environment such as a theater program in a university is a chance to get basic knowledge of the acting craft and the acting business, but a more vocational approach to acting can be achieved by taking classes specifically geared for working actors and/or preparing actors to work.

With good teachers, you have to audition for them. A lot of teachers are not very good and do more damage than they help. Sometimes, they're failed actors that are trying to support themselves. A lot of them present a very difficult audition process to make you feel like it is very hard to get in, and then they take everybody that auditions.

Talk with everyone that you know. Get recommendations. Be cautious. Find a way to expose yourself to the environment of a television or movie set, so when the big break comes, you'll know what to expect.

First of all, understand that there are no rules, there is no right or wrong way to do anything. What matters is what ends up on the stage or in film, and that it is right for what the writer and director intended. The way you go about it doesn't mean a hill of beans to anybody.

In A Chorus Line there is the song, "And I Felt Nothing". She sings about not being able to feel the imaginary skis and the wind going down the hill, and felt that it meant she didn't have any talent. That has nothing to do with it. There are a million actors out there who never feel the wind, never taste the ice cream, and they're brilliant. You have to experiment and do what you want to do.

The four A's (actor's unions) include Actors Equity Association, American Guild for Variety Artists, Screen Actors Guild, and AFTRA (the American Federation of Television and Radio Artists). Each union has its own eligibility requirements and benefits.

MUSIC

Music is defined as the "art of organizing sound so as to elicit an aesthetic response in a listener." Musical tastes are as varied as the possible harmonies within a tune.

The business of making and selling music is a complex process of creating and supplying sounds to satisfy the public's fickle demands. Some specialize in making "background music tapes" for use in offices, restaurants and elevators. Others write musical scores for motion pictures or TV shows. Some compose for the highly competitive popular song market. Still others work on classical compositions hoping to join the famed Bs (Beethoven, Bach, and Brahms).

There are five major types of careers in the music field:

- **Instrumental musicians** play an instrument in an orchestra, band, rock group, jazz combo, or solo. The type of instrument varies with the group—in the jazz field, for example, the trumpet, trombone, clarinet, saxophone, piano, bass, and guitar are common. Classical groups stress violins, cellos, and various woodwind and precussion instruments. Instrumental musicians are expected to provide their own instruments which may range from $3,000 to $50,000 depending upon the item and its relative quality.

- **Singers** interpret music using their knowledge of voice production, melody, and harmony. Most try to develop a distinctive personal style and their followers may easily identify them by their voice. Performed music ranges from opera and classical, to rock, folk, country, or western. Singers are classed according to their voice range: soprano, contralto, tenor, baritone, or base.

- **Composers** create original music including symphonies, operas, or popular songs. They use their knowledge of harmony, rhythm, melody, and tonal structure along with their aesthetic sense to produce music which is pleasing and, hopefully, saleable.

- **Orchestra conductors** lead orchestras and bands. They audition and select members for their organizations and direct rehearsals and performances. They use their knowledge of music, conducting techniques, and harmony to produce a distinctive type of music. In smaller organizations, the conductor may also perform many business related functions.

- **Choral directors** lead choir, glee clubs, and choruses. They also are concerned with auditioning candidates and selecting singers. They plan and direct rehearsals and conduct performances. As many members of choral groups are unpaid, directors must work hard to motivate the members to develop a good group spirit.

Music careers require talent, perserverance, and bit of luck. Around 500 colleges and universities operate music conservatories which grant bachelor's degrees in music. Many, however, enter the field directly from high school based upon their talents and prior experience.

According to the Bureau of Labor Statistics, around 192,000 persons were employed as musicians in a recent year. As in other performing arts fields, union membership is required or helpful for many. Many musicians hold other jobs, both in and outside the field, to help make ends meet. Often performing musicians teach privately. Some take jobs in nonmusical fields which meet basic living expenses and allow for musical activities in the off-work hours.

Talent and dedication are the two most important paths to success in this competitive profession.

JOAN JETT

Rock Musician

A young girl with wide dark eyes and black hair joined the crowd filling the concert hall. She had been looking forward to that night. When the house lights dimmed, there was a pause. Anticipation. Then, the lights splashed on stage and the air vibrated with rock and roll. The guitar was loud and she could feel the beat of the bass in her chest. She loved it. There was a sense of unity. As she danced with the thousands of people around her, and looked up at the performers on the stage, she could have sworn the lead singer deliberately tilted his head to look straight at her. She would never forget it.

Now, a pretty woman dressed in leather runs onto the stage, grabs her guitar, and looks out over the audience. It is dark past the eighth row. Flickering cigarette lighters are all she can see. Still, she looks. A guy in the ninth row swears that she is looking right at him. He loves it. He'll never forget it.

Contact. The high of human connection through music propels Joan Jett through the craziness of rock and roll.

> *The dream was to get in a band and be on stage and get the same reaction that had happened to me. I would go crazy at concerts. The dream was to be like another "Rolling Stones" and put together a band that would become huge.*

Joan Jett surged onto the music scene in the mid-seventies as leader of "The Runaways," the first all-female rock band. Weathering the bumps and bruises of the music business, she survived the disintegration of the trailblazing band and landed firmly on her feet with the determination of a dart heading straight for the bull's-eye.

Tenacity and faithful management joined with talent and energy to hold her steady through the ups and downs of a career in the music business. Hard work has paid off. With her band, The Blackhearts, Joan now tours the world, headlining for crowds up to 38,000.

Spending much of their time on the road, Joan Jett and The Blackhearts average close to 200 shows a year. While touring, the band's typical performing schedule is: four nights on, one day off, four nights on, one day off, then five straight nights on in a row.

> *The days off are always travel days, so they are not really off. A day off just means I don't have a concert.*

On the day of a major headlining performance in a big city, Joan is awake and dressed before noon, prepared to handle her press commitments for the day. Most often, "press" involves radio interviews to remind the listeners that she is in town, performing that night.

> *Usually, on the day of the show, they try and get me on the radio during rush hour so that when everyone is coming home from work, I am doing an interview saying, 'If you want to have a good time and hear some rock and roll, come down tonight'.*

The remaining day unfolds in charged anticipation of the night's show. She waits.

> *I get very wound up, very anxious. I want to say nervous but it's not nervous as in frightened. It's anxiety. I want to get on stage but at the same time I don't. If I could find a way to put it off for five minutes, I would.*

> *I don't get as nervous as I used to, however. Now, it's just bottled up energy.*

Frequent performances eliminate the need for rehearsal before a show. A sound check, however, is required on each new stage. In the late afternoon, the band congregates at the concert hall to play a few songs, check the equipment, and try to foresee and correct any potential problems.

Afterwards, Joan sticks around to watch the audience arrive.

I like to listen to them. It's a way to get to know your audience before you even go out on stage. Are they going to be crazy? Are they going to be really quiet? Is it the kind of crowd where we will have to work to get them to have fun?

A lot of times, certain towns have reputations of being hard to win over. I like to take it all in, it's a part of my routine.

As the time draws closer, the opening act prepares to go on stage. Joan watches them, ready to go when it's her turn. Prepared mentally and physically, her last regular meal was at 2:00 that afternoon, seven hours earlier.

I want to make sure my stomach is empty when I go on. I've been in a position where I've had a meal and you get on stage and get so hot that you get ill, physically nauseous.

It's time. The opening band is off the stage. The roadies have set up the equipment. The stage lights are dim. There is a split second of silence, a breath before the announcement.
"Ladies and Gentlemen. Joan Jett and The Blackhearts!"
Joan takes a breath and runs.

Usually when people see you run on stage, they scream and yell and you get a feeling for the kind of audience you have.

In a big concert, like 30,000 people, you can't really see anyone but you know they're out there because you can hear them. You can see the lighters.

That hour and a half on stage is what Joan Jett lives for. It seems endless, though it passes in the blink of an eye. The audience contact feeds her, replenishes her, reminds her why she chose this crazy life.

So many bands don't pay much attention to their audience. They do a song. The audience applauds. They do another song. The audience applauds again. There is no interaction.

I want to isolate every person like they are getting their own concert. I try and make eye contact with everybody. At a large concert, I just make sure that I am looking all around and covering every area where I know people will be sitting.

Performing is a euphoric feeling. There's no word to describe it. You can't say, 'Oh, it's like having three beers'. It's a rush, a feeling of power to a certain extent. To get 30,000 people to sing along with you, or clap their hands with you is the feeling of power. I think that one of the keys to get people to do that is to let them know you are a regular person just like they are.

The audience can make or break a rock and roll show. It is a symbiotic relationship, mutually beneficial. The band, having toured around the world, has experienced a variety of audiences.

In Tokyo, the audience is very polite. They're really watching you. They clap along to every song and scream and make a lot of noise during the song. At the end of the song, they applaud for a decent amount of time, then they get very quiet and wait. It's out of respect.

In the end, the language barrier is the only real difference to Joan as a performer. They know her songs, but she can't talk to them.

If something goes wrong, like my guitar is out of tune and I need a couple of extra seconds, I don't know how to say it. I don't have enough time to learn maybe five little raps when I need them. We play in so many different places. I can't learn Swedish, Norwegian, Danish, German, French, Spanish, and Italian. I just can't do it. I learn how to say, 'How're you doing?' and 'Goodnight'.

A large part of Joan Jett's persona is a certain innocent integrity that she brings to her work. A glowing letter from a fan will genuinely make her day, unfair press will make her angry. She is devoid of apathy. She loves to talk with fans. With her time upon the stage, she tries to ignite her audience just as the glimmer of their lighters excite her.

In a flash, it's over.

The crowd has demanded an encore. The band has willingly given it. The last chord is finally played. Now, Joan's primary concern is to change from her sweaty clothes and sit down for the first moment of rest since the show began.

> *Literally a minute after you've gotten off stage, some people will come backstage while you are sitting there exhausted, you can't perform like that and even think you can stand up afterwards, and they see you're tired and out of it and say, 'Wow. Are they ever stoned!' It's really annoying.*

Backstage, people are milling about waiting to meet the band, say hello, get an autograph. People come by from the radio stations that have helped with the concert, local record store people are there, people that the promoter might want the band to meet.

> *Usually after I am dressed and have cooled down a bit, I go out to the bus. If there are people hanging around wanting autographs and stuff, I sit there and sign them. I sit inside the bus, I'd get destroyed if I sat outside. There is absolutely no order.*

Joan Jett and The Blackhearts have tremendous fan appeal. This is one of the reasons:

> *If they are going to stand outside and wait a half an hour to see me, I'll sign my name for them. I enjoy it. I think it's fun when I have the time. I shake their hands, say hello, find out what they thought about the concert. It's a great way to keep in touch with my audience.*

> *You've got to face the fact that when you are as busy as we are, you don't have the time to hang out on the streets and find out what is going through people's minds. It's great to get a chance to talk to people. You get it right from the horse's mouth.*

> *The best part is, their feelings are just like mine. It helps to reinforce me.*

Reinforced, tired, elated, exhausted, Joan gets on the bus and heads for the next town.

As a general rule, if the next town is within a three-hour drive, the band will spend the night where they are. If it's longer, they leave. Anywhere from 2:00 to 4:00 in the morning, the bus will roll out of town while the band sleeps in the back.

> *You eat on the bus. You sleep on the bus. A lot of times it's your dressing room.*

> *Every once in a while we will fly. I will be too tired or my throat will be a little bit raunchy, or my muscles will be a little bit sore and I just want to take it easy and not go on the bus that night. Sometimes you can't sleep very well. So, I will stay over in a hotel and fly to the next concert. But, that doesn't happen very often. We usually travel by bus.*

A rock star. A woman. Oil and water? Joan Jett has successfully made the mix. A woman in this male-dominated business will draw the spotlight more readily than a man in the same situation. "But if you're no good, the advantage goes right out the window."

The rock and roll myth of the pampered rock star, indulged in destructive lifestyles, simply does not hold true with Joan Jett. It's a hard job, and she works hard at it.

> *It's a 'get your hands dirty' kind of job, 24 hours a day. You pretty much relinquish all of your privacy. You can't get angry with people for knowing who you are.*

The pressures of the profession revolve around responsibility. People are counting on you. You are counting on yourself. You don't want to let anyone down.

> *You have to take this very seriously. A lot of times people only last a year or two. You wonder, whatever happened to them? Maybe they couldn't handle the pressure, or they lived in the fast lane and went too fast.*

> *I look at it like an athlete looks at his job. You have to be serious and take good care of yourself. It's not easy to do on the road. We leave right after the concert and we're all wound up. It's not easy to go right*

to sleep, but you have to concentrate on keeping your health together. If my voice starts to get a bit rough, I try not to talk.

It is a lot of fun, but it's a lot of hard work.

Prepare yourself for rejection. Teach yourself to handle the verbal stab wounds that you will be vulnerable to as a public figure. Realize that there is nothing you can do about it but stay true to yourself and play the kind of music you believe in.

Rejection can come from the most unlikely places.

A lot of my fans like to show me how much they like me by saying, 'I don't care what my other friends say . . .' then they tell me all the bad things people say about me, '. . . I don't care. I'll love you forever.'

There will be people who couldn't care less about you, or who hate your guts. They are going to say what they want. It's all a part of this whole thing.

Let it roll off your back. Say to yourself, 'Hey, I'm doing what I want to do and that's what I am going to do. I am not hurting anybody. I am not hurting myself. I am having a good time. I am making other people happy.' If someone doesn't like it, they simply don't have to listen.

LES MC CANN

Jazz Musician

Jazz is native American music. Syncopated rhythm. Contrapuntal ensemble playing. A continuously evolving form of music with a unique sound. Normally weak beats in a measure are accented, a note is added to obscure a strong beat, independent melodies are combined. Jazz is living music, characterized by improvisation and individual interpretation.

Les McCann is a jazz musician. His music releases itself through his ten fingers and the air he exhales. A positive man, his eyes gleam with the indivation that he has seen all sides of life, and choose the even keel.

I play keyboards. I picked it up because I have a good ear. I always sang in the choir as a kid, and played in the marching band. I had formal lessons later. I never really knew how to read music. Mainly, my purpose for going to music school was to get away from Kentucky.

Les attended a music school in Los Angeles for a year, and spent two years at Los Angeles City College.

Around the end of that period, after playing at The Bungalow, causing riots, and things like that, I decided that I had to play.

Currently, he rises at 6:30 every morning. "I love to watch the CBS morning news." He lives in California and frequently has business on the east coast. The morning hours are the time to take care of telephone calls. "If I am having a good day, it means that nobody is calling me."

My manager calls me everyday to tell me what's happening and who I have to call. I try and finish everything before 11:00 am. That leaves me from 11:30 to 4:30 to play tennis. For me, tennis is a balance to all the other things.

Each day, Les practices his instrument, although, on the road practice time is a rare luxury.

At this point in his career, he can essentially chose how often he wants to work. He plays in jazz clubs, concerts, jazz festivals, and state festivals in other countries. He is on the road for approximately two weeks each month.

On this last trip we went to New Jersey. Since it was a cross country trip, we went a day in advance. I had a piano in the house and could practice. That was really a treat. I made my calls, but since I was in the east, I didn't have to worry about the evenings and my day was really free. I would go for long walks, eat ice cream, look at people.

The lifestyle on the road can be extremely difficult. You must take a hard look at yourself, establish your priorities, and prepare yourself for the stresses of physical and mental demands.

It got to the point where I couldn't wait to get on the road. You never know if you are trying to get away from your wife or get away from the things that you are not willing to face. When I was married, I was on the road sometimes nine months out of the year. Occasionally my wife went with me, but she had things that she wanted to do. It's very hard.

These last years have probably been the worst two years in the business, but I have enjoyea the time. When you are travelling with musicians, and you have other guys that you are responsible for, you can feel the pressure. I am the recipient of the stress. My doctors have told me that it's too much. I have learned recently to let go of all these things. I have faith in what I can do, and I have faith in what the band can do. I know that if they care about it, they will be there.

It's very important to get to know the business so well that you can direct someone to do it for you. You want to be free to play. The stress in the (music-side) of the business is enough. The key is learning how to speak up for yourself.

Les emphasizes the importance of taking a look at the people who truly mean something in your life. It's easy to isolate those you care about when dealing with your own stresses. Take conscious steps to avoid it.

I can honestly say that one of the most frightening feelings I have ever had was when I felt the success of a big album. It wasn't a million seller, but it was big, and I could feel what could happen. I don't know how I would have made it through that if it hadn't been for family and people I was close to.

The working environment in a jazz recording studio can provide stresses and satisfactions of its own. For Les McCann, his favorite time to record is at night when he's "a little tired, and a little relaxed".

I used to go into the studio to make a record and I (was terrified). I don't do that anymore. I go into the studio and play. I wish I had known how to do that then, but either I didn't believe in myself or I thought that I was going to make the best record ever. It doesn't work that way. You just have to go and do it.

Now, I am with a very small company, a one-man operation. Tight money, hope. Let's make a record and hope that somebody plays it. Most jazz musicians can't get a recording contract now because the business is rough. I am fortunate to be with this company, but he is the kind of guy who is constantly worried about what you do, even though he tells you to do what you want. Those kinds of things will always be there. You have to be strong and say, 'O.K., that's his problem.' You've got to know that the music is what you want it to be in the sense that you played it and played it well. You just do what you can and shut out the other things.

In New York on his last road trip, Les and his band were preparing to continue their scheduled tour to Japan. They were excited, looking forward to the gig. At the last minute—cancellation. In the midst of the disappointment, another offer came in. A record producer was in New Jersey recording an album with some jazz musicians. He wanted Les McCann to be a part of the album. He had received permission from the record company to use him, and Les agreed. He headed out to New Jersey to join in the efforts to put the album together.

It was a beautiful Frank Lloyd-Wright built studio. I could feel the old feelings coming up again. I was there by myself, with strangers. So I said, 'Hold it. Take a deep breath, pray a little bit.' I told myself that I was here because they wanted me to be.

A necessary and difficult phase of the studio process is developing a rapport with the other musicians.

Once it has been decided who is the semi-leader, you have to get along with different types of personalities. You are dealing with people's feelings all the time.

A producer, assistant producer, and engineer are in the recording booth in an adjoining room. The producer tells the musicians what he wants, but, "we're not in the Army. We are musicians speaking about art."

If it's a studio session where you are making a pop record, and everything is written, and you see what you have to do, there is no problem. This is a situation where they say, 'O.K., let's do a blues tune. Anybody got one?' Someone says, 'I got one, man.'

We try this, and teach the band that, and go and do it. Sometimes you get to a section where someone doesn't like the way everyone wants it played, or he doesn't have the ability. You can get mad and walk out, become a primadonna, or you can say, 'O.K.', and try and deal with it.

My main rapport is with the producer. I look over at him and see him smiling and know we are doing the right thing.

Time spent in a recording studio can be quite expensive. Like the range between an old Volkswagen and a Rolls Royce, recording studios vary in luxury from budget rate at about $10 to elegant, well-stocked studios at about $250 an hour. When the musician or band is signed to a label, the record company foots the bill and sets the tone for how a band will use the time. Some bands try to determine exactly how they will proceed before they enter the studio, others only have a general sense. "I have been in sessions where you sit around all day and try and think of something to do."

In looking back on his life as a jazz musician, Les McCann realizes that he was wrong to believe that the art is the joy.

It has to be the joy within your heart. When you are dealing with all these business people, you can hate what you do if you don't feel strongly about yourself and your music. It's a cold-blooded business, just like any other business in this country, and you get what you can. Agents and managers are like lawyers. They practice perfect lying. It's a game that they all live.

There are specific problems relating to black artists.

The black artists within a record company will only be handled by black people. They play politics. For example, if I come to Detroit, my audience is half black, half write. My music is played on college stations, jazz stations, and FM stations. My music is not played on Rhythm and Blues stations or on very black stations, but that's where they take me for an interview because it is the only door (the black promoter) can get into.

A misconception that people outside the music industry often harbor is the belief that musicians make a lot of money. The potential is there, but realizing that potential is a very different matter.

If you are a big star, you can make a lot of money by getting a big advance from your record company, or by having such a hit record that you make money from sales. It's hard to make money travelling and doing nightclubs. I have to take care of 19 people when we are on the road. It's expensive.

Quite often, Les finds himself in the position of having to turn down a job because his expenses would not be covered.

On the road, you are really just keeping your name going, and keeping the record promoted. Nowadays, the business is at the level where if you don't have a hit record, people don't want to hire you.

The record company takes back your advance from the sales of your record. So, if you get a huge advance, it's going to be a long time before you make any money off of that record unless you have a triple-million seller.

The other way to make money is to write songs. If you are writing, and your songs are published, you have a good chance to make money, especially if it's a hit.

Jazz, and jazz musicians are unique in the world and the business of music. Jazz cannot be taught. It is an expression of feelings.

Jazz is you, spontaneously speaking about something that you care about. It's your life and your expression. You can be taught how to play the piano, but nobody can teach you how to feel. That's how you get across great music. It's the additional feeling in the music, when that becomes one with what you are doing.

Master your instrument, but remember that the most important experience is to experience life, "without even thinking, you will speak from so many different places".

Now if you choose to make a living at it, that's another story. It would be great if you were rich, but I don't think you would suffer enough to get to the point where you have to play the painful parts.

HOYT AXTON

Country Singer, Musician

His dad sang all the time. He can remember hearing the beautiful, clear sounds around the house, in the yard, everywhere. Blues. Old folk songs. Country tunes.

His mom loved to write poetry, loved show biz. In 1956, she co-wrote Elvis Presley's first million seller, "Heartbreak Hotel."

"I saw how much pleasure she got out of writing songs," he recalls fondly, "then I saw those royalty checks coming in and I said, 'Wait a minute!' "

Hoyt Axton wrote his first song when he was 15.

I could sing three or four songs, and that was it. As far as playing guitar, I played with my thumb, very slowly.

Never having taken a music lesson, Hoyt learned to play from other people. In 1961, after a tour of duty in the Navy, he became a folk singer in northern California. With some old folk songs and songs that his father had sung, he sang for tips in a San Francisco place called "The Fox and the Hound."

I used to go the library and get the old folk music books and copy down the lyrics so I would have them right.

The next year, Hoyt co-wrote a song with a fellow he met along the way. The man had written a long song which Hoyt rewrote and played at The Troubadour in Los Angeles. John Stewart, a member of The Kingston Trio, heard the song and recorded it. It was called, "Greenback Dollar", and was a big hit for the Trio and big break for Hoyt Axton.

In this town, nothing succeeds like success, even if you don't know how you got it. I don't know how to make it happen, but I know how to recognize it when it is happening, and take advantage of it—sometimes.

Currently, Hoyt Axton and his band tour the country in an old Greyhound bus.

I have an airplane that I use on business, but not much when I am touring. We try and set it up so that no drives are more than 500 miles between shows, on a daily basis.

Typically, they roll into a town about 2:00 in the afternoon and check into the hotel. Hoyt immediately gets on the phone to see what's going on.

I manage myself, and do about half of my bookings through my own office with my secretary. I lost a couple of million dollars back in the late 60's and early 70's from what I consider to be crooked management, crooked involvement by people. In 1975, I took it over. They sure weren't earning what they were taking.

It's not a job that I wanted. I am not a businessman, I didn't study business, but I wasn't going to end up making millions of dollars over a thirty year career, and end up in the old musicians' home.

Cheeseburger in one hand and phone in the other, Hoyt ties up all the loose ends for the next day or the next week while the band does the sound check in the arena where they will play that night.

My guitar player has a low voice, so he gets up and impersonates me. They all think that's funny and have a good time.

Once they have set the equipment up, and got everything ready for the show, they come back to the hotel, clean up and have a cheeseburger. Then, we go over and do the show.

Stage performance is always more complicated than it may appear.

The major thing, believe it or not, is that there is a split sound system. The bane of any singer's live performance is trying to get a sound on stage through the monitor system, that doesn't feedback, or rumble, or make noises, one where everyone can hear each other and perform their best.

Hoyt enjoys performing in front of a live audience. He has a tremendous amount of respect for the fans that come to hear him play.

Whatever following I have is not necessarily because of any hype program that went down in the industry. It's because I just continue to get out there on that stage, as I have for 25 years, night after night. I've built up a following of people that appreciate that I may not be the most velvet-voiced son-of-a-gun around, I may not be a consummate musician, but they know that after they have put in their twelve hour day, if they go out and take their hard-earned money to pay for it, I am going to work as hard as I can.

After the show, as the crowd files out the door, they load everything back on the bus and return to the hotel to clean up and grab another cheeseburger before hopping on the bus to drive another 500 miles.

The bus is like a mini-home. There is a toaster oven, coffee pot, popcorn popper. Most often, the band spends the night atop the many rolling wheels that carry them into the next town.

Usually a road trip will not extend longer than three weeks at a time.

In 1974, I was on the road 325 days out of the year. I travelled over 100,000 miles on the bus that year.

Though Hoyt Axton earns a major portion of his income through songwriting, performing pays well.

I earn a flat rate. I don't believe in getting a percentage of the door. There are too many ways to be hustled. There are too many doors in some of those places.

Six years ago, in 1979, Hoyt Axton started his own recording label, "Jerimiah Records". The decision to go out on his own grew from the belief that he wasn't getting an honest and fair shake from the labels he had been associated with previously. It was time to take some action.

You need almost unlimited funds. You have to be careful. You have to know something about the business, how it functions, so that you know whether it is working right or wrong for you.

We have had real problems with collecting our money. We have no muscle. We can't say to a distributor, 'Pay us what you owe us', because we are about 30th down the line. All we have to muscle them with is the next nebulous record which may or may not have a market.

Songwriters and publishers are in a better position than in past years. In 1910, records sold for 10 cents. Big, thick records. The writer got a penny, the publisher got a penny. The price of records went up to about $1.30, and the situation remained. The writer continued to get a penny, and the publisher got a penny. It didn't change for sixty years. Currently, however, royalties have caught up and increased to about 4 cents. Additionally, the music business has become fast-paced and complicated.

For example, Arlo Guthrie sells an average of a couple of hundred thousand albums. He has a following out there. Warner Brothers dropped him last year. They aren't really interested if you don't sell 400,000 records, or don't have an organization behind you that is willing to spend $300,000 under the table to have a hit record.

With my last album, I tried to sell it in the United States for six months. It's a good album. I couldn't sell it. I sent it to Europe, and they took it in one week. It's doing very well over there. It would have to do extremely well in Europe, a million units, to bring it back and sell it here.

It's a rough business. Opportunities for shady wheeling and dealing abound. There are no absolutes in an industry that changes as rapidly as music. It responds to a multitude of pressures and directions, economic, social, etc. Prepare yourself. Pay attention. Keep your eyes open and your head clear.

When I canned the Beverly Hills crowd that I had going, the top management, Lear jets, the whole trip, and went out on my own, everyone in that group, business manager, attorney, managers, agents, individually came to me and said, 'Listen man, you're right about those guys, maybe you don't need them, but you need me'.

Their consensus was that I was just another hillbilly from Oklahoma, and that I would be down the tube in six months. I thought, 'They are full of beans'. I had made a couple of million dollars, and they were telling me that I was broke and in debt.

Now, I have one secretary, and a tax man who comes in when I need him, and is paid on a daily basis plus expenses.

For aspiring songwriters, there are publications, like *Songwriter*, that are excellent informational sources. There are services and information sheets that come out bi-weekly or monthly that let you in on some of the tricks of the trade.

Song Plugger, out of Tennessee, provides information on the people who are recording and looking for material.

You won't spin your wheels and send material out to people who either write their own, or have access through other means.

Hoyt underlines the fact that to remain in the music for any length of time, the artist has to love it. "Blind love, like the love a puppy has for his mama. Everything else is up in the air."

Go to college if you are in a position to. A good course to study is accounting. A working knowledge of business can be invaluable in keeping tabs on the flow of your hard-earned dollars.

Play music. Test your songs to live audiences. Work gets work. Study the music of people who really excite you. Stay aware and alert. Don't be paranoid, be watchful.

Looking back on it all, has Hoyt Axton's life as a musician been pretty good?

It's treated me better than I've treated it.

CHRIS COTÉ

Pop Band Singer, Songwriter

He looks like a rock star. Jet black hair falls just above the shoulders of his sleeveless tight tee-shirt. Styled. An earring shines from the right lobe. Weight training has given him upper body strength, performance stamina. He stands tall and commanding upon the stage, the microphone sending lyrics from his original songs out to eager ears. Young women would die to meet him.

His wife makes coffee. Cream and sugar?

His year-old daughter makes an appearance. Daddy?

Kissing them both, he smiles with the pleasure of his family. They are the important ones.

Chris Coté is a songwriter, singer, and keyboard player for the pop band, Max Bonding. He is Max Bonding. "If I left the band, they couldn't use the name."

He is no stranger to the music business. Max Bonding formed after another original band, Avalon, split up. The history of Avalon remains in his memory as a learning experience. It began in 1979. Chris and a songwriting partner were writing music for television. As they worked toward getting their songs covered, they were told that they needed to put a band together. They did. Avalon was born. Chris Coté on keyboards and lead vocals, his partner, lead vocals, and a bass player and drummer.

Exposure is the crucial next step. How do you get someone to hire you to play in a club? It's a catch-22.

They ask you, 'Have you worked anywhere?' You say no, and they say, 'Well, you're not working here.'

There are, however, certain clubs that will take a chance on a new band. You've got to find them.

Most original band clubs offer music six or seven nights a week and they must fill all of their time slots. A new band can usually get a midnight slot on a Monday night, or some other unpopular time. If they like you, and if you draw a certain number of people, they will book you earlier. Have a good attitude, a professional presentation, and get all your friends and acquaintances to come out and see you play.

Avalon played for about a year and a half. They built up a following, drawing crowds of two to three hundred people. The next step was to get a record deal.

We got hooked with a producer, signed a production deal with him, and did four songs. It was with those four songs that we did our final assault on the record companies. We pressed it up on vinyl and sent them to everybody.

It was called a spec deal. The producer's time was out of his own pocket, but instead of paying for high priced studio time, they arranged to use a recording studio's down time.

It's available time that isn't being paid for anyway. If anything happens with the album, the studio will get a piece of it, and the producer will get a piece of it for his time.

A professional package was the goal. The band had a photographer shoot a cover photo for the album which they joined with the record, a resume, and a biography to complete the package.

You can't just drop a tape off in your blue jeans and expect them to say, 'Oh great! We've been waiting for this!'

One week after their last good gig, Avalon was offered a record deal with Capitol Records.

A few snags began to surface.

My partner didn't want to play anymore. We had almost fired our drummer twice, and were going to fire our bass player, too. Each time we had been about to fire them, someone came along and said they loved the band and we didn't want to appear unsettled. Then, we got the record deal and couldn't fire them.

Essentially, the producer of an album is like a film director. His job is to work with the band or the artist, pick the right songs for them, or take songs that have been written and make sure they make sense. His job is to make the song and the album come alive.

A producer will generally want to hear all of your songs. He may hear a little nugget in one tune and suggest a rewrite around a particular section.

A certain amount of rewrite is fine for an artist to accept, but there are certain changes that become strictly gratuitous. The producer wants to put his little imprint on it.

Avalon's record deal stipulated that the A and R (Artist and Repertoire) man at Capitol Records who had signed the group, would also be the person who produced them.

Chris and his partner spent six months getting out of their old production deal, a long and harrowing experience, and signed with Capitol on Christmas eve of 1981. Within a month, the producer told them that he couldn't work with the drummer and the bass player.

We had to break the news to them that they weren't going to play on the album. They got advance money, but it was a very depressing situation.

The album was not the success they had hoped. One of the major problems centered around management.

We were signed to the record label by the same man who was producing us. He told us we didn't need management at that point which we realized later was very self-serving. He didn't want a manager around to get in his way. Also, in a way, he was right. You don't need a manager if your have no product, if you aren't playing around. We were stuck. We had nobody to turn to when we felt that things weren't going the way they should be going.

Another thing is that we didn't have a strong, good relationship with the record company because we didn't have a manager to schmooze the people, the secretaries, the head of the departments. The band can do that, but only to a certain extent.

You are like a product. They don't want to talk to the product, they want to talk to the handlers.

Avalon eventually dissolved. With the experience behind him, a bit older and a bit wiser, Chris formed Max Bonding and began again.

Each morning, Chris wakes up to an exercise routine of weight-lifting or running.

It's important, especially if you are a singer, to be in good physical shape.

For the following hour and a half, he is on the telephone calling members of the band, publishing people, A and R people.

I call people I know who are producers and tell them what's going on. If I have a gig, I tell them where we're playing. If I don't have a gig, I tell them that I have a tape that they should hear. It's called schmoozing. It's called making contact. You are reminding them that you are here. There are a lot of people out there trying to get ahead.

Essentially, Chris is performing a managerial function for the new formed band.

It's unfortunate, but true. When you are in the 'up and coming' stage, it's hard to find a manager, and you need one. It's important to have somebody. A lot of careers have been made or broken because of management. It's another catch-22. You can't get a manager until you are good, and you can't get good until you have a manager. I sit in that crack. I am waiting to get somebody.

From 11:00 in the morning until about 2:00 in the afternoon, the band rehearses. They try out new songs, polish old ones, and tighten up the arrangements. Afterwards, Chris is back on the phone, or meeting with people, or writing new material.

On days when the band has a gig, the idea is to lay low and save up their energy. There is always a sound check, so the band gets to the club early, with all the equipment, to get it loaded in so that there will be no surprises later. They play a few songs in the empty club to make sure it sounds right, then leave to rest before returning that night to play.

In most original band situations, you don't make any money. It's maybe ten bucks, not even gas money. At the club we are playing in tonight, we are getting forty bucks a man. The only real purpose of the gig is to get people to come out and give positive or negative criticism.

Chris sees Max Bonding as at the end of phase one. Phase one: perform the music, make sure the personnel is right and everything gels with the band. Phase two: tighten up on the arrangement and try and get into a studio and record.

Right now I have one song, averagely recorded with the band. We need three or four really well-recorded songs, the arrangements tightened up, then we can start playing for industry people.

If you are a member of a band when you make a record, you are called a royalty artist. You play and sing on the record, and are paid once per tune, union scale.

Now, for example, if I were a royalty artist, and everyone else was just a part of the band, they would be paid for every minute they are in the studio. They would get maybe three or four times union scale. It's a question of whether you want to make the royalties or not. Sometimes it's good, sometimes it's bad. You can wait around forever to make your money.

Specifically with a band like Max Bonding, should the band be offered a record deal, Chris would not have the choice whether he wanted to be a royalty artist or not, but the members of his band would.

For example, our bass player has said that he doesn't know if he would sign a record deal. He would rather just make the money and not be tied up and pay legal fees and all that.

For beginning musicians, this is something to think about. You may want to work in a band as a royalty artist, or may choose to become so good at your instrument that you will be hired to play on the road or in the studio with another band.

If you concentrate primarily on playing and not really on writing songs, it is a sure sign that you will become a hired hand. There's nothing wrong with that, but it is really stiff competition.

If you spend a good amount of your time writing, getting good at your instrument, but concentrating on writing and singing, you will probably have more luck (becoming) a wealthy artist. Anybody can luck into a great song with the right breaks.

Chris emphasizes one point: the only way to be successful in the music business is to know the business side as well as you know your music. You have to be willing to put in time to read *Billboard Magazine*, keep your ears open, find out who is who in the business, and remember who is who. In this rapidly changing business, keep up, and stay in touch with what is going on at all times.

As you proceed toward success in the music industry, watch for snakes in the grass. "Anytime there is a chance to make big money, there is the chance to be taken by sleazy people, even in the reputable companies."

When the record with Avalon was done and coming out, I had a sneaking suspicion that maybe it wasn't going to be successful. I went to a family reunion back east and it brought home the fact that family and friends are what matter anyway.

On the other hand, that feeling passes and you say, 'Yeah, that's great, but I still want to have a hit record.'

PAUL JOHNSON

Freelance Drummer

He taps his fingers continuously, unconsciously. He lives with a beat in his head and his mind on the business. A drummer. It's all he ever wanted to be. As a freelance drummer, he takes on the responsibility of familiarizing himself with all styles of music. He can play anything, everything. A newcomer to the southern California music scene, he says "Yes" to any type of call that comes in. Work gets work in this business, and he is willing to pay his dues.

Last week I did an Iranian dance. They got my name through another ethnic job I did.

Paul's father was a drummer. As a kid, Paul was always playing. It was natural for him to study music in school. He never thought about alternatives. He was a drummer.

I went to music camps as a kid, then got a music scholarship to Arizona State University. I studied for two years, then hit the road with The Four Freshmen, The Four Lads, and some nostalgic vocal acts.

The bands hired Paul through an agency he had worked for. An agent there referred him because he could read music and play shows. His experiences on the road with the bands put him in contact with a lot of people who would later be instrumental in connecting him with people in Los Angeles.

Has the move to Los Angeles improved his career?

It has improved my playing. The environment in Los Angeles is rich with musical talent. The inspiration and motivation to practice are here. A real motivation is paying high rent and not getting very many gigs. To me, that is motivation to practice and get really good.

Morning is the time to get on the phone and make contact with people who are in a position to hire him. Often, Paul has been at a club the night before where he came across someone who told him about someone who needed someone to play.

They might tell me that this person does shows and needs sight readers, for example. The names and phone numbers are usually scribbled on napkins or the back of my business cards.

Nighttime in a nightclub is time to be seen and to politic yourself. Let people know you are still alive and playing music.

I go out and grease the wheel, as they say, supporting other musicians, and making contacts if I can. I follow up the contacts with a phone call to check in and say, 'Hi, I am a friend of so and so and if you ever need a drummer, or if your regular one can't make it, give me a call'. With the phone calls, I am trying to line things up, maybe get an audition with someone new.

There is a hodgepodge of people at different levels of advancement trying to get work. Eventually you meet them, become part of that scene, and they take it for granted that you can handle it. That's when they'll call you, and you're on your way. It takes time. You have to jump in the ocean and swim around for awhile.

Each day, Paul practices his instrument. At the very minimum, he spends one hour with his drums. More often, Paul practices for two to five hours each day.

If I hear something exciting on the radio, I'll write it down or run in and play it on the drums right away. I like to be able to play it as well (as the drummer on the radio).

Aside from practicing, I spend a good portion of my day listening to new records, and the radio. I don't just listen passively, but am aware of exactly what they are doing so that I can duplicate it myself.

Most of Paul's gigs (jobs) are at night. Sometimes it's every night, sometimes, once a week.

Generally, freelance and studio agents don't have agents. The artists are a part of the musician's union and are protected. When musicians play a union job, they file a contract with the union and will be assured that they get paid.

For an average four hour dance, like a wedding for example, Paul's salary may range from a minimum of $60 to a more desirable $125. It's usually between $85 and $100. A steady engagement where you work six nights a week will generally pay a little less per night.

I am trying to get into studio recording. That involves television, movies, jingles, radio, or anything that is recorded and has music.

If you get hired to do a session, and the producer likes your work, he's apt to call you back. If you prove yourself to be capable and likable the first time, chances are they will call you again.

They like professionalism. A lot of times they will ask you to do things that you wouldn't agree with as a musician. That producers don't necessarily know, but you have to just smile and do what they say.

It's a matter of waiting until you meet the right people. It takes time, so in the meantime, you do the work you can, and do what you have to to support yourself.

Our society requires a lot of capital to be comfortable, and it is often hard to meet that. You have to compromise once in awhile. But, the joys of playing my instrument far outweigh having to eat Spagettio's once in awhile.

Paul points out being a musician, being a great musician, isn't your ticket to prosperity. The very rich musicians are the star entertainers. For example, David Bowie is rich, but his drummer isn't. Neil Diamond is rich, but his drummer isn't. The musicians, while they are making a handsome salary, aren't rich. It's just a good gig, great exposure. If you've worked with David Bowie, you're never going to be out of work after that.

As far as the business end of it goes, trying to solicit for myself gets a little depressing. But, I have learned so much and am playing better, so my attitude is good. Having a good attitude helps you get gigs. People don't want to hire a bully or a sour person. The next guy is just as good. It doesn't pay to be a downer or a drug addict. They'll just forget you and hire someone else.

JACK ELLIOTT

Composer

American pride was renewed that summer. Skeptics warned of traffic grid locks, terrorism, unruly mobs of spectators. The excitement in the air overrode the worry. Thousands of people, hot dogs in hand, sat in the Coliseum and cheered and cried for the Olympic athletes.

As each event concluded, the three best stood still while the now-famous music filled the air with notes of pride, sharing, and unity. It brought the crowds to their feet, silenced the home viewers, and expressed the magnitude of the event.

Jack Elliott conducted the Olympic orchestra. He has written television scores that bring forth recognition in an instant. He is currently the head of The Foundation for New American Music, a non-profit organization to raise money to commission people to write for The Foundation's performing arm, The New American Orchestra. A plaque on his desk remembering the 5th annual concert at the Dorothy Chandler Pavilion reads, "With gratitude, appreciation, and respect for following the 'dream'."

With a voice of deep resonance and a handsome face beneath an epicurean gray beard, Jack is a man of confidence and talent. He graduated from the Hart College of Music, now a part of the University of Hartford, Connecticut, with a degree in composition. For the next year he taught, then continued his education toward a masters degree.

> *I moved to New York. I made a living teaching, playing piano in groups, and playing the organ in synogogue while I studied composition. Writing was always my main interest.*

From New York, Jack crossed the Atlantic to spend a couple of years as an accompanist and a music director in Europe. He worked in a record company writing arrangements for singers. When he returned, he was offered a job in a theater as dance arranger on a Broadway show.

> *That led me into television as a dance arranger on shows like "The Ed Sullivan Show," "The Perry Como Show." And in 1963, to come to Los Angeles as an arranger for "The Judy Garland Show."*

The years of writing for variety television led to jobs at Disney, then television work at Universal Studios, then movies of the week, then series television. It has been a career much like a winding trail of dominoes. One thing leads to another. Work begets work.

> *I've done a little bit of everything. I've (conducted) the Grammys ever since they've been a live show. I've done the Emmys, Kennedy Center Honors, The Academy Awards, and at the same time, I continue writing the background scores for television.*

Jack's initial launch into a career in music was a combination of playing and being heard, and his own initiation. Listen to my stuff! Hear me play! What do you need? What can I do musically that can fit in?

> *Today, a lot of work comes from people who know me. That is a result of age. You are helped a great deal by your friendships and your peers, and people you have worked with, for, or around. You have to be very aware of what circles you travel in.*

Making connections is a way of life, a technique for living.

> *You don't look at it as what people can do for you because that is extremely transparent and easy to pick up on. My friends were musicians and we were all pretty much involved in doing the same kinds of things. We would always work together. If somebody called me to do something that was conflicting with what I had to do, I would always recommend a friend of mine, or people that I knew.*

> *I've had no objection to calling up someone and telling them that I am looking for work. I think that it's part of anyone's education to be aware that your friends are going to be what you've got to count on.*

Although he spends most of his days in his office at The Foundation for New American Music, Jack continues to write musical scores, most often for television.

For the beginning television score composer, it is a chicken and egg situation. You will need to develop a demonstration tape because no one knows what you have done before. However, demonstration reels and tapes tell the listener only what you have done, which may not be right for them. At the same time, you probably won't get a job at all without a tape.

At this point in Jack Elliott's career, with a string of successes behind him, who makes the decision regarding his musical score?

It could be anyone from the garbage man to the executive producer. You hope that it's the producer and the director. I've seen strange things happen on scoring stages. I've seen producers come in and go over to the fellow who's pouring the coffee. There's a 60 or 70 piece orchestra playing over there, and he'll ask him, 'How do you like it?'

You have people with diverse backgrounds that have managed to put projects together. They want to get it on, make the deal. Many times, they don't have too great a knowledge of what they are doing. As they get more successful they begin to believe that their success is tied, not in the ability to administer and make the deal, but to a creative situation. You find lawyers who put deals together, now start talking about what the score should be. It's very difficult to deal with.

As soon as you begin to believe that your past successes will insure future success, the table can be turned on you.

As you get older, one of the problems is that producers don't want to deal with you because they figure you are going to do what you do, and they can't change you. I have a theory that people don't hire you for what you do, they hire you because of what you've done, so they can tell you what to do. The more established you are, the more vulnerable you are in many respects. They want to get some fresh blood.

You must know exactly what you want out of the profession of writing television scores. If you are looking to make a lot of money, the potential is definitely there.

The more money you make, the less likely you are going to have control over what you are doing. People become more and more specific as to what they are paying you for.

It is a collaborative business. You must have a personality that can handle collaboration.

You don't have the ability to say, 'This is what I write, this is the way I want it to sound, and this is the way it's going to be.'

The best line I ever heard about this business was that there is no other business where you can make so much money and have so much time off to sit around and bitch about how bad the business is.

You need a tremendous amount of enthusiasm and talent for the work you are producing. Additionally, you need to develop an ability to be completely indifferent as to what happens to it after you do it.

That can be tough to handle. This is an art form, only in certain aspects. Basically, it's a business. You are providing a service, and if they don't like it, they'll go somewhere else and get a different kind of service.

Fill your background with as much education as you can get your hands on. Sooner or later, the education will help.

There are some people who don't need it. You want as much knowledge as possible, but the way you get it is another story. You can go to school for it, work for it, or a combination of the two. If you're a terrific piano player who never learned how to write music, go and learn how to write and put it together with your ability as a player.

But remember, no one can teach you to be a composer. They can teach you technique, but they can't teach you what to write. As you do more, you're going to get better at it.

DIRECTING

The theatre lights grow dim and the opening credits flash on the screen. You glance a minute to note the stars and the key supporting players. Then, you turn to your companion or reach into the barrel for popcorn. With the exception of directing superstars like Steven Spielberg or John Houston, few people remember the off-screen artists who put their favorite films together. Yet, of all the professionals associated with the production of a motion picture or television show, the director is considered one of the, if not the most powerful player. He or she is in charge—involved in selecting actors, approving costumes and sets, staging rehearsals and choosing camera angles. The stakes are high. Weak direction can result in financial and professional disaster.

The same principles apply to stage and radio performances. The role of director is so important that in some productions, the director is selected even before the script. When asked why he wanted to try his hand at directing, a famous actor replied, "Which would you rather be, the player or the pawn?"

As defined by the Directors Guild of America, the director has sole charge of and makes final artistic judgments during these three basic phases of making motion pictures, and television productions on film, tape, or live:

- **Pre-production.** The director makes hundreds, even thousands of decisions on the final script, sets, props, special effects, locations, and schedule. The director must balance artistic consideration with financial limitations.

- **Production.** The director rehearses the actors, fine-tunes their performances, places the cameras, determines which take, of many takes, will be printed, and otherwise composes the scene. The principles to be utilized are similar whether the director is directing a theater piece, feature film, a television show or special, the evening news, the Super Bowl game, or even a soap commercial.

- **Post-production.** The director, along with the producer, makes decisions about the project which includes editing, dubbing, scoring, and other final procedures that bring it to the point where it may be previewed or broadcast. The director, along with the editor, selects the best shots, taking segments from one filming and splicing them with another. Often, the director will supervise the re-recording of entire scenes if the sound quality is inadequate.

However, directors are not kings. They work under producers who are concerned with both the artistic production and other aspects—particularly marketing and finance. So, directors may find themselves caught between actors and actresses with strong convictions about the drama, and producers who feel that marketing or other factors make their idea difficult to execute. But, a good director can sell his or her ideas to producers, actors/actresses, and crew to really control the process.

The director is the storyteller. His or her vision of the script is what audiences see on the screen or stage.

This power of control and artistic decision have attracted many into the elite profession of director.

RICHARD DONNER

Film Director (Lethal Weapon, Ladyhawke, The Goonies, Superman I, The Omen)

He began as an assistant director for live television, one of three assistants on the show. Then, assistant directors were like traffic cops—there was urgency and excitement. Live television was much like theater. Richard's job as AD in New York resembled a floor manager's job. At 6:00 a.m. he was taping the rehearsal floors to the dimensions of the set. He put chairs where the beds and couches were. Hopefully, with a little imagination, the actors would feel like they were rehearsing on the actual set.

For the rest of the day, the assistants were at the beck and call of the director, ready to do anything and everything he needed.

Probably the most exciting part of it was that you tried something new each time. I think the thing I learned most from that experience was how to work with actors. Also, I picked up the ability to improvise at the last moment.

In New York, around 1954, Richard Donner inaugurated his career as a director working on commercials, documentaries, and industrial films. But, feature films were always his goal. Whatever he did, from a 60 second commercial to a 60 minute documentary, he imagined that he was making a movie. A commercial was a tiny movie that was over in a minute, a documentary was a special kind of movie with a specific subject. They were stepping stones. He was working his way up—paying his dues.

People say that you pay your dues, well I have never paid my dues. I have been so lucky and so happy with what I am doing that I don't believe it. I've had a lot of bumps. I have had guys be heavies on me and mean and tasteless people have used their power wrong, but it was still a thrill that I was directing them, that I was making a movie.

Over the course of his successful directing career, Richard Donner has had the thrill of directing *Lethal Weapon*, *The Goonies*, *Ladyhawke*, *Superman*, and *The Omen* among many others. He is still childlike in his love of the work. It is a contagious enthusiasm, the aura of a man who knows who he is, what he wants, and how to get it. When he reads a script, he asks himself a question: Would I like to see this? If the answer is "yes," he makes it, and lives the craziness of a director's life for the year it takes from script to final answer print.

Casting is a vital portion of the director's job. The combination of cast and crew can be the life or death of your picture. With his actors, Richard Donner begins the casting process by attempting to acquire a sense of their personalities. When an actor comes in to read, or to meet him, Richard is looking to see what he or she is like, and if their personal character is right for the part in the script.

Once an actor is hired, Richard prefers to have him or her present when he is nearing a decision about another actor. That way, "it becomes a homogenous group."

I cast the crew like I do actors. I want to surround myself with not only a competent, exciting, creative group of people, but a group with a good temperament, a nice sense of humor, and an enjoyable personality. It's a family for the next couple of months, and you want to come home to a nice family every morning. I have often not taken the best man at his job because I have not liked his personality.

Once the cast and crew have been hired and the script is ready to go—rehearsal.

I always have at least a week, sometimes two, where we live, eat and breathe the characters. We walk it through, talk it through, and try and resolve all the problems beforehand. It's insanity to resolve problems on the set when you are shooting. I try and make sure that everything is delineated well in advance. Of course, it never is. Once you start looking through a camera and bringing something to life, it takes on a whole new life.

In the studio, a feature director's working week is five days long. On location, it's six days, "which means that you are working seven days a week because on the seventh day, you are preparing, going to the editor, looking at locations."

Typically, a shooting day begins at 8:00 a.m. Richard is on the set by 7:00 or 7:30.

The morning is the best time for me. I never take it home with me at night. I try and get it out of my head totally, go home and have my own personal life, a good night's sleep. When I wake up in the morning and my mind is fresh, that's when I really attack the day's work and the previous day's work. It's very difficult, but I find that I have to do it or I won't start fresh in the morning.

On the set, Richard acknowledges that he never really feels like he's in charge though everyone comes to him for an answer, and he is the only person who can give the answer.

It's a funny feeling. I have never been one to be a commanding officer. I am pretty laid back and easygoing. I always feel that people will do their job on their own, they just need guidance and direction.

I am surrounded by subjectivity, the actor who sees his role the way his character is, the special effects man, wardrobe, make-up, everybody. I take a lot of subjectivity and try to transpose it into an objective thought. That's the way I try and make my movies. I try and give everyone their own space and realm. I'm willing to listen to anything that anyone has to say. I love contributions. But when it boils down to it, there can be only one person directing a film. You cannot make a movie by committee.

While a shooting day may end by 6:00 p.m., the director's working day extends far into the evening. Dailies (film shot the previous day). Mechanical problems. In a picture with a lot of special effects, Richard might call key people for a meeting at the end of the day in an attempt to foresee any problems with the next day's shoot.

Then, usually, just before I go home, I may stop in and work a little bit with the editor. I see what he has done, what he is putting together, if I have to add anything to my day's work.

Richard is rarely home before 9:30 or 10:00 at night.

For that period of making a motion picture, your life is not your own. It's crazy time. Unless you live with someone who understands it and can live with it, it is almost an impossible deed. Your lifestyle is so erratic.

Final cut. Directors want it. Studios are afraid to let go of the control. A director with final cut is in an enviable position, it means that the studio has extended a vote of confidence, the director will have artistic control over his or her film. Thankfully, Richard Donner has reached the point in his professional life where he has the final decision of how his picture will be presented in the theaters.

However, he cautions that, as a new director, you cannot do much to protect your cut. Instead, surround yourself with good people who respect you and your directional abilities, do your best work, and hope.

You've got to look at the studio's point of view. They are giving you a minimum of two or three million up to 20 or 30 million dollars to make a movie. Unless you have proven yourself, I can understand them saying, 'Hey wait a minute'.

It's a very difficult position to be in, negotiating that final cut. It's called, as in Shakespeare, the unkindest cut of all.

In the course of most successful director's lives, there will come a time when he or she will be directing a major star. When you know that you will be working with a star, prepare yourself for what you will be getting into.

You know that you are working with the same ego that you have. You know that you are working with the same insecurities that you have. You also know that you are working with a very talented human being. That's why you're doing it.

You have to enter into that relationship knowing that there will be a lot of pain, a lot of hurt, a lot of grovelling, and a lot of giving. If you don't, you are fooling yourself, hurting your picture, and hurting the eventuality of a good relationship.

Know that it is going to happen to you and be prepared to handle it.

To prepare yourself for a career as a feature film director, you can take classes to learn about the technical aspects of the job, you can work in some capacity on a movie set, you can enter from the acting profession. Whichever road you chose, Richard Donner stresses the importance of preparing yourself for life. Look around you. Look at reality.

There are probably eight million people thinking the same thoughts, and getting off a different bus at the same time. It's probably stupid to come out (to Hollywood) and be naive, but it is probably the best way. If you're not naive, you'll never come.

I think that this is a town where if you analyze things, you'll fail. Go by the seat of your pants and be instinctive. Go by your gut instinct and take a crack at it. It's a drug. It's a terrible addiction.

The stress of a director can be enormous. You are always surrounded by people waiting for an answer, a cast and crew waiting for direction—and a studio waiting for a picture. The responsibility is on your shoulders. The art lies in assuming the responsibility, but allowing it to rest lightly.

I'm the big boss. I am ringleader. It's got to be that way. It's nice. I don't use it to dominate. I use it to try and keep the proper control on a picture. The end result of a motion picture belongs to the director. If it's good, everybody takes credit. It it's bad, it's 'Well, the director sure messed up'.

I always say that my car is pointed toward the gate. As long as I am secure and happy enough with myself, and confident about what I do, I am prepared to go only to a certain point. But no further.

ALLAN ARKUSH

Music Video, Film and Television Director

In the mid-60's, he was a high school student with an interest in film. He thought about graduating and going to film school. At the time the best known film schools were UCLA, the University of Southern California (USC) and New York University (NYU). He spoke with his counselors.

"What direction should I take?" he asked.

"What is film school?" they inquired.

Allan enrolled as a freshman at Franklin and Marshall College in Pennsylvania, in the psychology department. A year later, he transferred to NYU film school to study under Martin Scorsese.

One of the things I have found is important in any field, but especially in film, is to have an inspirational teacher. It can make a big difference.

In 1970, Allan Arkush graduated from NYU with honors, and made a student film that won second prize in the National Student Film Festival.

While at NYU, Allan took every possible opportunity to make films. He found that the more he worked at it, the better he got. Film history was an important part of the film school curriculum. As a filmmaker, a background in film history provides the vocabulary that you'll use and carry with you throughout your career.

Within the film industry, there are mixed opinions about the value of film school education versus a hands-on apprenticeship in a film studio.

It depends on what area you are going into, and whether you are going into the film business to make money or to make good movies. Oddly enough, that first year at Franklin and Marshall was the most helpful. I got a very good education.

In film school, I was very motivated by my classmates. They are people that I still work and deal with. Also, you can make student films that are stupid. It's really important to embarrass yourself when you are making student films. It's primary. You may never ever get another chance to make something that is so personal.

It's kind of sad when I see film students go in and all they want to do is make a little short film to show to movie executives to get them a job. That's not the purpose of film school.

Film school can, however, be a means by which your talent as a filmmaker can be recognized. The movie business is a relatively small one. People know each other and continuously rely on a little help from their friends.

Scorsese, my teacher, started working with Roger Corman doing an exploitation picture called Boxcar Bertha. *Roger asked Martin to recommend some good film students because he was doing a series of nurse's movies and needed people to direct them. A friend of mine got the job, and he invited me out. I got a job in the editing room of New World Pictures with Roger Corman at $75 a week. That was in 1974.*

Allan soon started directing for Roger Corman. His career began to bloom after he co-directed a movie entitled, "Hollywood Boulevard".

We did it for $75,000 in ten days. I got paid $85 for directing it, and it went on to gross a million and a half.

After directing a few more films, Allan formulated an idea for a high school musical. He knew the rock scene. He sensed that his idea would be a success. Eventually he got the green light and directed *Rock and Roll High School* which has since become a big cult movie.

Right around 1980 or 1981, rock videos started coming along. Everything I had done had a lot of music in it. I did an interview where I mentioned that I wanted to do a music video, and I got a phone call from the manager of Def Leopard.

The manager had loved all of his movies and had read the interview. He picked up the telephone, dialed information, and asked if they had a listing for Allan Arkush. Minutes later, he had Allan on the phone. He told Allan that he was managing a new group and was looking for a director who understood what they wanted to do.

So, I sat down with the group at a concert and asked them, 'What do you want to do?' They told me what they wanted, and I told them that it was no problem.

One thing led to another, and soon Allan's resume expanded to include the direction of several rock videos. It was a natural combination of his love for music and his knowledge of filmmaking.

Most video shoots are one or two days. The pre-production is vastly important. With a short shooting schedule and a tight budget, the planning and pre-production activities increase in importance.

Inexperienced people cut down on pre-production as a way of saving money, and all they do is lose that money. They have thrown it away.

The first task of the director is to find the best location and the cameraman. The shoot has been thought through, so that when the director looks at the location, he or she is able to take the shot list and transpose it to the reality of the room.

I walk through the whole shot list with the cameraman and simplify things and figure out which shots will be in which direction. The pre-production takes about two to three weeks on the average.

In the case of the Elvis Costello video I did, I met with Elvis, we had dinner together and we talked about the video. I sensed what he wanted and didn't want to do in terms of his performance. Then we shot the next day. It was a 7:00 a.m. call.

As the director, Allan is on the set, ready to work early, while the crew is still setting up. He knows that he will be pushing everyone to their limits, and feels that it is best to take a few hours out of your sleep and be ready to work the minute the crew is ready. It shows a commitment. You are also available to handle any small problems that might come up.

We didn't get our first shot until about 11:30 in the morning. We worked straight through and didn't finish until about 2 or 3 a.m. By the time I went home, it was 4:30 or 5:00 in the morning. It's load-in, shoot, load-out. That's what video schedules are like. It's really hard work. I often hear about video shoots that last for 36 hours straight because nobody really knows what they are doing.

Allan has had the experience of working with both actors and musicians. He finds it easier, in a production situation, to work with actors.

Actors know what is needed of them. They understand the nature of the performance. Rock bands are not trained as actors. The director has to talk them through each scene, give them line readings, things you would never do with an actor. Sometimes I have even had to show guitar players how to play their guitars in an exciting manner so that it looks interesting.

Most musicians are familiar with the microphone but not the camera. They have no idea what they look like when they are singing. They are used to performing for the back row of an arena, not the close lens of a camera.

They really can't act. The best you can hope for is some charm from them, or a certain amount of lack of inhibition.

In essence, the band is the producer of the video since it is coming out of their royalties.

They have a lot to say about it. They have so much control, but are not always the best people to know what is best filmically. This isn't true of Elvis Costello or Bette Midler or any of the really good people, but many times there is a sense of cliche. They want it to be like another video they saw. The similar format that you see so often in videos comes from the bands. You have a similar subject matter, you have people who want to look like other groups, and you get a similarity of vision.

Can you make a career out of directing rock videos? Allan doesn't think so. The budgets aren't big enough.

When I say career, I mean a 20 year career. Someone can certainly make videos for five years and make a living at it. To do it for $3,000 a video, when it is so much work, doesn't pay your time. When you consider what the DGA (Directors Guild of America) minimum for a director is, doing a video is like doing it for free. Of course you move up, and eventually get the big jobs—and you can certainly make a living at that.

Making videos can be a sideline or can lead to other things. Someone who does videos can then do commercials, but I don't think that you can move from videos to features or television.

Allan sees the music business as having more respect for the artist than the movie business does. They are treated well and not interfered with artistically.

In the movie and television field, if they could do without a director, they would. The executives in the music business seem to come from a background where they are not musicians. They can't sit down at the piano and write a song like Elvis Costello can. So, the attitude throughout the industry is that the artist knows something that they don't know. They want to give them as much rope as possible.

This has transferred over in the video field. It is why they have been burned a lot, but it is also why it is often very pleasant to work for these record companies. They will let you take a big risk. Of course, it is not as big of a financial risk as the movie business, but they are willing to go with you.

For the beginning filmmaker, videos are a great opportunity. The film student can take a local band and make a rock video and there is a chance that it will be played.

On the other hand, with a dramatic short film, your only hope in the industry is an Academy Award nomination, and even that doesn't necessarily lead to another directing offer.

With a video, you have a chance for exposure, and you can deal with people who have a similar amount of experience as you.

In this business of one-thing-leads-to-another, the artist can find him or herself pigeon-holed. You are offered jobs based on your previous work. People will hire you because they want someone who has experience with a certain type of style.

I thought that I would be able to do things in the video area that I wasn't able to do in the feature area. I thought I would be able to do much more experimental work, things that are more in line with some of the interests I have like non-narrative story-telling and visuals for their own sake.

I used to love underground films in the late 60's with the techniques of painting on film and abstractions. Those are the things that I wanted to get into, but I am not offered those videos. I am offered the videos that are humorous, that demand a really good performance from the musician. It's hard for me to get something that is dramatic or to get a certain kind of artist to go for what I want to do because I don't have film to show them.

Find a band in your high school. Borrow a video tape camera. Most high schools have some sort of audio visual society with two tape decks. Hook up the two tape decks and edit it afterwards. Try anything you can think of. It may seem embarrassing or silly, but the more you do it, the better you'll get. Build up a reel of different videos and then take them to a record company and say, "This is what I can do." They are always looking for new people.

You can also submit your rock video to MTV. They will accept "basement tapes," unsolicited tapes, and will watch them and pick the ones they like. MTV invites various people in the video and music business to look at the tapes and give them a grade. The A tapes will be shown, and bands can end up with record contracts.

Other avenues include local television shows. "I'm sure that some of the local area shows will air local videos." Contact the television stations in your area to see if they would be willing to screen your three minute video for possible placement on their show. It's good exposure. A video is something that you can produce with minimum expense, unlike the difficulties of putting a film together. You will have something tangible to show people.

A lot of video companies need people to go out and bust their backs and do these kinds of videos where there is not much profit margin. It's mostly perspiration that gets it done.

It's a 'hands-on' business as opposed to movie making. You can't walk on a movie set, no matter who you are, and start moving the props around. In a video, you can pick up the table and say, 'Put it there!" That's really satisfying. It's rolling up your sleeves and actually working.

The video business is in a state of flux. It is still new enough so there are people in record companies who will look at your tape. If they like your style or an idea that comes across in the tape, they may think of you for a regular video.

I think the business will expand because it is now getting into concerts and regular programming. Everyone is talking about long form video tapes. You go in and buy a tape for $29.95 that is an hour long. There is the chance for it to really expand where an album will come out on video tape before it will come out as a regular record. With all the cable stations showing videos, there is certainly a demand. It's not just rock groups that are going to need videos, it's country bands and middle of the road singers. Not all the big video companies want to do a country video. If you can find an area where there is a need, go to it.

There aren't very many Roger Cormans around anymore who will let you do a feature. It's harder now. I think that the video way is a better way.

BILL PERSKY

Television Director (Kate and Allie, Movies of the Week)

He stood, smiling, before the tuxedoed crowd. His colleagues applauded. The television cameras zoomed in on his left hand as he raised the golden Emmy award in appreciation.

Best Director.

"Kate and Allie".

Bill Persky would remember that evening. He would think about it on the plane back to New York to continue working on the hit show that he directs, writes for, and produces.

Bill initially got into directing through writing. He didn't feel that the directors were conveying the same messages he was writing, so he decided to do it himself.

Most directors of half hour television shows don't have a lot to say. They are really traffic cops. It's all the producer/writer. The only reason our show is different is because I am a producer/writer who also directs.

Bill received his bachelor's degree from Syracuse University. He studied some communications, but looking back, feels that none of it contributed to what he would eventually do.

In a way, the more diverse information you have, the more you benefit. In terms of the actual work, you learn it all by doing it.

For example, I have a kid working for me as a gofer. He went to college and television school, and he's learned more in the past six months by getting sandwiches for people and hanging around than he ever learned in schools.

However, an important point to note is that in the competitive business of film and television, the competition for every job, even gofer, will be stiff.

You do have to start cutting people off somewhere. So, I guess there is a tendency to hire someone who has gone to school and studied, and has paid some dues, rather than a kid who never went to school.

"Kate and Allie," like most television comedy is an in-studio, tape show. The average show is on a five-day week schedule, normally Monday through Friday. However, Bill Persky's experience is more complete than that of a director who isn't also producing the show.

There are writer/producers. Every comedy show in television is produced by a writer because ninety percent of the work in the show, and what keeps the show going, is based on whether your scripts are good. So, in television comedy, being a producer involves dealing with scripts. Also, the producer does the editing and things like that, so normally, the director isn't as involved as I am.

Monday morning, 8:30. Bill is at the studio to begin editing the show that was taped on the previous Friday.

When you shoot a show, it's long and there are mistakes. You do two shows; a dress rehearsal, and an air show, and you take the best performances and shots from each. Tape is really edited as you go along, so I am really just refining it.

Monday, noon. The network executives and the cast have arrived. They sit around a table and read the show that will be taped in the following week. It is important to hear the spoken script. This allows the opportunity to make any necessary rewrites before it goes into production.

Occasionally, the cast and network people will make comments or suggest changes, however, "there is a lot of trust in me and Bob Randall, so they know we are going to fix whatever doesn't work. Our scripts have been inordinately good, which is a very unique situation."

Afterward, the cast reads the script of the show that they will be rehearsing that week. It's already been rewritten but some changes may still be suggested and made.

Monday, 1:00 p.m. Lunch break. Bill returns to the editing room to continue editing last week's show.

Of course, our show is different again, because I am a writer. I make most of the changes on the set which cuts out a lot of the problems that normally occur.

Monday, 2:00 p.m. Lunch is over. The cast is back at the studio, and Bill leaves the editing room to begin blocking the show. Blocking is the process of determining the movement of the actors within the set and deciding which camera will cover that movement.

We will generally block about half of it by 6 p.m. Then, everyone goes home, and I go up and finish giving my notes to the editor who has been working on the notes that I gave him earlier.

With this particular show, Bill generally figures out the blocking as he goes along. Over the weekend, he might mull over particular problems, but it's essentially a process of thinking on your feet.

After you have done five or six shows, everybody has sat in every chair on the set, and everybody knows what you can and can't do. It's like living in your own house. How many different things do you do? You come home and sit down. That's what happens in a show.

Generally, high production cost and union restrictions don't allow the flexibility to shoot a television show in and out of the studio. Location shots are expensive. Bill does, however, include some outdoor shots in the show, but they are the exceptions rather than the rule.

Tuesday morning, 10:00. Rehearsal. Rehearsal continues throughout the day. By about 4:00, and after the lunch break, the network people arrive, the writers descend from their offices, and the cast and crew run through the entire show. If there are any glitches, any parts of the show that don't work, this is the time to fix it.

I write a lot during rehearsal. We don't have the vast changes that most shows have after the run-through. Most shows will have three to four hours of rewriting after a run-through. I am in a position of control, so I don't have to get anyone's permission to change anything. I don't have to call upstairs and wait for the writer's stuff to come down. It's an atypical situation.

The network has the option of saying that they like or dislike a part of the show "But, we've had no problems with them. They love everything with minor exceptions."

When the run-through is completed, the group takes a look at the edited first cut of the show. If there are any changes to be made, the editor will stay that night and make them.

Wednesday, 10 a.m. In any given show, there are approximately 250-300 shots. Each shot has to be marked. The marked script is then given to the cameraman and technical director so they know when to cut. On Wednesday morning, there is rehearsal until 1:00, when the cast is released and Bill has the chance to mark his script.

Afterward, he takes a final look at the show from the previous week to see that it's finished and fine, and he files it in the back of his mind as completed.

Thursday morning. The cameras are there and the entire day is spent blocking the show with the cameras, getting every shot and every movement to coordinate. At about 5:00, there is a run-through on camera for the network. Everyone has the chance to see it again, and see exactly how it will look when broadcast into the public's living rooms.

Friday, 10:00 a.m. The final run-through. The run-through lasts until 1:00. It is a time to refine everything, prepare for the taping. At 4:00, the audience enters the studio, the warm-up person talks with them, gets them in the mood to laugh, and prepares them for what they may expect at the taping.

We then do a dress rehearsal. It's a full show which we record, and it's over by about 6:00 p.m. We let the audience go, and have a note session. I get notes from the network and from the other writers, then I go with the cast and give the notes. At 6:30, we do the show again, and are generally finished by 8:00.

There is an audience both times the show is taped.

I personally don't like an audience. I feel that I would rather just shoot it, get it perfect, and put it behind me. With an audience, you are always worrying about the entire show the whole week long. But, there is a certain vitality for the cast. They get ready, and build toward the performance, then it happens.

The entire process begins again the following week.

Kate and Allie is taped in New York. Most television shows are taped in Los Angeles.

Los Angeles is built to do these shows. The stages are better. It's easier to do a show in Los Angeles. Even the unions are different. In New York, you are working in theaters that are under the jurisdiction of live theater contracts so all of the rules are different. For example, your prop department are all stagehands. In the theater, the guy might have been a prop man on one show and something else on another. In Los Angeles, you are a prop man, period. There is more experience in Los Angeles.

Basically, in Los Angeles, the whole town is set up for television. In New York, you need to build almost all the scenery you need because nobody stores anything. In Los Angeles, you can rent anything.

Directing, for Bill Persky, is like writing. In place of a piece of paper, he has people to work with. You must enjoy, and have the ability to work effectively with actors and direct the cameras in a dynamic and capable manner.

A lot of writers have no interest or no ability in that direction. There are a lot of technical things that you have to know, and you either enjoy it or you don't. A lot of writers aren't necessarily that visual.

Of the many careers in show business, directing is one of the most difficult to break into.

If you want to be a writer, you can sit down and write. Getting someone to look at it is another story. But, if you want to be a director, you need an awful lot of expensive stuff to do it. It's very hard to get started.

Talk to any director. The way he got there is different from anyone else. Some guys start off as actors. There are a lot of guys who were on a series, hung around the set and said they would like to direct one. If it turned out good, they directed another one. Then, if the series went off, they were already directors. Some guys are writers. Some guys are assistant directors who gradually worked their way up. Nobody just falls into it.

Has Bill Persky's professional life changed since he won the Emmy?

The truth is, I was getting the same offers before as I am now.

JOAN DARLING

Film and Television Director (Magnum P.I.; First Love; Mary Hartman, Mary Hartman)

It was wonderfully theatrical. Poolside in Palm Springs, Joan Darling was paged. After viewing the pilots that were her directorial debut, Grant Tinker, then the producer of three hot television shows, wanted to book her for the entire season.

Her first thought was, 'Thank God I can finally earn a living'.

Joan's face and body emit sparks of expression. She is alive with a genuine appreciation for life's intricacies and her place among them. A woman of priorities, Joan exhibits the intelligence and judgment to charge after challenges, then slip from the mire of Hollywood to replenish herself at her Colorado home.
At Carnegie Tech and the University of Texas, Joan studied acting.

I used to direct scenes for people in class but I didn't like it because, strangely enough, I felt too masculine.

Years later, as an actress and writer, Joan sat across from producer, Norman Lear, trying to convince him to produce a 90 minute movie on the life of Golda Meir, starring Joan Darling. Joan had written for Norman, and he knew her in the roles of writer, actress, and acting coach.

He called in his associate and had me tell him the concept for the movie again. Then, the two of them nodded at each other, and Norman said to me, "Do you want to be a director? I said, "I'm not a director." He said, "I think you are." He gave me the pilot scripts for Mary Hartman, Mary Hartman.

After reading the scripts, Joan visualized a concept for the show that she felt confident to handle. She phoned Lear.

I told him that I felt Mary Hartman *was more than a satire on soap operas, but really a satire on how Americans presented themselves to themselves, and the damage it caused. He loved that, so he said, 'Go to it'.*

Joan's writer's mind and her ability to deal effectively with actors were the qualities that Norman Lear sensed as a solid foundation for directing talent. He was confident that her technical expertise would soon catch up to her natural abilities. That first directing job was in 1974. Currently, Joan has two feature films, three pilots, and 17 television episodes to her directing credit. She has learned a lot in this past decade.
First Love, Joan's first feature, was instrumental in providing the experience needed to avoid some directorial pitfalls.

Once you deliver the director's cut, you have nothing to say. I didn't know enough to insist upon a paid public preview. What you really need is a director's two paid public previews. Then, the arguments stop.

With two paid public previews, the director has the opportunity to show the film to an audience, pragmatically see what works and what doesn't work, and re-cut the picture. There is the chance to correct the mistakes, and bring it back into a preview house. The audience's reaction provides the leverage needed to persuade the producers of the validity of your choices.
As a director, Joan trusts two things. She trusts other people's skills, and she deeply trusts her ability to get people to do their best work, happily.

With editing, for instance, I really know a lot about editing, because I have worked with a very good editor. But, to lay down the basic pattern so that it's elegant and rhythmical, and correct, is not a skill that I would ever want to learn. It's not just a skill, it's a deep talent.

I feel I have an ability to know good work when I see it, and connect up with the people, and give them the scope to do their work without getting in their way. At the same time, I get what I want. I am always interested in what someone has to offer.

The profession of directing is almost entirely dominated by men. There can be additional difficulties for women to overcome.

I can think of only one difficult experience on a set with a crew member. I generally have no problems, and that is partly because I choose the people. With that one problem, I think that he was reacting to the combination of the fact that I am a woman, and was inexperienced. However, I won that battle, and by the end of the show, he liked me a lot. I was tough, tough, tough about it, and just hung in there until I wore him out.

The place where I have the most problems, I feel, is with studio executives. I think they have the most problem with the fact that I am a woman. It wasn't until this year that I realized, and really admitted to myself, that there are certain men who don't like women when dealing with them on a one to one basis.

Joan sees the advantage to directing in terms of the stimulation drawn from the challenge of performing a job that is unique. It's fun.

The toys are fabulous. You get to play with toys, even in a sit-com, that are extraordinarily exciting.

Now, at last, I finally feel grown up enough not to carry the anxiety I used to carry. I really have my skills.

A disadvantage is the obsession required to do the job right.

Not only does it become an obsession, but you are like a junkie. When you come off a job, you have to really know how to bring yourself out of that job, or you'll go nuts. After you come off of a job, all of a sudden it's over, the pressure of what to do with yourself for stimulation is really bad.

I don't know how any woman who directs consistently could be married, unless they were married to my husband. You have to be with a man who understands the nature of the job, and knows that you will be back in a year.

There are several ways to break into directing, and certainly Joan's method was unique. It is important to take the necessary steps in preparation for the day when someone says, "Here, kid. Direct."

Develop as many hobbies as possible, directing-related hobbies such as going to museums, looking at films, reading, and listening to music. Develop an appreciation and sensation for all of the arts.

I don't know anything about the film schools. My feeling is any organized school for commercial art is always very political and a waste of time. I think that they should get an 8mm camera and go out and start shooting movies. You start with super 8mm and move up to 16mm. They should force themselves into a hands-on frame of mind.

I would say to get a really good liberal arts education and make movies. I think they should study acting to find out what those problems are. I think that they should try and write something. They should engage in all of the things that go into directing. I think they should always be directing, plays, films, anything. Totally get your hands into it. One, you'll find out if you really like it, and two, that's the way to develop a skill. I got all my skills backward. I was really lucky.

JOURNALISM, REPORTING

In the mid-1970s, a popular film entitled *All the President's Men* attracted throngs of movie-goers to neighborhood theatres across the United States. Adapted from the book of the same name, the film told of how two reporters for the *Washington Post*, Woodward and Bernstein, used journalism techniques to cover, and uncover, the true story of the Watergate scandel. The two reporters met with secret contacts, such as the famous unknown, "Deep Throat," to unravel the story. As a result, the Nixon Presidency was doomed—and the reporters received the Pulitzer Prize for Reporting.

Shortly after the film's release, newspapers and magazines reported an increase in employment applications. Journalism schools across the country received record numbers of candidates for admission. High school and college newspaper staffs raced to outscoop each other for the lead by-line story in their next issue.

Today, journalism is still a hot career with a wide range of opportunities, for example:

- **General reporters** who investigate, develop, and write stories which run the gamet from international conferences to meetings of the local PTA.

- **Special reporters** who work in areas such as sports, finance, entertainment, fashion, food, or real estate. They become experts in their areas and cover activities like sports contests, film openings, theatrical productions, or fashion shows. Others prepare the day-by-day articles which make up the financial or real estate sections. Still others work for weekly sections of major newspapers devoted to themes—food, home, or local activities—which are often tied in with special advertising sections.

- **Editors** who give assignments to reporters, review and improve copy, make basic page layout decisions, and generally supervise the collection and dissemination process.

- **Broadcast journalists** who make "live reports" from the scene of newsworthy events, rewrite stories for audio and visual presentation from local sources and press news services, and appear on local and national news programs. In small stations, broadcast journalists may also serve as announcers, writers, or even advertising hustlers.

- **Correspondents** may prepare articles for magazines, collect news from observation, research, and interview for a newspaper, a press service, or a television or radio network.

- **Columnists** are generally experienced journalists who write or broadcast commentary. Some specialize in finance, minority affairs, politics, women's issues, or humor. Major papers often have an "op ed" page filled with short columns.

There are around 10,000 newspapers in the United States and even more periodicals. They range from small town weeklies to stock national publications—*The Queen Anne's County Record* to *Vogue*. Some hire dozens of new staff members each year whose jobs are highly organized and (usually unionized). Others hire infrequently and prefer persons with a variety of skills.

Many prepare for the field by taking a bachelor's or master's degree in journalism. However, the necessity of a journalism degree is debated by professionals. In a recent year, 17,200 received degrees. Of these 56 percent took jobs in the media field (17 percent with newspapers, 11 percent with radio or TV stations, 9 percent in public relations firms, 9 percent with advertising agencies, 3 percent with magazines, and 7 percent with all other media jobs). Only 25 percent took jobs outside of the media field.

Today, women and minorities are an important source of new hires in the journalism field. Women now comprise 60 percent of today's journalism students.

In a recent year, women accounted for 45 percent of newly hired newspaper journalists, and minorities accounted for 17 percent of new entry-level hires.

Journalism is a field full of possibilities for both men and women interested in a career offering the potential to travel, encounter all kinds of people, and stay at the forefront of current events.

ELIZABETH TAYLOR

Magazine Correspondent

The Chicago Bureau of *Time* magazine is the base for six correspondents and a bureau chief. Unlike the busy city room of a metropolitan newspaper, each correspondent has a private office. There is a feeling of camraderie, team spirit. The group is proud of its magazine and of their abilities as top-notch journalists.

Elizabeth Taylor has been a *Time* correspondent since June 1983, originally hired for the summer only.

I had intended to return to graduate school the following September. On the eve of my departure, however, I was offered a full-time job as a correspondent with the magazine.

Initially, I worked there to test the waters, to see if I liked being a journalist with a newsmagazine. In two weeks, I was convinced that this was what I wanted to do.

A graduate of Mount Holyoke College, with a double major in history and politics, Elizabeth had always been intrigued by the world of politics. "When I was 16, I was the first girl from Pennsylvania to become a Congressional page." Her senior honors thesis brought her down from the hills of Massachusetts to a senior citizens home in the Bronx. Elizabeth interviewed Jewish immigrants and fell in love with the process of obtaining oral history.

I realize now that there is a very strong similarity between what the academic world calls oral history, and what we call reporting.

After a year of graduate work in American history at Yale, Elizabeth left to work for *Time* magazine. How did she get the job? She chose a name off the magazine's masthead, wrote a letter with a resume, and was called for an interview two weeks later.

Not to be misleading, however, I spent five years acquiring experience which I thought would prepare me for a newsmagazine. In 1980, I worked for a journalist as his research assistant. Bit by bit, on my own, I tried journalism, doing freelance work for whomever would pay me to write. I sustained my freelance work by working full-time in Washington as a legislative aide in the U.S. Senate.

A newsmagazine wants people who can not only report the news, but analyze it. My training in writing and history prepared me to be a journalist who not only reports, but also interprets and analyzes events and trends.

Originally hired in New York, Elizabeth was reassigned to the Chicago bureau. Chicago is the fifth city she has moved to in five years.

For anyone thinking of going into journalism, it's important to think about how often they want to be uprooted.

Time magazine, unlike many newspapers, doesn't require much "beat" reporting; reporters that regularly cover only a specific area or subject. The midwest bureau is responsible for a fourteen to fifteen state territory.

I cover Kentucky and West Virginia. I read their local newspapers and am always on the lookout for anything that is either a trend story or a news story. I have developed some sources, so that if the local newspapers don't report a story, I can still ferret it out myself.

Generally, Elizabeth's working day begins at 9:00 am and ends at 7:00 pm, with a multitude of variations in between. But, the variations usually stretch the working day rather than shorten it.

On Thursday and Friday nights, when the magazine closes, we wait around until the copy comes back for us to comment on and correct. So, Thursday and Friday nights are frequently very late nights. There have also been nights when I don't go to bed, but work straight through.

Occasionally, a correspondent can take the computer home and have the story sent through an electronic mailbox. Elizabeth prefers to wait, it's safer to see the story in print.

In essence, a reporter is always working, one way or another. They may be out on a story, in the office, or looking for something new, but it doesn't stop.

A reporter, whether for a newspaper, magazine, television, or radio, is required to bring a journalistic eye to life and everything he or she sees. There is always a part of me that is thinking analytically. I think it makes life much richer.

The bureau chief is responsible for distributing work and assigning stories. The correspondents also regularly suggest stories in a weekly conference. The suggestions are sent to the New York office where they are approved or turned down.

Sometimes an editor will say that it isn't quite the right time, or that it will be a part of a larger story. Sometimes a story you suggest completely fits in or is completely at odds with a story suggested by another correspondent.

Although there is competition for a story within the Bureau, and among other journalists, Elizabeth finds that the world of journalism is not one of heirarchy. The concept of seniority isn't as prevalent as it is in other businesses.

In business, for example, someone might be automatically promoted if they put in three years. Here, if someone is a star after six months, he or she will be getting better and better stories. Someone else could be sitting in the same chair for six years, not doing anything very imaginative, and will sit in that same chair. Promotion is based on performance.

The best, and most productive atmosphere is one of sharing.

I have found that journalism works best when there is a climate of collegiality and a sharing of sources and a story.

Out on a story. Glamour. Travel. What is it really like? If the story is small, Elizabeth will have a stringer do it. Stringers are part-time correspondents who are usually employed by local newspapers. Their names do not appear on the masthead of the magazine.

With other stories, Elizabeth takes a flight out of Chicago, arrives in the city where the story is breaking or has broken, and at times, doesn't even have a chance to check into a hotel. Most often, she arrives prepared with the names and phone numbers of the people she needs to contact. She may phone them, meet with them, or run into them while she covers the event.

The worst thing that ever happened to me was while I was covering a demonstration at an Army base in upstate New York. I had a kidney stone. I was in the middle of nowhere. I didn't know a soul. I ended up having to report part of the story by phone from the bed, then the doctor let me out. I couldn't drive, so I had to have someone drive me around. I covered the story, and went back into the hospital that night to pass the kidney stone.

It ended up that there wasn't enough space for the story, so it was shorter than we had thought.

The amount of travel can vary from bureau to bureau. Elizabeth has travelled more since she came to the Chicago bureau, partially because she wanted to see parts of the country she had never seen before.

Yesterday, I had to interview the Governor of Nebraska. Perhaps I could have done it by phone, but I had never met him and I wanted to see Nebraska. It was a very quick trip, but I got a chance to explore a bit and watch the Governor operate.

Unlike a lot of people, travelling isn't exhausting for me, yet. I enjoy the constant stimulation.

As a reporter, you will invariably come across people who are reluctant to talk with you. The type of reporting you do, and the reason for the interview will determine the degree of unwillingness. Most people are open and willing to talk with Elizabeth. Some are not, and diplomacy is required.

Vanessa Williams (first black Miss America) didn't really want to talk to me, however, her mother was very nice and invited me in to look at family pictures. I have found that people in the Midwest are very open. I think it's partly because they are less barraged by journalists than people in the Northeast. On the East Coast, there is such a high concentration of newspapers and television that journalists are often regarded as nuisances. Here, we are considered more interesting and trustworthy.

Elizabeth finds it most stimulating to talk with people who don't normally talk with journalists. Ordinary folks.

I think there is a tendency on the part of many journalists to forget them. I am trying to bring the wisdom of ordinary people to the pages of Time.

Different reporters have different qualities. Some investigative reporters have the tenacity and type of personality that disregards how offensive they may be to get the scoop. There are other reporters who bring a story to life on the strength of their beautiful writing.

At times, the shy and unassuming journalist can elicit warm, human emotions and truth from someone reluctant to talk with a more aggressive person.

Some of the best reporters I know are very quiet, and seem almost deferential. They are really very patient people who will just wait for the story to unravel.

I think that people can learn how to write, can learn how to find out stories, but curiosity is very hard to teach. If you are naturally curious, you can use that quality to make yourself a really good reporter, and a very good journalist.

Elizabeth has found that her stress level is as high in this job as anywhere else.

I think that you bring stress to your work. You must be able to work under a deadline, but we have a little more time, particularly at the beginning of the week, than newspaper people might. The pressure is less than you might think.

When I was growing up, I was always very intimidated by journalists. I had an image of reporters as harried, ruthless characters who abandoned their values in pursuit of a story and glory. Those folks exist, but it is possible to be a good, caring reporter.

The biggest advantage is the pleasant surprise of discovering that your job is fun and stimulating and a great way to spend the day.

I hadn't imagined that someone would pay me to run around, find out things, think, and tell stories. There is a wonderful feeling, a high, when you are working on a really good story.

You have the chance to reflect on society and the changes it is undergoing. You are constantly learning. There is a constant struggle. They say, 'You are only as good as your last story.' For me, it's fun to compare where I was three or four months ago, and see an improvement or a different style in my writing. You always have to work at that.

If you are a woman or man who is interested in raising a family with the stability of a permanent home and neighborhood, journalism may not be for you. It's hard. There are periods of time that you can take off and have a child, write a book, or do something else, but the lifestyle for a journalist requires travel, relocation, and long, uneven hours.

If you are someone who needs structure, I wouldn't look to this kind of work.

Another disadvantage to working for a magazine such as *Time* is the lack of a by-line system. The system is one of cooperation. You won't see your name in print every week. The by-lines that you see in the magazine credit the major contributors to the story. However, there are usually about five people working on a story. There are also reporter researchers in New York who check facts. They assist the writers, but their names don't appear. Editor's names don't appear. It is a group effort. There is recognition at the magazine, but not by the rest of the world.

At a magazine like Time, *you have to forego the ego gratification that one might receive at a newspaper or on television.*

If you are thinking of a career as a journalist, prepare yourself by writing constantly.

Write articles, news stories, features, op ed (Opinion/Editorial) pieces, reviews. Even if you have another job that has nothing to do with journalism, if you are waitressing or working in a car wash, you can still write constantly. People will be impressed with what you can show them and you will also be learning the trade.

The pros and cons of opinion regarding the value of a journalism degree vacillate with the person. People who have gone through journalism school think it's great, people who haven't, think it's a waste of time.

I was cautioned not to go to journalism school, that I could get in without it.

It is getting tougher and tougher to launch yourself into the field. Elizabeth advocates attending journalism school if you feel that a degree will give you more confidence, or a certain "leg up." However, many feel you must be a star in journalism school to equal the value of experience gained by working your way up through a small magazine or newspaper, or writing freelance articles and compiling a substantial portfolio. Each individual must decide how he or she would feel most comfortable and most prepared for the realities of the profession.

There are two bits of advice that I have been given. Someone may not like what you write, and may wish you had never written the story, but if they can say that they were given a fair shake, then you are doing your job. Objectivity is extremely elusive. Everyone has their own version of an event. Choosing a story is making a subjective choice.

Secondly, I read about someone who worked for a blind editor who told him that the story had to make him see. I think about that a lot. 'Write a story that can make a blind person see.'

MICHAEL GOLDBERG

Magazine Writer

Rolling Stone, a leading magazine of pop culture, boasts a circulation rate in excess of one million readers. The faces of past, present, and future stars of music, film, and television grace the biweekly covers. Madonna, Julian Lennon, Bruce Springsteen, David Letterman, Clint Eastwood. Hot performers are invited into the prestigious spot underneath the magazine's stylized signature.

In a play on words of the famed New York Times heading, "All The News That Is Fit To Print," *Rolling Stone* adds a touch of humor with their caption, "All The News That Fits." Stories, profiles, and reviews by Michael Goldberg have been a regular part of the magazine since he joined the staff in 1984. Since then, he covered the behind-the-scenes wheeling and dealing of the controversial Jackson's Tour among other assignments.

As a high school student, Michael was arts editor for the school newspaper as well as publisher of his own music magazine. Continuing the journalistic trend, he attended the University of California at Santa Cruz and wrote for the campus paper and a local, underground newspaper. Remaining in the Bay Area, he relocated to San Francisco to study journalism at San Francisco State University. In conjunction with his wife, Michael wrote a weekly music column for the *City of San Francisco* magazine, published by Francis Ford Coppola.

My wife and I knew a couple of writers who contributed to the magazine. I showed them an article we had written, and they let us mention their names in a cover letter that we sent with the manuscript to the magazine's arts editor. She liked it and published it. After that, the editor wanted more articles, and before long, we were writing the column.

Before earning a degree in journalism, Michael left San Francisco State. He was faced with a decision.

As it happened, one of my classes coincided with the day I had to be in the office wrapping up the column for City of San Francisco. *For some reason, the instructor couldn't see that working on the column would be an important "real life" learning situation. So, I decided that the actual experience of working on a magazine column would be more useful.*

For the next several years, he wrote freelance articles for *Rolling Stone*, *Esquire*, and other publications. After establishing himself as a competent and dependable freelance journalist, he let his *Rolling Stone* editor know that he was interested in a staff position should one become available. Pleased with his past work, they hired him to fill the next vacancy.

In his home office in San Francisco, or the *Rolling Stone* office in Los Angeles, Michael's day begins on the telephone. He calls musicians, attorneys, band managers, record producers, and other music industry sources to obtain information for the story or stories he is working on. The remainder of a typical day is spent conducting "in-person" interviews, attending musical performances, listening to records, and, of course, writing.

Lots of writing. I am usually working concurrently on five or six stories. For example, one week I wrote about John Fogerty's first live performance in 12 years, the making of the superstar USA for Africa We Are The World *record, REO Speedwagon's comeback, the death of Gavin Report founder, Bill Gavin, a lawsuit against Led Zeppelin, and rock radio.*

There is a subtle seniority system at *Rolling Stone*. The senior writer has first choice on a story. Generally, the music editor will discuss various stories with the staff writers and assignments are made. Location and other story involvements will also determine which reporter will get a story. If the story breaks on the east coast, a reporter from the New York office will usually cover it.

Approximately 50 percent of the story ideas come from Michael's editor, and the remaining half are generated by Michael himself. Coming up with ideas is the important part of the job. As soon as the editor approves a story idea, Michael proceeds. At least every other week, he travels to Los Angeles.

When I was working on a major profile (2,500-4,000 words) I'll spend three or four days hanging out with the subject, at her or his home, the recording studio, backstage, etc. I'll also interview friends, business associates, former band members, producers and girl or boyfriends.

In the profession of reporting, there is an inherent challenge: the reporter must have the ability to get people to talk to him. Michael is quick to point out that the challenge is more difficult than one might think. Attorneys are generally reluctant to talk to reporters. Most record company executives are difficult to get on the phone, and even harder to get on-the-record.

As for the stars, even if people want you to write an article about them, they want a flattering article. In most cases, that kind of article is boring. I try to write a realistic portrayal, a well-rounded profile.

While reporters feel the responsibility to maintain an objective view of the person they are writing about, it is important for them to release themselves from the worry of what the subject may think of the article.

If you do worry, you aren't going to write a very accurate or interesting story. You have to go with the truth. If the subject is nervous, shy, and awkward, you're doing your reader a disservice if you don't mention that in your story.

Michael loves music, loves to write, and loves to be in the middle of things. Reporting for *Rolling Stone* provides the perfect opportunity to indulge all three interests.

The job takes you to some interesting places. I spoke with James Brown inside San Quentin prison once. I got inside the gates at Michael Jackson's home in Encino, rendezvoused with sources around Venice Beach to document the last days of Beach Boy Dennis Wilson's life. It's exciting. There is never a dull moment.

Long and odd hours are the norm for a good reporter. Sources may call at night or very early in the morning. You may have to interview a musician after a performance as the clock ticks towards 2:00 a.m. You must have the type of personality that thrives on unexpected, ever-changing time demands if you are to truly enjoy your work.

Research and preparation prior to an interview are factors that contribute to the separation of good reporters from bad. Good reporting is an art of effectively combining a variety of skills.

When I was young, I didn't have an idea of how much work was involved in reporting. I thought that if you could just sit down with Mick Jagger, you'd get a good story. In fact, what you discover is that just getting to the point where you can sit down with Mick Jagger is difficult. And, once you have access, there is a lot of skill involved in getting a good interview. It takes years to learn how to write a good story. There is nothing easy about being a writer.

Again, write, write, and write some more.

Learn how to write great stories. Learn how to dig for the kind of material that will make a good story. Write the kind of stories that Rolling Stone *publishes. Get your work published.*

Results are what count. From my own experience, I don't think a degree is important. Newspapers and magazines want skilled reporters who can deliver good, accurate stories.

I think that most editors are looking for well-written articles on subjects that are appropriate to their publication. An unknown writer can get published, but it does take persistence. You are entering a field already overpopulated with experienced writers. At the beginning, don't worry about where you place your articles, just get published.

RUTH ASHTON TAYLOR

Broadcast Journalist

Over 30 years ago, a young and ambitious woman set her sights on a career that was almost entirely dominated by men. She refused to let the odds sway her. In New York, she attended Columbia University's School of Journalism and charted her career.

My professor of broadcast journalism was the head of CBS news. He hired me out of school and that was that. I always say that I was born and raised at CBS.

Ruth Taylor was working for CBS before she graduated. She continued to work while she completed her education. Upon receipt of her master's degree in journalism, she was ready to take on the full time challenge of working as a journalist.

Education and journalism walk side by side. While the debate over the formal degree continues among students, journalists agree that a broad education, including a good foundation in English and History, will provide a scope of what the world is all about. Knowing the world around you is a key to successful journalism.

I think a liberal arts education is a very good idea. You have economics and a smattering of the whole history of civilization. As a journalist, you will dip into every aspect of life at one time or another. I do stories that involve economic theories, history, politics, and the arts.

Certainly, you should know how to write, although, I must say, at times modern journalism doesn't seem to put the emphasis on writing that I think is important.

The field of journalism has passed through various phases over the years. Currently, Ruth sees the profession immersed in a superficial phase. A phase that will most certainly pass, she cautions. "You don't prepare yourself for the worst. You prepare for the best."

Specifically in the specialty of broadcast journalism, there appears to be an emphasis on people who have energy, personality, acting ability, and a certain look. Writing ability appears to be taking a back seat.

In broadcast journalism, when someone is hired as a reporter, there is very little concern over how they write. Writing is basic to telling stories. As far as I have ever understood journalism, a journalist is a storyteller. It may be a factual story involving economics, or a human interest story with emotional appeal. You need to know how to manage words to be able to make a story as effective as it can be.

I was supposed to give a keynote address at a writers' conference, and I asked one of our news directors how important a part writing plays when he chooses reporters. He said, 'None. Production skills play a big part.'

If you are talking about professionalism, I think that writing skills are very important.

Ruth stresses that this superficial trend is not limited to one challenge or one particular station's broadcast journalism. Committee reporting at every station is a contributing factor. Several people collect the facts, and someone else writes the story. This type of reporting can lack a journalist's inner feeling about a story.

But, you can have an inner feeling about a story, and if you don't have the craftsmanship to write it and tell it, you'll never get it out there where someone else can be effected by it.

There is one constant in a career in broadcast journalism. There are no typical days. Each day is different and always will be. Each story is different than the one you covered the day before.

In the morning at CBS News, the producers, news director, and assignment editors get together and decide what news of the day they will cover. Then they assign stories to different reporters.

A reporter may be following a story with demands of its own and that will be considered and treated as an assignment. Many of the reporters specialize, or have a particular beat. The advantage to specialization is that people will call you with information, or you will be notified before or when things are happening.

Rather than a specialty, I am inclined to be given long stories. For instance, when the school desegregation case was before us in Los Angeles, I was assigned that. Therefore, that was a story that kept me in education and politics and all of the ramifications of that case for a period of two or three years. That was my story to keep hold of, to know before it happened what was going to happen, so we could be ahead of the story.

One of our executives from New York said, 'Oh, I understand you are following the desegregation story.' I said, 'No. I am hoping to lead the story and be ahead of it.' You want your audience to get first-hand news earlier than other people. You want to be able to tell them what is going on, very quickly.

Time is always the biggest restraint on a broadcast journalist.

You've got to get the story, and get it shot and written and edited and on the air at a particular time. The restrictions are built into the business. Nobody stands over you with a club to get you to work. If you miss your deadline too often, you won't be around very long.

Specifically with television journalism, the reporter needs a good knowledge of pictures. What pictures will be enhance the story you are telling? What kind of pictures do you want your camerman to get to help tell the story?

There is also an important sense of professional team effort. The cameramen, because they are good at their craft, will have ideas to contribute. It is important to maintain communication, cooperation and respect for the team as a whole.

During the day, Ruth Taylor is out of the office more than she is in it.

That's what I like about this kind of work. I don't like to sit around in one place. I write fast. I write in the car, in the truck. I compose in my head, and have to do a lot of things while I am moving around. You are usually out of the door very soon after you get in it.

During the long and successful years of her career, Ruth has worked weekends, evenings, six-day weeks, you name it. She works until the job gets done. However, it's essential to establish priorities early in your career as a journalist. You can become easily obsessed if that is your choice. If not, the career can be molded to include other aspects of life.

I have three children. I have a stepson that I have raised since thirteen. My two daughters are grown, and I have a grandson. You need to make good provisions and make sure that your family is in good care. You also have to make certain restrictions on yourself, things that you won't do. I won't take long trips too often that will take me away from my family. I chose not to work at night in terms of a nighttime show.

My priority is my family, and I have been able to balance the two. If it comes to the question of whether I should take an opportunity that might not be so good for my family, or miss it, I would miss it.

The high point to the profession of journalism is the excitement. Things are happening all around you. There's never a dull moment.

There's no question, if you don't have energy, don't try and do this kind of thing. If you want to be comfortable, don't do this. You are going to have a lot of uncomfortable moments. A lot of times you have to work late or get up early, or go places that are wet or cold. If you like adventure, and if you like learning things and you have a lot of curiosity, this is endlessly different. You stay alive, because it's fun to go to different places everyday.

Be aware that you will be taxed as a person, energetically and mentally. You will not have a good day everyday. It's hard work and you cannot do it unless you are prepared.

Most often, you will need to know the background on a story. If it's a murder, you need to know about the people involved. If it's some kind of an economic or political story, you've got to read in depth about that particular story. It's like cramming for an exam. I cram so much on different aspects of the news that ultimately I have read deeply about most subjects.

In the competitive field of broadcast journalism, job security begins with security in yourself, your craft, and your ability to do your job well. When you have a solid background, you know that you are specifically trained to do what you are doing. Talent and competence will always be in demand.

It's not a question of feeling secure in your job, in fact, I used to quit every Friday. You don't want to feel too secure in your job if things are wrong, if somebody tries to make you compromise your conscience and do something you don't believe is an honest approach. If you have to depend on the security of the job alone, and not the security of yourself, you are in a precarious situation.

Someone will say, 'I am taking drama, will that be helpful?' Well, it won't hurt, but it's not going to be what you will fall back on.

Start out by getting the best possible education. Acquire a rounded set of facts and depth of knowledge. You will be in a business where you will constantly draw on your mental and physical resources.

A part of the excitement to the profession stems from the fact that you will have the ability to directly use what you learn.

Keep in mind what you want to do, and ultimately, you will head for the crafts that will help you do it.

Train mentally in as broad a fashion as possible. Education is exciting if you think of it as preparation for doing exciting work. You will be learning about the world we live in, and finding out what kind of world it is. You've got to know where it all came from.

WILLIAM F. ENDICOTT

Newspaper Bureau Chief

In 1881, the circulation of the first issue was less than 1,000 copies. In 1885, the editorial staff consisted of four people.

The lobby of the home base of the *Los Angeles Times* newspaper breathes tradition and commitment to truth through its marble grandeur in commemoration of over a century of quality publishing. Where a linotype once set seven to nine lines a minute, the computerized phototypesetter now produces actual type at a rate of 2,000 words per minute.

The commemorative photographs chronicle our lives. Baseball player Jackie Robinson waves from the dugout, Robert Kennedy lies slain at the Ambassador Hotel, Michael Aldrin plants the American flag on the moon.

The newspaper has bureaus that stretch across the country and the world, tributaries that flow into this main office. The Sacramento Bureau of the *Los Angeles Times* consists of eleven people who cover state government and state politics. William Endicott is the Bureau Chief. He makes the assignments on the news that the paper will cover, does the administrative work for the Bureau, edits copy, and writes primarily analysis pieces.

Much of the kind of thing I write, as opposed to straight reporting, is to some degree subjective. I base what I write on my own knowledge, background, and experience, plus conversations with the people involved.

In college, William majored in political science. He knew then that he wanted to be a journalist, but opted to enter the field with a liberal arts background. Twenty eight years ago, he began his career as a reporter for a newspaper in Lexington, Kentucky.

William began as a general reporter, then worked with the wire editor. He handled all of the wire copy that went into the newspaper. After a short time in the Marine Corps, he returned to land a job as sports writer for the *Louisville Courier Journal*. Transferring to California, William worked on a few small papers before moving over to the *Los Angeles Times* in 1967.

In today's sophisticated newspaper reporting, an advanced degree is not necessary, but it can prove to be a valuable asset.

The way reporting is done, and the issues we deal with are more complicated. I wish many times that I had more background in economics, for instance. It's a bonus if you have it.

As a journalist for a newspaper the size of the *Los Angeles Times*, you can forget the certainty of 9 to 5 working hours.

Many times when you get to work in the morning, you have no idea how your day will end up. Events evolve, things come in, you hear about things that you want to pursue.

Much of the reporting through the Sacramento Bureau includes in-depth reporting, extensive profiles. This type of reporting is very different that the coverage of events as they are happening.

We have a reporter now doing an extensive profile on the Governor's Secretary of Health and Welfare. We will lay out his week built around the idea of having the story done by the end of the week. He will do interviews and research all week at his own pace. We free him up to do whatever he needs to do to complete his profile.

There is a daily log. Each morning, William's secretary checks the datebook for happenings of the day, and places the appropriate information on her boss's desk before he arrives in the morning. The Governor may be having a press conference. There may be a hearing on a bill of particular interest to the paper. There may be reports that will be released by a state agency.

From the log, William makes assignments as he determines which stories are worth covering. The assignment is made and the reporter gets to work.

After the reporter is finished with his piece, he or she gives it to the Bureau Chief. William reads the story with an eye for offering suggestions, pointing out holes in the piece or areas that need to be pursued further.

I am looking at it for content, to make sure that there are no unanswered questions in the story, and all the elements are covered.

When the story is done to the reporter's and the Bureau Chief's satisfaction, it is shipped down to Los Angeles to be added to the rest of the newspaper.

William's boss is the Managing Editor in the Los Angeles office. They speak to each other about two times a month.

I am left to run sort of an autonomous operation here. If we got too far out of line, I am sure I would hear about it, but there is a lot of independence.

A fundamental talent to reporting is writing. The more you write, the better you become. It is a talent that can only be perfected with constant use.

I look back at stuff that I wrote in college and high school and am appalled at how bad it was. At the time I thought it was great.

I still try and improve my writing. I believe your thought processes get better and you become more conscious of how to phrase things, how to make a point better. Anyone who thinks that they have reached a pinnacle and can't improve is badly mistaken.

As Bureau Chief, William sees the need to stay on top of what is happening in the world and in other newspapers. It's a part of remaining effective in his job.

I regularly read the New York Times. *I read their coverage of Governor Cuomo with interest because it sometimes suggests ideas for things that we ought to be doing. It's interesting to see what is going on in other parts of the country in state government.*

William feels a deep sense of satisfaction in seeing a concept for a story evolve into a good, readable piece. Conversely, there is a lot of pressure involved in the inherent nature of the job.

Deadline pressure doesn't bother any of us very much. I guess we are used to living with that. I feel the pressures of being on top of things, being concerned that I am doing the right thing and presenting things in the proper context.

Despite the criticism, I think there is a tremendous amount of integrity in the press. We are concerned that we don't distort events or blow things out of proportion. It is self-imposed pressure more than anything else.

There is also a certain degree of pressure from Los Angeles that things run smoothly, and so on.

William Endicott has been married for 28 years and has three children. Although he has managed to enjoy the pleasures of mixing family and professional life, it can be very difficult, requiring a great amount of understanding from spouse and family.

In campaign years, I've covered the presidential campaign and maintained my responsibilities as Bureau Chief. That's hard. In 1980, I was gone almost all of the year.

There are a few specific ways to land a job on a major newspaper like the *Los Angeles Times*. The classic method is to work your way up from small papers. A small newspaper can offer a variety of experience and the chance to learn how things are done in the many aspects of newspaper reporting.

In most smaller papers, salary advancement is achieved with the move from reporter to editor. You become an assistant city editor, city editor, managing editor, and so on. On larger papers, however, salaries, for the most part, are competitive in editing as well as reporting. Both groups are well-paid. A reporter who wants to continue writing and reporting can do so without passing up the salary increases that he or she deserves.

The ideal with my job as Bureau Chief is that I can do both. If I decide that I want to spend a week sitting in the office, dealing with other people, I can do that. If I decide that I want to write, I can do that, too.

Other avenues include internships on major newspapers, or through reporter trainee programs. Apply directly at the newspaper.

After three or four years as an intern, you will ultimately get on the main staff.

A small newspaper is still a good way to go because you get such a broad range of experience. You almost have to do everything.

Female journalists need not feel the discouragement of years past. Where they were once pigeon-holed as society or feature writers, they are now offered the same opportunities as men. "In fact, there is quite a drive on at most major newspapers to recruit more women and minorities."

Don't major in journalism. Explore a liberal arts education, with perhaps a minor in journalism. If you are so inclined, get a master's degree in economics or another field of interest, to broaden your base in the subject. Obtain as much practical experience as possible.

Then, start sending out resumes and try and get a job. It's tough. The field is pretty crowded right now. Particularly right after Watergate, when reporters were so glamorized, the journalism schools really filled up.

It's almost always possible for a young person to get a job on a small daily in a small town. They don't pay much, but you will gather practical experience. There is a high turnover on the small papers.

Much of the success of landing a job with a newspaper lies in the person's talent of being at the right place at the right time. Make it the right time by sending your resume out frequently. Continue to write and stay prepared. Persistence will make it happen.

JIM MURRAY

Sports Columnist

The National Association of Sportscasters and Sportswriters named him "America's Best Sportswriter" 14 times. In 1982, he received the "Red Smith Award" for extended meritorious labor in sportswriting. He is the author of two books chronicling the sports world as seen through his observant and knowing eyes. Jim Murray has been a writer all his life. He joined the staff of the *Los Angeles Times* in 1961 to write the sports column that has won him a loving and loyal readership.

I started to write professionally when I was in college in 1941. (As my career progressed), I worked for Time *and* Life *and other publications. I wasn't only doing sports. I was a regular, legitimate writer for the first 20 years.*

At the present time, Jim Murray's sports column appears in the daily newspaper four days a week. He began with a six-day column, reduced it to five days, then three days when serious eye problems interfered with his work. Now, he is comfortable with his working schedule. He initiates the subject he wants to write about, and goes out and gathers the material for his column.

Mornings at 7:30 will find Jim at the breakfast table in his home reading the newspaper. The computer waits downstairs in his home office. Breakfast completed, he descends, boots up the computer, and sits down to write the column. The remaining day is spent canvassing prospects for the following day's column.

Yesterday for example, I got up, wrote the column, then went to Anaheim stadium. I arrived there at about 5:00 and interviewed an Angel player until 6:00, then went over to the other dugout and interviewed a Toronto Blue Jay player.

I approach the players cold. I know some of them, and some I don't know. I walk up to them and say, 'I want to talk with you for 15 or 20 minutes when you get a chance. We can go sit in the corner of the dugout.' He'll say, 'Fine, wait until I bat,' or 'I have to do a T.V. interview,' or 'I have to call my broker, how about in an hour?'

Some guys don't want to be interviewed, but I usually get positive responses. Most players accept journalism as part of their business. If they didn't get all of that media attention, they wouldn't get all of that money. But, it is their accommodation.

As a lead columnist, the newspaper expects you to attend sporting events and cover them. Some travelling is involved for major events.

The sports editor will suggest things, or tell me that, for example, starting Monday we will be writing about the Olympics and getting a special edition out each day. I am an employee at the paper. I do what I'm told.

The time it takes to do the column varies. There are days when he knows exactly what he will write about and it flows as fast as he can move his fingers. Other days, the process may take hours. There is also the consideration of thinking time, interviewing time, and time to review your notes.

For Jim Murray, the advantages and disadvantages can be summed up simply:

The major advantage is that you are gainfully employed and you get a paycheck every week. The disadvantage is that you have to sit down and write whether you feel like it or not.

To aspiring journalists and columnists who are interested in sports journalism, Jim Murray suggests they try electronic journalism first. The rewards are greater. What is electronic journalism?

Howard Cosell.

MEDICINE

Misconceptions regarding the lives of physicians are as varied as the illnesses they are trained to cure. There are no secret elements, no magical cures, no phone booths into which medical "Clark Kents" disappear to prepare for miracle feats.

However, the lives of physicians are often highlighted because of the role they play in helping people stricken by disease or other health problems, their relatively high levels of income and prestige, and the growing number of questions today about medicine (high costs, malpractice suits, foreign-trained doctors, prepaid medical costs, supply-demand for doctors, etc.).

The number of physicians in the United States increased

from nearly 300,000 in 1975 to over 500,000 today and the ranks of practicing physicians are steadily growing. A majority render patient care through a medical speciality. According to recent statistics, 87 percent of physicians are male but this figure should change as women now constitute from 30 to 40 percent of many medical school classes.

The average American male visits a physician between four or five times each year. For women, the figure is slightly higher, around six per year. These add up to more than one billion visits a year, with the accompanying need for trained doctors to meet these patient's needs.

Typically, undergraduate pre-medical education is four years of study in core science courses, physics, chemistry, and extensive mathematical preparation. There are exceptions. Some students complete the pre-med requirements in three years, and are accepted to medical school without a bachelor's degree. Any type of degree may be acceptable providing the prerequisites are met.

The information in your undergraduate education is designed to prepare you for your medical school education, and is also a means for identifying students who will commit themselves to steady and rigorous study.

Marquis Hart, M.D.

In the final year of undergraduate education, the prospective medical student must pass the MCAT exam (Medical College Admissions Test). Once you are accepted to a medical college, the first two years are devoted to the basic sciences, and are essentially an extension of your pre-medical education. The last two years are the clinical years, with an introduction to the various medical specialties.

A computerized system is available called "The Match" to help you select your residency.

In my case, the summer of my third year was when the process began. You go out and visit a number of residencies, and rank them on a scale of 1-10, or 1-5 depending on the number of residencies that you see. You get an appreciation of the hospital's strengths and weaknesses. They, in turn, rank you among the hundreds of applicants that they see. On one day, all the numbers go through the computer system, and you end up with one hospital designated for your residency.

Marquis Hart

Some students and some programs don't get matched. In that event, the student's advisor will make phone calls to programs that haven't matched, and attempt to arrange the needed residency.

The winter months went by, and in the spring, close to the end of my fourth year, the computerized results came out. It's a long process of waiting.

Marquis Hart

The first year of post-graduate training, internship, is usually a part of the "on-the-job" training of residency. Residencies span three to six years, depending on the specialty. At the completion of residency, the MD becomes board certified and is eligible to practice.

In addition to the MD degree (doctor of medicine) there are two other degrees which are recognized by the American Medical Association; The first is the DCM (doctor of chiropractic medicine) and the second the DO (doctor of osteopathic medicine).

LESLEY BLUMBERG

Gynecologist, Gynecological Surgeon

Dr. Blumberg announced her intention to move her office on pink stationary.

My first name, Lesley, is a man's name too. I figured that a man wasn't going to use pink stationary. I got a lot of one and two-time doctor's referrals because doctors have patients who are asking for a woman gynecologist.

On the third floor of a three story medical plaza with dark windows, her private practice office overlooks the busy boulevard below. Angry honking and the screech of burning rubber are inaudible within the beige walls of the waiting rooms. *Mademoiselle, Time, Newsweek.* They are current and neatly arranged. She wakes each morning with the sun, jogs, and takes breakfast at the hospital before rounds. Eating beside her are other physicians. It is their time to relax before the day, and be seen. "Out of sight, out of mind. You don't get referrals."

Including residency, Dr. Lesley Blumberg has been in practice for 12 years. She practices gynecology and gynecological surgery.

I wanted to be successful as a surgeon. I knew general surgery was overfilled, and didn't feel like doing urology, neurosurgery, or cardiac surgery. I couldn't think of anything surgically I wanted to do except maybe orthopedics. At the time, 10 years ago, it was very tough for a woman to make it (in that specialty). So, I liked gynecology.

I think there was more community need. I was convinced by someone in the community that as a woman it would be better to go into OBGYN. I was the only woman gynecologist in my city for two years. It was very unusual.

In addition to the office practice, Lesley works out of four hospitals, primarily two. If a patient is hospitalized, she sees them everyday unless it's necessary to arrange coverage by another physician. 7:30 am is her ideal time for scheduling surgery. Each succeeding case might possibly be delayed by the length of the prior case, so the optimum time is the first slot of the day.

The private office practice is four full days a week. After rounds, she arrives at the office, clears her desk of phone calls, and starts seeing patients, ending the day around 4:30 or 5:00. On the fifth day she does surgery, catches up on paperwork, and makes more phone calls.

You really do have a lot of extra stuff that goes along with the regular practice. I'm on the phone all lunch hour so I can get out earlier. My day off gives my nurse an opportunity to restock and clean the office, and catch up on her correspondence work.

Lesley has opted not to deliver babies. She wants a more normal lifestyle. Her emergency calls average several times a month as opposed to several times a week in obstetrics. "It's not a big part of the specialty anymore. People aren't having huge families."

Emergencies in GYN include tubal pregnancies, ruptured cysts, abscesses, or women who believe they have appendicitis and a determination must be made as to whether it's truly appendicitis or a pelvic infection. Occasionally she'll deal with a miscarriage though she refers her obstetric patients to other physicians.

Any doctor has to put up with emergency calls. The degree depends on your specialty. You can be interrupted at times when you would rather be doing something else, whether it's the theater or the ballgame. You have to leave.

It's hard when you're dating. It's more socially acceptable for a man to say, 'Sorry, honey. Gotta go.'

Two other physicians share her group of offices. They have a form of practice called an association. Each physician is financially independent, but they share the responsibilities for salaries of the office manager, bookkeeper, and receptionist. The rent and basic fixed expenses are divided, one third each.

The amount we earn depends on how much we want to work, how much work we get, and the kind of work we get. This is probably what enabled me to give up obstetrics. If the three of us had been partners, they would have wanted me to do it. As a partner, some of what you do is going to be dictated by the other partners.

In an association, you pick up your own charts and go. It's like the difference between living together and being married.

My impression is that associates are more amiable in the long run. With a person just coming in, it's sometimes difficult because you don't get as much up front. You aren't being salaried by the partnership, so you have to be more like an entrepreneur, go out on your own merit, and struggle a lot harder the first year. In the end, I think you end up ahead.

In a primary care specialty such as gynecology, most patients come by word of mouth. Gynecologists get their patients from other patients. There are occasional surgical referrals from other physicians, but the bulk of surgery comes from within your own practice.

Some physicians have specific referral patterns, people that they are able to work with themselves. You hear the joke that if everyone golfs together, they are going to share patients together. You tend to know the people you refer patients to more socially, but it's not true in all cases.

I try and find someone that my patient will like. If you refer a lady to have a breast removed, she would want a surgeon that she felt wasn't a sexist and was going to be sympathetic.

It took two to three years for Lesley to build up her practice to a comfortable level. Most physicians take at least five. It is a slow starting process to build up your patients and referral patterns when you start with nothing. A business organization called, "Women in Business" was helpful. She affiliated herself with the organization, and they gave her tips on the best methods for avoiding some entrepreneurial pitfalls.

One of the misconceptions Lesley had about a doctor's life was the belief that it was going to be very, very glamorous.

I think it's more just a lot of hard work. However, I have had so many gratifications through what I do, and recognition in the community, more than I anticipated.

Malpractice insurance in the OBGYN specialty is one of the highest of all specialties. It is the first or second biggest expense in running a practice, up to a fourth of the patient's bill. It's fixed. It doesn't go down. Dr. Blumberg pays $36,000 a year in malpractice insurance.

There is a lot of emotion related to pregnancy, abortion, natural accidents, and children that are born defective. People won't be happy with anything less than a perfect result.

There is also a tremendous amount of government infringement in terms of abortion and sterilization. There are all sorts of regulations that pertain to this specialty that you wouldn't find in other specialties. People just starting out won't find the same freedom that we had in medicine 10 years ago. It was like being your own boss, then. Now, you have a lot of bosses in a sense, people infringing upon your rights to do what you want to do.

A misconception concerning physician's income plays a part in most medical student's education. Most surgical specialties earn over $100,000 a year, but many physicians do not.

Think of it. Anyone who only has time to sell, can only sell the amount of time they have. If you make a product, the sky's the limit. I think that a modestly successful businessman can do as well as a physician.

The problem in business is that many people go into it and fail. Doctors almost always succeed.

STEVEN DUBIN

Psychiatrist

A locked door leads into the unit. A small meshed window allows a view into the hallway. The sounds of nurses and social workers fill the silence. They laugh, chat, and continue with their work. A room with a square couch and a few chairs sits unoccupied, with peaceful paintings of the sea decorating the walls.

Dr. Steven Dubin is a psychiatrist. He currently runs a ten-bed psychiatric crisis unit affiliated with a University of California Medical Center. His warm and approachable manner contrasts the beige walls of his office. His medical degree is in osteopathic medicine.

A DO is the same thing as an MD. I am board certified by the American Medical Association as a psychiatrist. DO is a degree, but I do the same thing that MD's do. I got my degree from an osteopathic medical school, did my internship in an osteopathic hospital, but did my residency training at an MD institution. For me, at this time and place, it really has not made any difference at all.

Steven went through four years of undergraduate education, was undecided in his career direction, got a master's in physiology, then decided while in graduate school to be a physician. Medical school was a three year shot for him, continuing straight through for 12 months a year. After a year's rotating general internship and the decision to go into psychiatry, he trained for three years in a psychiatric residency, completing the sum total of 13 years of training after high school. He has been with the crisis unit for four and a half years.

It's a three day crisis unit. On a Monday morning, I'll come in and there will be eight people, the following Thursday, there will be a whole new group of eight people, and the following Monday, another new group of eight people. We wind up seeing anywhere from 80–120 people a month.

The crisis unit has a staff of 35, including residents, interns, social workers, and nurses. They keep patients for three days of intensive evaluation and therapy.

People who come here are either suicidal, homicidal, or acutely psychotic. For example, their thoughts may not be very clear. They may have delusions or auditory hallucinations. Because of their symptoms, they are unable to take care of themselves.

The day begins at 8:00 a.m. From 8:00 to 8:30, he reviews charts then joins the team and eight patients for an hour of group therapy. The purpose of the group session is to see everyone and determine if there have been any changes from the day before. It's a team approach. There will be anywhere from three to six staff members for the eight patient group.

The group is also good because we do what we call a mental status. For example, people who are psychotic, we treat with medication. We want to see if they have gotten better, worse, or stayed the same. We look to see if they are thinking clearly and coherently.

Someone may come in with the delusion that they are Jesus Christ, or that the FBI is out to kill them. Some people believe that someone is talking to them. They can hear the voice, but no one is there. The voices may tell them what to do, make comments about them, and say that they are bad people. It can be extremely painful to the person.

People play a large role in causing their pain. Ideally, we want to take a look at what they are doing, because we all play a part in what happens to us.

Afterward, there is a staff meeting to discuss the patients. It is at that time that a decision is made as to who will be assigned to work with whom, what direction they want to go with the patient, and what they think is important to be done. Ideally, the patient will have art therapy in the afternoon and an individual session with either a psychiatrist, psychologist, or social worker. Family, friends, and lovers are encouraged to come in and spend time with the patients.

162

For the remainder of the working day, ending around 4:30 or 5:00, Steven supervises the staff, teaches, and maintains the responsibilities of his university appointment which include research, writing and publishing.

The patients are brought to the hospital by friends, family, the police, or other hospitals.

We wind up getting a huge assortment of people, anywhere from a lover, friend, or husband who left a marriage, then attempted suicide, to transients, bag women, and people who come off the airplane from foreign countries and become acutely psychotic because of the change. We see almost everything.

We work intensively. I think that in three days, it's not so much that you change the person, but they can benefit tremendously. In three days, we take a look at what they are doing, and hopefully get some understanding of how it came to be.

Being in a psychiatric unit, you are in a place where you can't run from your problems. You spend time working on them, beginning to understand them, and getting some control over what has been happening to your mind.

About half of the patients will be discharged or sent home after the three day period. The rest will need further hospitalization which is arranged at another facility in the county, or an in-patient unit at the hospital. The stresses in this type of psychiatric facility can at times be overpowering.

I have chosen to work in the area of the sickest of the sick in the sense that they are the ones with the most problems. The sadness can be overwhelming.

At times, one of the things I question after four years, is if this will be my last year. It's very rewarding. We laugh and have fun together, but it is very stressful.

Steven believes that in medical school, the realities of psychiatry are not taught well. He feels that the problem centers around the difficulty of talking about the subject of mental health.

It's easier to talk about a heart attack than a manic-depressive illness. They are bogh biological illnesses, and yet people can accept that you have heart disease. If you have schizophrenia or manic-depression, people don't know what to do with that.

The field of psychiatry has markedly changed. People do get a tremendous sense of relief. In fact, I think that patients get better quicker in psychiatry than in a number of other areas of medicine. I have no question about that. I can have someone in an acute psychotic state, and in three days, they can be totally changed. Their behavior can go from totally inappropriate to appropriate, 180 degree change in just three days.

The whole area of biological treatment of psychological illnesses only started in 1954. Unfortunately, there are still misconceptions about psychiatric illnesses.

Another problem lies within the medical profession itself, specifically with physician prejudice against psychiatry.

Quite frequently, the person you are treating has the same issues that you have. I think it's easier to talk about sodium and potassium, than to talk about death and dying. It brings up your own issues about death and dying.

The potential for job burn-out is high. To circumvent the fatigue of similarity, a variety of experience is available in psychiatry. You can work with families, do group therapy, and also practice medicine. A psychiatrist can have a hospital practice, private practice, see out-patients, and have the opportunity to act as supervisor.

One of the advantages to working at a University-affiliated hospital, and also, a training hospital, is that you are in an academic position. There is the sense that you are not working alone. You work with the staff and fellow psychiatrists. It's a place where you combine clinical services, teaching and research.

A drawback to his specialty lies in Steven's belief that psychiatry isn't paid as well as some other areas of medicine. "Someone can do two years of training in anesthesia and make $300,000 to $400,000 a year."

Back on the plus side, the malpractice insurance is relatively low, and the profession can be structured to deal with a minimum of off-hour emergency calls.

If you are working with in-patient care, then you have a lot of weekend work, a lot of phone calls, but if you are working with outpatients, your weekends can be free.

I think it's an extremely worthwhile field. It's wonderful to see someone get better. It is a field that is just beginning, in a sense. You are talking about human behavior. It's a field of potential growth, individual growth. You learn a lot about yourself, and a lot about others.

JIM PAGANO

Emergency Medicine Physician

Jim Pagano was a guitar player. He has a youthful face and a vulnerable, trusting presence. His dark eyes have seen innumberable medical emergencies. As an undergraduate, he had been interested in science and social studies. A career in medicine floated through the back of his mind. He considered it, took several pre-med courses, then dropped out after two years to play music jobs. The frustrations of the music business lead him back to school.

I was back in college and found out that all I needed was three years of college credit to be eligible for medical school. I applied and got accepted. I had an A-average.

While in medical school, he was undecided as to the specialty he would find enjoyable and acceptable. A choice had to be made.

I met this fellow, an emergency physician, saw what he did, what his lifestyle was like, and the hours that he kept. He wasn't soliciting people to come to him. If they had a problem, he took care of it. They went about their life, he went about his.

Jim graduated from medical school in 1978. He completed an internship in internal medicine, and a residency in emergency medicine. He is currently a practicing emergency physician, a medical specialty that has only reached recognition in the last few years.

A small room with a television and a bed constitutes his office at the hospital. The ER is covered 24 hours a day, seven days a week. He works out of two hospitals, on a 12 or 24 hour shift. As his shift begins, he prepared himself to handle whatever comes through the door. In a normal 24 hour shift, he expects to get about 4 hours sleep. Some nights, he doesn't sleep at all.

It's the kind of job where it could be dead quiet one minute, and chaos the next. You don't have the luxury to sit back and relax. You don't have 15 minutes for a coffee break and a guaranteed hour for lunch. There are days when you might not even have the chance to sit down.

There are a lot of quick decisions that have to be made. Generally, you don't know your patients. You haven't established any kind of relationship with them. They are coming to you in a stressful situation, and you are put in the position of having to quickly assess the problem, run through a list of possibilities, and determine what is most likely wrong with them. Then you pick what you think is the best thing to do about it.

Stress is a factor to be dealt with.

You adopt a different way of looking at it. The emergencies aren't horror shows as much as they are problems that you are specifically trained to deal with.

The process of learning to deal with illness and injury on a detached clinical basis starts in medical school. The first time they present you with a cadaver, and you start cutting it up, everyone is completely appalled. Gradually, you become more used to doing things. You are less afraid, less emotionally involved, and more able to put things in perspective. You look at it like a challenge. If you don't take care of it, no one will.

At the end of a shift, you can completely remove yourself from the stresses of the profession. There are no calls in the middle of the night, or beepers to carry around for unforseen emergencies. It allows a process of recuperation from the tensions of everything from colds, sore throats, and minor injuries, to heart attacks and automobile accident trauma.

Jim sees emergency medicine as an exciting and useful profession. The emergency physician has the opportunity to intervene in the course of an acute problem. Most of the patients that Doctor Pagano sees will be able to carry on with their normal lives after he has treated them.

The other side of the coin is the lack of continuity of care. You are not likely to see the same patients again, or develop a relationship with them. You don't even get the opportunity to witness the results of your work.

Jim sees misunderstanding among other physicians towards emergency practice. He has found that physicians tend to be protective of their patients. They don't want you to perform services that they would be equally qualified to render.

> *In one of the emergency rooms in which I work, we have to call the patient's private doctor to tell them that their patient is in the emergency room, and ask them if they want us to take care of them or not. Unless, of course, it's a life-threatening situation. Some physicians will come in themselves, most will tell me to take care of them and send them to him the next day. In most cases, that's O.K., but if I've just spent an hour and a half doing a plastic repair on someone's face, and never get to see that patient again, it's a little frustrating.*

The malpractice insurance is intermediate, higher than a general practitioner, but significantly lower than surgical specialties.

In most emergency rooms, billing has changed in the last few years. In the past, most ERs were run by physicians contracted by the hospital. The hospital would guarantee the doctor a percentage of the gross physician billings, and would assume the task of collecting.

Currently, Medicare has stated that they will no longer reimburse hospitals for Medicare expenses if the hospitals are taking part of that money to reimburse hospital-based physicians. As a result, several emergency groups have reluctantly moved into billing and collecting. They must develop or hire a billing service and wait the three to four month turn around time. In other words, they are not paid by the hospital, but from their own billings.

> *It's the kind of practice where you don't get to pick and choose whom you see. The amount of bad debts that exist are generally higher than in private practice.*

The specialty of emergency medicine is unique and relatively new. It attracts physicians with the temperament and ability to enjoy this kind of working style.

> *An emergency physician is someone who is definitely not a traditionalist. He doesn't have his roots based in traditional concepts of medical practice. You have to be willing to be very flexible in terms of your schedule, willing to work nights occasionally, and long hours.*

> *We like to have things moving quickly, like to be put in pressure situations, and like to make quick decisions. Most of the people who were involved in it while I was training, were also people who did other things, like musicians, writers. Emergency medicine suited them because it enabled them to get away from medicine for days at a time. I still have musical aspirations. For me, it's important to do a lot of different things.*

JOSEPHINE ISABEL-JONES

Pediatric Cardologist, Medical Teacher and Researcher

The UCLA Medical Center, overwhelming in size and reputation, is a highly regarded teaching institution. Dr. Josephine Isabel-Jones, a pediatric cardiologist is involved in research as well as patient care. She works out of the Marion Davies Children's Clinic, the interior waiting room designed with bright colors, playful paintings, and children's books. "Just follow the yellow line to the physician's offices." Small offices of private practice physicians. A sense of discovery is in the air, cures, vaccinations, breakthroughs.

Josephine is a walking example of a woman who has it all. She speaks with the sense of peace and relaxation that comes from a person fulfilled. Her four children know her as a nurturing mother, her husband sees her as a loving wife, and her colleagues appreciate the dedication she displays as a physician. Three demanding professions rolled into one. A woman ahead of her time, she hyphenated her maiden name long before it was fashionable.

A month earlier, Josephine celebrated her 20th class reunion from medical school. She completed her undergraduate pre-medical education in three years, then continued her medical training at Meharry Medical School in Nashville, Tennessee.

When I was in medical school, there was a quota of four women per class. My admission class was about 70. We've gone from the statistics of about 3 percent of people entering medicine being female to around 33 percent at UCLA. That is fairly proportional to the number of applicants.

After obtaining her MD, Josephine did a year of internship and two years of residency in pediatrics.

At that point I was board certified, or at least eligible to practice as a pediatrician. I chose, however, to sub-specialize in pediatric cardiology. I did an additional two years of post-graduate training called fellowship, specifically in pediatric cardiology.

Currently, 80 percent of her time is spent caring for patients. Almost all of her patient activity is also teaching activity.

I think I chose this setting because my particular needs were quite varied. I needed the patient contact, but I learned that I enjoyed dealing with students in a teaching situation. I am involved in research and student affairs as one of the assistant deans. This is a perfect setting for that variety of interests.

In more recent years, the research I have chosen has been patient related. Early on in my career, I did more bench-type research, but I find that because I have a very strong patient orientation, clinical research is the best area for me.

On a typical day, Josephine arrives at the office anywhere from 7:30 to 8:00 in the morning. Often, there are early morning conferences or teaching sessions. The morning activities include seeing patients in the office, or making rounds to hospitalized patients. She's also involved in different laboratory procedures.

At least 25 percent of her time is spent with student affairs such as counseling, interviewing candidates for medical school, and writing dean's letters. Her day usually ends about 5:00 or 6:00 in the evening. With her administrative duties, meetings are often scheduled in the evening after the clinical activities are over.

In my division, we divide up our clinical responsibilities (among seven doctors), and that includes taking emergency calls. That is an advantage to being in a group-type setting. We have access to the records on an emergency basis of any patient carried by a member of our group. It works very well, and helps to relieve the problem of always being on call.

There are certain patients that I know better than anyone else, and under those circumstances, my colleague would call me and say, 'We have Susie or Johnny, and this is what's going on. What would you advise?' Chance are, I would come to see that patient even though I'm not on call. There are situations where you establish a certain rapport with the patient or the family and it's important for you to be involved. That happens occasionally, but not enough so that it is an interruption.

Doctor Isabel-Jones doesn't find it additionally stressful dealing with children's medical problems.

I think that the thing I have found rewarding and attractive about pediatrics is that you help most patients to get well, to establish a reasonable quality of life. I think I would have difficulty in medicine dealing with patients who have so many complaints and are not likely to ever be well.

In pediatric cardiology, for the most part, we have something to offer children. For most of the legions that require surgical intervention, there is a procedure that can be offered. I feel that the medications and behavior modification programs are realistic in reaching the goal of helping patients reach a reasonable quality of life and to grow up to be adults.

A career in medicine was an early goal. The closer she worked towards obtaining the goal, the more she was convinced she had made the right decision. As a mother and a wife, there have been times she would like to spend more time with the family, times when her absence demanded her children's adjustment. Their flexibility was an essential ingredient in her success. It works.

I think I have always been open to adventure. I had no preconceived ideas as to what my lifestyle would be. It's busy, and in order to work in a career that is demanding, in terms of time commitments as well as a lot of energy, I think it means that maybe you just work a little harder. The important thing is that I am able to satisfy the needs of practically all of me.

She does. At the times she feels the pressures, she stops and thinks, "Do I really want to do all these things? Is there another way that I would choose to live my life?" At this point, I don't think that I would like to change anything."

For Josephine, the biggest bonus to the medical profession is the opportunity to satisfy her need for a service-oriented career. She needs the interaction with people, the feeling of giving what she has to offer, and truly being of help. It is a continuously challenging profession. There are always new techniques and a new body of knowledge coming forth from the medical science portion of the profession that directly influences changes in private practice medicine.

An advantage of medicine, in general, is that it is a very flexible kind of career. There are so many different kinds of careers in medicine that a person can adapt a lifestyle to their own needs and still fulfill their other needs as a person. For example, the situation of being a mother. There are so many opportunities in organized health care delivery. A person can set hours and be salaried and not be bothered by the business aspects of medicine. You can have a lifestyle that is comparable to any other working person.

At times, it is tiring. There is a feeling of being overwhelmed by the stresses of the career. Specifically to women thinking of entering the medical profession, Josephine emphasizes the importance of feeling that a career in medicine is not impossible. "Don't feel inhibited by the length of the training period and the time commitment." It passes quickly.

I think that if it is really what you want to do with your life, then it is worth the time commitment to get there. Once you are there, there is enough flexibility that you can enjoy your career and do other things. You can be a mother and a wife and do a lot of other things.

For both females and males, I think that if you have a great interest in family, the important thing is to try to find a spouse that is sympathetic and supportive of your career needs, just as women usually are for their spouses. I think that you have to have that kind of sensitivity in choosing a mate.

STEPHEN COOPER

Plastic Surgeon

In the bright white light of a hospital room, a crowd of nurses and doctors gather around a bandaged person, preparing for the unveiling. We see the surgeon's backs, and the swirling of unravelled bandage. A beautiful blond emerges, then screams in horror when she sees her face. The operation had failed to make her look like the aliens who surround her.

"The Twilight Zone".

It was a memorable episode, but fortunately far removed from the realities of the modern day specialty of facial plastic surgery.

Dr. Stephen Cooper is an ear, nose and throat physician, with a sub-specialty in facial plastic surgery. He decided on his specialty by the time he was a senior in medical school, and received his MD in 1968.

> *When I finished in 1968, my field in surgery was still fairly open, and not too competitive. So, I didn't really base my decision on the demand for my specialty, but rather, on my desire to be an E.N.T. (Ear, Nose and Throat) specialist.*

All plastic surgeons are not E.N.T. specialists. There are two separate specialties. Ear, nose and throat includes regional specialization, meaning that these surgeons sub-specialize and do plastic and/or reconstructive surgery of the head and the neck. They confine themselves to facial and cosmetic surgery, but don't do other areas such as breast or hand surgery.

Stephen Cooper performs surgery three to four days a week. His day begins at 6:00 a.m. He jogs, exercises, and arrives at the operating room by about 7:30. The operations last anywhere from one to three hours, depending on the amount and the type of surgery scheduled for that morning. After surgery, he goes to his office to see patients until noon. Following lunch, he continues seeing patients until 5:00, when he makes rounds at the hospital. "I don't stay late if I can help it. I try and get home and spend time with my family." On a typical day, Stephen can make it home by 6:00 in the evening. The office practice is Monday through Friday, and "I don't take Wednesdays off."

In this particular specialty, emergency calls are rare, it's an average of once a month.

Elective plastic surgery at times involves counseling patients.

> *I think that the job of the surgeon is to exercise judgement, to know if you can help a patient surgically. If you can help them, you recommend the operation. If you don't feel you can help them, (you make the judgement) not to do the operation. There are some patients who come in requesting a procedure, or wondering if they need a procedure, that I will say 'no' to. The bottom line is that you want to help your patient. You want a happy patient, you want a successful result when you are dealing with a patient whether it's medical or surgical. You want to satisfy the patient. If they don't need an operation, it's your job to tell them no.*

Stephen's father was a general practitioner, and he grew up with basic knowledge about a doctor's life.

> *Frankly, I don't think I am quite as busy as I thought I would be. Doctors, and in general, sub-specialty surgeons, are not as busy as they used to be. There are a lot of other surgeons in our specialty in the area, and there are only so many patients to see. But, I think that's O.K. I don't know that I mind that.*
>
> *I am certainly making a lot more money than I thought I would ever make. My father being a G.P., was a middle-income doctor, a low to middle-income doctor as far as doctor's incomes go. As a sub-specialty in surgery, I am making more money than I thought I would ever make. I am living a lifestyle beyond what I would ever have conceived I would be living.*

The specialty has changed since Stephen was in medical school, and he also handles head and neck cancer. In years past, these cases were referred to general surgeons. Although he has to keep up with current advances in the specialty, he hasn't found it to be extensive.

Our specialty is a little stagnant right now, probably has been for the last ten years. We have small new procedures that come around and are tried and tested and discarded or kept, but it is not terribly difficult. I read a few journals, and go to a meeting or so a year to keep current. It's not too hard. Radiology is really the field where there are tremendous advances in science and technology in the last decade or so.

In terms of the business side of a medical practice, Dr. Cooper's past experience in a partnership helped prepare him.

My first private practice experience, the first four or five years, was in a partnership which included myself and four other specialists. We had a business manager, and one of the doctors in the group was a pretty good businessman. I learned a lot in those years. I wouldn't have been very well-prepared had it not been for that. Then, when I opened up this business, I was extremely well-prepared, and I have run an extremely efficient business operation.

There are pros and cons to a partnership situation. It depends on the individual. In Stephen's case, they had a salaried situation that was based on their productivity. If you were a big producer, you took a larger share of the salary pool. "I found partnership satisfactory for the first three years or so, then I really grew to find that I wanted to be on my own."

An advantage that Stephen finds in his specialty is that you are doing work you love, and getting well-paid for it. He can't conceive of work that could be more interesting or challenging.

It depends on how you practice, where you practice, and the nature of your medical community. If you are out in the boondocks all by yourself, you might stagnate intellectually. But, when you are in a big medical center like this, and you are surrounded by other good caliber physicians, there is a constant influx of ideas and challenges which really make it fascinating.

One of the disadvantages of a solo practice is that when you are not there, the bucks stop, and the practice stops. You are under a certain amount of time constraint. You can't take time off whenever you want to and expect to maintain your lifestyle and your income.

Another disadvantage is the change in the public's attitude towards men and women in the medical profession.

Until the last several years, I think the medical profession was very highly respected in this country. I think that has changed somewhat. I don't know whether I would call that a disadvantage, but it is a source of some frustration and anxiety on the part of doctors as a group, that we're not held in the same esteem by the public.

Some reasons for the change include malpractice suits, the high cost of medicine, and people not being able to afford the kind of care they need. Physicians are under pressure from insurance and governmental organizations to work for less, take patients that don't pay, have their fees set, and see patients that they may not want to see. Stephen's medical malpractice insurance is $13,000 a year.

What I am saying, in essence, is that I think doctors as a group have lost some of their independence. In the 10-12 years that I have been out of residency and in the field, I have felt the change. It's distressing, somewhat. There's not much I can do about it, but do a good job myself.

The best advice he could give to someone thinking of entering the medical profession is to do well in medical school.

Doing well in medical school will determine whether you get a good residency. You don't have to be brilliant to be a successful doctor, you have to be a hard worker. You have to have reasonable intellect, you have to be personable, but basically, you just have to work really hard.

MARQUIS HART

General Surgery Resident

A doctor's hospital lounge. Respect and silence fill the mid-day air. There are no physicians sipping coffee and holding X-rays up to windows, or the blur of white coats hurrying in to make a phone call. Instead, it resembles a community dorm room. A doctor sits uninterrupted in a corner reading a medical text, another peacefully stares out a window.

Marquis Hart decided to go into medicine when he was in junior high school. At Stanford, completing his undergraduate education, he took an anatomy course which led to his desire to practice surgery. He graduated from Johns Hopkins Medical School in 1983, and is currently a second year resident at a Los Angeles Medical Center.

When Marquis began working at the medical center, he would arrive at the hospital at 5:00 in the morning, and leave around 7:00 in the evening on the two days that he was not on call. On the third day, he spent the night at the hospital, taking admissions in the emergency room and caring for patients with surgical problems.

As a second year resident in the general surgery service, he arrives at the hospital at about 6:00 in the morning and stays until 6:00 at night. He is still on call every third day. The general surgery service is the most time-consuming of the specialty services.

Other second year activities include research responsibilities and the running of medical conferences.

Usually, I get in, see my patients, then go to the operating room. Between operating (times), I call for lab and pathology results. In the evening, I go on rounds and see all my patients, and try and give instructive points to junior members of the team. It's basically an apprenticeship. You try and bring younger doctors up, and senior members are bringing you to a higher level.

You split your time between assisting and operating. It's essentially the clinic patients that we operate on. The private patients don't come here to be operated on by the residents. The amount of surgical responsibility depends on your year and your ability. In your first year, you are doing smaller cases like hemorrhoids, and inflamed appendixes, but as you progress, you start to do hernias, and gall bladder surgery. There is always a senior resident, or senior attending physician who is guiding you through the case.

(At this point), I have already observed the particular surgery several times, and have proven that I know all the steps. It's a gradual situation. You've seen the operation in your clinical years in medical school, and as an intern. As a second year resident, you go in with the same assistants, but this time, they let you do more of the case. You really do know what you're doing by the time you have the scalpel in your hand, and if there is a question, it's obvious, and the senior surgeon will take the scalpel out of your hand.

During his first two years as resident, Marquis must spend one to two months a year working in the emergency room of his hospital. He must familiarize himself with emergency procedures, take care of the patients, and prepare them for the operating room. He starts off by seeing the patient himself, creates his own clinical impression, and then presents the case to the attending physician who examines the patient. Between the two of them, they work out the best possible plan for the patient.

If an emergency room patient needs surgery, he would then call a senior, or third year resident, to evaluate the patient's need for surgery. In acute cases, the patient would be transferred to surgery immediately. If the case were not acute, the third year resident would call the chief resident to evaluate the patient before a decision is made.

After five years of training, including the chief residency year, the new surgeon must pass the surgical boards. Once he or she is board certified, the surgeon then can operate independent of another board certified surgeon.

As a second year resident, Marquis is the primary surgeon about two to three times a week. For the remaining times, he is the assistant surgeon.

A disadvantage of residency is the amount of hours the resident must spend in the hospital. It takes time away from friends and family, and according to Marquis, tends to narrow your view on life.

You tend not to be as well-rounded as other people with respect to social and political events because you are at the hospital and don't get exposed as much. I go home, eat, catch a few minutes of the news, spend some time with my child, and then go to sleep.

During the residency years, it is a mistake to think that you will be making an excellent salary. Considering the number of hours required at the hospital, a resident makes an average of $2 to $3 an hour.

To think that all you have to do is put in four years of medical school, and then you'll be in the money is a mistake.

Even after you get out into practice, you don't make a lot of money. After you are out in practice for five or six years, (you can make good money). But by that time, you are going to be 40 years old.

The working environment for a resident can be extremely stressful in terms of the work that must be completed each day. There is the stress of losing a patient, although the successful cases outweigh the unsuccessful ones. Deaths and complications are handled as a means for learning.

You are rushing around to see your patients, to get to the surgery on time, and to collect data in between the operations. Once you get out of the operating room, you have to call the lab to find out the results on the patients you have on the floor, and then you have to coordinate a lot of small activities. Basically, you are a data gatherer during your first six months of internship, and then that information has to be presented in a concise manner to your chief resident. The interaction between you and your senior members can be stressful if you don't have the information.

For Marquis, any negatives to the medical profession are overshadowed by the fact that he has the opportunity to practice medicine. There is an interaction with patients and a continuous learning process that is unique to the profession.

When I first came here as a medical student, there was a patient who was impacted. She was unable to defecate because her rectum was like a hard rock. Although that is thought to be a procedure that most people wouldn't want to do because you go in and put your finger in the rectum and pull out the feces, here is a patient that hasn't had a bowel movement for four or five days. So, you go in there and disimpact them. The lady started crying and hugging me, and it was very rewarding. It makes you feel good.

Spend time in a hospital while still in high school or college. Get a first-hand view.

In terms of education, a good knowledge of math and biology are essential. Spend your undergraduate years in a university that also has a medical school. This will allow the opportunity to interact with medical students.

By going to a university that has a medical school, it will be easier to get into that medical school than it would be to get into other medical schools. It will make you a more likely candidate.

Go to the most prestigious university you can because the competition is stiff. It definitely matters. Try to go to the most prestigious medical school also, if it fits into your other needs.

I wouldn't let the fact that you don't like the sight of blood keep you from going into medicine. It's something that you will be conditioned to as you go along. A lot of physicians don't like the sight of blood. You can go into a specialty that has nothing to do with operating. You can go into psychiatry, and you will never see blood. If you have a weak stomach, you can direct your specialty to whatever is comfortable for you. At some point in anyone's medical education, you are going to have to see organs and blood, but that doesn't have to be what you see after you're finished.

SPORTS

Play ball. Those two words, a simple sentence, bear major significance for professional athletics. Most professional athletes began playing for fun in their early years. Now they are participants in a multibillion dollar business, with the accompanying level of stress from one of the most competitive professions in the world.

Today, soccer, tennis, golf, horse racing, marathon racing, and countless other sports are performed at the professional level. The three sports, however, that continue to attract the most spectator attention are baseball, football and basketball.

Baseball attracted nearly 50 million fans in a recent season, up from 30 million as recently as 1970. Around 350,000 fans attended a recent World Series while countless millions tuned into the games on their radios and television sets.

Baseball talent is sought out by scouts for major league teams, who don't confine their efforts to the United States. Professional baseball players may be drafted from high school but more and more now have four years of college experience.

The newly-drafted baseball player usually enters the minor leagues which are organized into three levels—A, AA, and AAA. Advancement is based purely "on the numbers"—the player's batting, fielding, or pitching statistics. A minor league player may be called up to the majors at any point—or returned just as quickly. Some players are never called up at all.

Minor league play is a process of intensive and continuous practice, a time to finely tune abilities as a player and to prepare for the tough competition and tensions of the majors.

Statistics from the National Football League report an attendance of over 14 million in a recent year. Postseason games, such as the Super Bowl and the Pro Bowl added another 600,000 spectators. Even the short-lived United States Football League attracted nearly 4.5 million fans in its first year. Four more million regularly watch football games on television.

As with all professional athletes, football players were the best of the best in their schools. The cream of the athletic crop. Most professional football players are drafted from college but a college education isn't essential. The current rules state that if you don't go to college, you are ineligible to play professional football until your would-be class graduates.

> *They are trying to encourage kids to go to college. Professional foot-*
> *ball is very physical. They want kids to mature, grow, and be bigger.*
> *Size, strength and quickness are big elements to this game. They want*
> kids to have four more years before they get into the league.
>
> *Mark Wilson, Quarterback, L.A. Raiders*

An additional reason for the ruling is to avoid potential tampering with high school and college aged young men. The competition among teams for the best players is as strong as the competition among players on the field.

Making the move inside to the basketball court, around 11 million fans attend professional games each year. Four quarters of action. 15 minutes long. 94 feet of court to traverse. Basketball is a game of stamina as well as skill. Although height will announce its presence early, basketball talent doesn't necessarily show up by the high school years.

There are some people who are late bloomers. You have players that don't develop until they get into college. In high school, they are average players, then they go to a good school, and in a couple of years they are all of a sudden one of the best players in the country. They get to the pros and continue.

Byron Scott, L.A. Lakers

Some players, however, have star quality from the first time they dribble the ball.

Americans love their spectator sports and, hot dogs in hand, continue to enjoy and support them in increasing numbers each year. Professional athletics is an elite career for athletes with the ability and determination to make it to the top.

BILL RUSSELL AND MIKE MARSHALL

Professional Baseball Players

Little League ballgames. Blistery afternoons in the sun. The family piles into the station wagon. These are the memories of many young men and their families. From splintered bleachers, mothers and fathers watch their sons in stripped knickers awaiting their turn at bat. A time to shine. Or a time to slink back to the bench.

Big League ballgames. Dodger stadium. Dodger dugout. Ballplayers chew gum and joke with their comrades. Practice commences. The manager watches. Millions of dollars hang in the balance.

Bill Russell, Dodger shortstop, has been on the team for 16 years. He is a pro in the truest sense of the word. In a profession fraught with injury, early retirement, and traded players, Bill Russell has lasted, a valuable asset to the team.

At 17, just out of high school, Bill signed with the Dodgers. He is quick to point out that his is an unusual story, most major ballclubs sign players out of college. "They don't have to put a lot of money into developing you in the minor leagues." Still, wherever the talent shows up, high school, college, or an empty lot in Brooklyn, a scout will be there.

A family man with a wife and two daughters, Bill appears calm and confident, with the experience to know that he can handle anything. After 16 years on the ball club, the pressures of replacement have eased. He has played shortstop for twelve of those 16 years, and until recently, didn't feel there was anyone to take his job. A part of his confidence stems from the knowledge that he can play other positions and help the team.

One thing you have to keep in mind is that you must play to the best of your ability and not play over your head. You can't play any better than you are. The sooner you realize that, the better off you are going to be. I've given everything I have, and that's it.

When the Dodgers play at their home stadium, Bill can sleep late in the morning and take care of errands and family business until it's time to drive the short distance to Dodger stadium.

When I get to the ballpark at about 3:00, I go through my mail. I get fan mail, and answer them. I read the paper. If I have an injury, I go in for therapy for that. I start hitting at 5:00. We hit in different groups, so you have to be here early enough to get your work done prior to your hitting time.

A veteran with the wisdom of experience, Bill stresses the importance of handling stress.

The pressure in this game is that everybody has the fear of failing. Consequently, you are going to make mistakes, and you are scared that you are going to make mistakes. You have to grow up in a hurry, and fight it within yourself. There is always someone looking over your shoulder.

When you first come up, the old cliche is that it's easier to get here than it is to stay. You have to be able to handle the crowds, the media attention, and everything about playing in Los Angeles. It's not easy. You have to go out there and perform and do a job. I've seen a lot of people come and go, and I feel very fortunate to have stayed here this long with one team. The sooner you can deal with the pressure, the better off you are going to be.

In the United States, there are approximately 600 major league ballplayers. The competition is staggering. Bill strongly recommends a solid college education before entering, and stepping out onto, the field.

These days, you need an education to get any kind of job at all. If you are good enough, you can still play after college.

In my case, I was lucky, but that's just one out of millions of people. In this game, you can get hurt, and have nothing to fall back on.

In a one year period of a baseball player's life, the season occupies six months, with the team on the road for three of those months. Although there is a four month break during the winter, the lifestyle can be tough on family life. Adjustment and flexibility are the key elements in successfully combining home life with home plate.

Over the course of the season, my family travels a couple of places with me. They have a rule that your immediate family can fly with you if they are 14 or older, so my wife and oldest daughter go on a couple of trips with me.

The rules remain the same, the fans continue their loyal support, but through the years Bill Russell has seen his profession change.

Everything has changed. The ballparks are bigger and better, the players are smarter and bigger, the salary structure is a lot better. Traveling accommodations and food have gotten better. Everything about the game has changed each year since I got here.

In the fluctuations and mutations of different aspects of baseball, there is one constant: a successful career requires a basic security in yourself and your abilities. With that foundation, you can change and grow as a ballplayer and enjoy the longevity of a career like Bill Russell's.

* * *

Mike Marshall emerges from the sacred clubhouse standing tall and commanding in his Dodger uniform. An intense young man, he is serious and professional. His dark hair matches dark, watchful eyes that are constantly alert to changes on the practice field. He reads a lot, carrying bestsellers with him on the road.

Drafted from high school, Mike signed with the Dodgers and played in the minor leagues for nearly four years.

I was first called up (to the majors) in 1981, and played about 5 weeks. In 1982, I was called up just before the All-Star break and played better than half a season. In 1983, I was here a full year, and I have been here ever since.

As a relative newcomer on the team, the absence of job security and the pressure of performance were his daily companions. The crowds watched expectantly as he stepped up to the batter's box, they inhaled collectively as a high fly ball heads toward him in the outfield, they booed his success in an opponent's stadium.

The ability to effectively release yourself to play your best baseball separates the pros from the amateurs.

You have to perform for 50,000 people a game, and the TV audience. There is pressure involved there. I am looking forward to this year because this is the first advantage I've had as far as the contract goes, whether it be going into arbitration, or being able to sign a five year guaranteed contract which many of the younger players are doing. So, maybe when I get that security, the pressures and the tensions will ease a little bit.

Mike was among many minor league players who held the mistaken belief that once they hit the big leagues, they had it made.

I work harder now than I did in the minor leagues just to stay here. I take more batting practice, I spend more hours at the ballpark, I worry more. So, once you get here, it isn't a better road. It's a lot of work and it's hard maintaining it and staying on top of things.

Media attention and interviews provide additional stress.

I think that it's very, very important for people to understand that we are human beings too. I'm not in a good mood everyday. I like being alone a lot, and there are times when I just don't want to talk.

I do have the choice, however. I can tell someone that I don't want to do the interview that day. It doesn't happen very often. For the most part, I feel that it's an obligation to the organization. It goes with the territory.

Getting there and coming back are a big part of every ballplayer's professional life. Travel and professional baseball go hand in hand. Most often, a travelling day is provided to fly, arrive, and relax before the following day's game.

While on the road, Mike's day begins at about 11:30 when he wakes up and eats a good, solid lunch. "Lunch is an important part of the day." For a night game, the bus leaves for the ballpark at about 5:00, so the day is free to do what you like.

> *Some of the guys bring their wives on the road. We are a close team on the field and in the clubhouse, but off the field, we don't hang around that much together.*

Mental preparation is as important as physical preparation, they are connected and intertwined. Mike sees it as a continuous process.

> *It's different than football, or maybe hockey where you get a lot of days off. In baseball, it's day in and day out. The concentration is in being prepared, and being 100 percent, both physically and mentally. To play 162 games in 180 days or 190 days, is quite demanding on the body. You have to stay on an even keel physically and mentally and be prepared for each day.*

Shining brightly through the layers of stress is the reason ballplayers play baseball. They have the rare opportunity to spend their days playing a game that they love, and reaping the substantial financial rewards that come with the job.

> *If you stay healthy, you can secure your family for the rest of your life.*

Another plus to the profession is the time off during the winter months. Relax, maintain your physical condition, and prepare yourself for the coming season.

Mike's advice regarding a career as a professional baseball player is straight forward and direct, like the man himself:

> *I don't think college is the total answer to anything. Just work hard at whatever you decide to do. I know a lot of people that have graduated college and are looking for jobs.*

> *I remember Chuck Tanner, the manager for the Pirates, said an interesting thing. He said, 'Make them take the uniform off you. Wait until they tear the uniform off you. But when they do, be ready to do something else.'*

JAY TIBBS

Professional Baseball Player

A ball of pink bubble gum rolls up and down inside his left cheek. His eyes are fixed on the batting practice. He makes mental notes, gauges each player. Perhaps an inside curve might throw him off. Fast ball, swung on and missed. Strike one. His young face is alive with anticipation. He can't wait to get out on the mound.

Jay Tibbs was called up from the minor leagues two weeks earlier. "I was drafted right out of high school. It's not rare, but it's an honor."

Jay graduated high school in 1980, and played in the minor leagues for four years. His lifestyle as a starting pitcher is different than players in other positions. He pitches every fifth day. Though he must keep himself in top physical shape at all times, Jay's preparation intensifies the day before he is to step out on the mound.

I start thinking about the game. I sit and watch. I watch the hitters, look for their weaknesses and their strengths, and try and store it away to use later. It's little things, like maybe, the left fielder has a weak arm and can't throw.

It's not unusual for a rookie to step right up to the majors as a starting player. If the ballclub needs a position filled, you'll be placed there. You have to be ready. "Most importantly," Jay smiles, "You have to have fun."

You can't put too much pressure on yourself. You have to go out and have a good time. But, there is always pressure on you to do well. You come to the park, and you're thinking about the game even though you try not to. It's a difficult situation to be thinking about because when you get between the lines, that's when you start working.

As a rookie player, the sheer numbers of people watching you perform requires the adjustment that experience alone will bring. There is no advance preparation other than the warnings that you can't let it get to you. Ignore the crowd and cameras. Play your best game.

When you're out there pitching, you can't really hear any one person, you can't define what anyone is saying. I try and block them out, have fun, and pitch my game.

Some of the changes from minor league baseball to the major leagues are obvious. Stress. Pressure. Crowds. Media attention. The tensions of trying to stay, and to live up to your potential. In terms of the player's ability, Jay doesn't see much difference between the top players in the minors and those we see on television and in our big league stadiums.

I thought the players would be so much better than in the minors. As far as the surroundings, however, it's like night and day. The tension is so much greater.

As far as the players go, I think the only difference between a triple A and a major player is that the majors are a little bit more consistent. Pitching-wise, they are around the plate more, hitters will hit your mistakes more. I had more difficulty pitching in triple A because the guys there are hungry to get into the majors, so they try and really swing the bat. They are more aggressive at the plate. These guys here are just waiting for their one pitch.

A pitcher in the major leagues. Jay grins. It is a dream that few realize. The odds are against you every step of the way.

My first goal was to try and get a college scholarship, but I got drafted from high school. The money was right, but it doesn't happen that way for all the good players in high school. You can be drafted in high school but if you aren't a high round pick, and the money isn't that good, you'd be better off going to college.

Get your education in, and if you are good enough, you can be drafted from there. I was just in a situation where the money was right and I felt like I could play, like I made the right decision.

Work towards perfecting the position in which you feel most confident. If you are a strong pitcher, develop it. If you have always played outfield in high school, chances are you won't be drafted to play first base. The competition is stiff. Only the best will be considered. Find the position that showcases your talents as a ballplayer, and work at it until you are exceptional.

NORWOOD VANN

Professional Football Player

At home one evening, during his freshman year in college, he sat watching a *60 Minutes* segment on athletes. Many of them couldn't read. They had gone through high school and college on athletic scholarships and couldn't even read when they got out. He immediately went and picked up a book. "I said to myself, 'Man, I'm not going to let this happen to me!'" And he didn't. Though football was a big part of his college life, he was determined not to let football be the only part of his life. He used his North Carolina football scholarship to its full advantage educating himself while preparing for pro ball.

Now, Norwood Vann is an outside linebacker for the Los Angeles Rams. A dream come true. Pro prospect. He made it. The grounds of the practice field, tidy and green, look like a posh elementary school. The sounds of grunting and clashing padded bodies fill the silence. Beautifully spiralled passes fly through the air, weightless men jump to catch them, frozen for an instant in mid-air. Each day, Norwood still learns more about pro ball.

When I first started playing football, I was a running back. In high school, I was a quarterback, and in college, I was a tight end. When I got here, they moved me to outside linebacker.

The scouts came around school when Norwood was a junior in college. They watched, timed players. The team played it's best football. Afterwards, a scout approached him and said simply, "You are a pro prospect."

Then I thought I wouldn't mind playing if I got a chance to. I wasn't really thinking about it. As my senior year progressed, I was doing well and got better each game, and the opportunity arose.

The generally recognized belief is that a player stands a better chance of making it in pro football if he comes out of a college that has a well-known tradition of winning. "It has a lot to do with the amount of publicity a person gets coming out of college."

Norwood was a tenth round draft pick. Number 253. His lucky number. 252 players were picked before him. The next step was training camp.

Pro football training camp is a six-week process of elimination. It is a tense and difficult experience, and preparation planning is impossible. It changes year by year.

We practiced twice a day. I didn't know the system, the players, or the coaches. I thought, 'I'm going to go wherever they tell me to go, if they tell me to jump, I'll jump.'

They bring in about 100 rookies and put us in dorms. The rookies come in a week early and try and learn the system. The veterans come a week later and they go over the same thing with them that they went over with the rookies so the rookies will get a double dose of it. Then they start the process of elimination.

They put you in situations to watch you play. If you looked good, you would make it through the week. Each week, there was a cut. It started with about 100 guys, and by the end of the week, they had to be down to maybe 80, then the next week, 70 and so on.

It's hot, and you are trying to learn things, and you're doing things wrong, especially my situation. They just moved me into a new position, so I didn't have the foggiest idea how to play the position.

Out of all the guys that came in, they drafted ten. There were six rookies on the team then, I was the only one to make it. they cut some guys and then brought them back. But, I was the only one who stayed from day one all the way through.

It came down to the last day of cuts, and the night before, I couldn't sleep. To make it this far, and get a bus ticket home, that would be bad. There was a lot of pressure.

He made it. As a rookie, Norwood plays in each game on special teams; the kick-off returns, for example.

You have to pay your dues. Very seldom, a newcomer will come in and start, unless something tragic happens. I am learning from just sitting back and watching.

The practice day begins at 9:30 a.m. The team meets to discuss the plans for the day.

It's very relaxed. Then you break up and go to your individual meetings. You watch film on your opponent, and on yourself. After that, we have lunch.

About 30 minutes of additional meetings await the players after lunch. Then, it's time to hit the field and practice for two solid hours, ending the day at 3:00 p.m. Friday, they get a break. Team practice begins at noon and ends an hour later.

Each practice is specifically designed to prepare for the team they are about to play. Some Rams wear the jerseys of the opposing team as part of the preparation.

On game days, we go to the hotel. (The reason we stay at the hotel) is mainly for meetings and stuff so everyone can be at one place and nobody has to worry about someone not being on time. The next morning, we get up for the pre-game meal, some church services, and meetings.

We like to associate with each other on and off the field. We go out together and party together.

Football is one of the most physical sports of professional athletics. The risk of injury is ever-present, and occasionally frequent. As an outside linebacker, Norwood is in direct physical contact with the opposing team's offensive line. His risk of injury is great, but to play his best game, he cannot allow the interference of fear.

I get hit all the time, but I never worry about it. My mother always said, 'If something is going to happen to you, it's going to happen to you and there's nothing you can do to change it.' So, I don't worry about breaking a leg or really getting hurt.

I broke my hip playing football, and a finger playing baseball, so I have had injuries, but I think it is better for a person not to worry about it.

A working life in the public eye has its pros and cons. As a role model to young men, Norwood sees the opportunity to continuously better himself. Conversely, the notoriety and public attention can be tiring. Fans await autographs. Professional athletes in America have reached star status. "Sometimes you think, 'Oh, not again!'

Most often, football talent for the potential professional level will show itself by high school at the latest. The high school athlete has at least an idea that he might make it in the pros whether he is heading in that direction or not. To all who dream of a career in professional football, Norwood offers one piece of advice, "Get a good education."

A lot of people say that when you play professional football, you are going to go and get hurt and then what are you going to do? I see people that are in a wheelchair, and can't walk or can't talk, and they're driving their wheelchair with their little hands. They go to school. I know good and well that if I break my leg or something, I can make it. I can go to class on crutches.

Keep your goals in perspective.

My goal is to be the best I possibly can, and to get better each day. I just want to play football until I get tired of the game, until I get up one morning and say, 'I don't want to practice anymore.'

MARK WILSON

Professional Football Player

Quarterback Mark Wilson stands tall and slender compared to his defensive line. Soft-spoken and genuine, Mark is a family man with his home base in Seattle, Washington. He was drafted into professional football in 1980 from Brigham Young University.

In football, either you make the big time or you don't. Before the season begins, we go into training camp with (about a) hundred guys, all the draft picks. We only have 12 draft picks, and they'll sign maybe 50 players that are free agents. The coaches evaluate the players based on their performance in practice and the pre-season games, then they select a 49 man team. The other players are released.

The regular football season begins in September and ends in December. Play-off games begin about a week after the season ends, with the team who wins the first play-off moving into the second, and the team who wins the second, moving into the Super Bowl. The Raiders play four pre-season games. For the regular season, they will play eight home games and eight away games.

During the season, Mark is awake at 8:00 a.m. enjoying a good breakfast before leaving for the practice field. By 10:00, he is at the field and his working day begins.

Because I am a quarterback, I have more meetings than most players, so I am in meetings until 1:30 or 2:00.

Mark's physical practice commences at 2:30 when he practices with the team for close to two and a half hours. Each evening, at home, he studies film on the team. The camera's eye records the strengths and weaknesses of the team. The quarterback watches each play over and over and returns the following day to start the process again.

Some days are more involved than others. As you get close to Sundays, our game days, you taper off a little bit to try and rest yourself. We have Tuesdays off.

On game day, we have a special pre-game meal about four hours before the game, and don't eat until after the game.

When the Raiders play a game away from home, they always return that night.

Even if it's a night game, we'll get on the plane and fly back. It's really nice for a family. I'm gone only two, or at the most, three days during the week, and it's only every other week.

A few of the surprises that Mark found as a professional football player were the schedule and the intensity of play.

For some reason, I had it in my mind that everyday you'd 'go-out-there-and-kill-each-other' type of thing. The whole perspective is in preparing yourself for the game, so it would be counter-productive to kill each other during the week, and show up ragged and tired for the game on Sunday.

Don't put all of your eggs in one basket.

When I went to college, we had 30 guys there on scholarship. In my class, we had a very good football team. We finished ninth in the country, but only had two guys drafted into professional football. There were some guys who just pointed everything towards pro ball and forgot about their schooling. When it didn't happen, they were left wondering what they were going to do.

Go to school. Get the best education possible while playing your best football. If you are a good player in high school, powerhouse colleges will actively recruit you.

I think the best situation is to go the best and strongest football power. If you can play and be competitive on that level, you can probably be successful at the professional level. Certainly, the scouts will notice you more. Also, the level of competition will be a lot greater in the bigger schools, so I think you'll improve.

But, I think if you are a good player at a small college, they are going to find you. The scouting system now is so diverse that the good players will be found, but the level of competition won't be the same.

BYRON SCOTT

Professional Basketball Player

The Forum in Los Angeles, home of the Los Angeles Lakers, seats 17,505 basketball fans. The Lakers play 41 of their regular season games to that maximum crowd. For a rookie, it's his chance to shine.

At the beginning of the 1983 basketball season, the Lakers traded a veteran player for another veteran and a rookie. It was the rookie's time to show what he could do. The media's eye was upon him from the moment the controversial trade was made. Byron Scott didn't let them down.

The dream began in junior high school. He wanted to play pro basketball, didn't want anything else. Byron's father was a basketball player. His influence and inspiration affected young Byron's decision to pursue basketball as a career.

My father played his basketball in Arizona, and the only thing that really stopped him was that he got into a car accident before he got drafted. I set my goals on doing the things that I know he wanted to do.

A star player in high school, Byron Scott led the team in scoring, rebounds and steals for three years in a row. He played forward until his junior year, when the coach switched him to guard in preparation for college. A basketball scholarship seemed the natural next step. Arizona State University offered. Byron Scott accepted. He played guard on the university's team for three years, left before graduation, and was drafted by the San Diego Clippers. At the time of his departure for ASU, Byron didn't know where he would play professionally.

I had people who were working with me and giving me a lot of information on where I would go in the draft, what pick I would probably be, and where I would end up.

I was 4th pick in the draft by the Clippers and we couldn't come to any agreement as far as contract, so I just had to sit it out until the end of October when the Lakers and the Clippers made the deal.

Byron Scott currently plays guard for the Los Angeles Lakers. On a game day, he is up at 8:00 in the morning fixing himself a light breakfast. He arrives at the court at about 10:15, gets himself taped, looks at film, and gets out onto the court to practice shooting for about half an hour. The team practice lasts from 11:00 to noon.

At 12:00, I come home and fix what I call a "pre-game meal". It's something like steak or Lasagna. I eat that, and about 1:30 or 2:00 I try and get a couple of hours sleep. I wake up, take my shower, get dressed, and am at the Forum by 5:30.

Byron is generally the first player to arrive at the Forum. The extra time allows a period of relaxation.

We have a tape recorder in the locker room, and we have players that bring their music, and I bring my music sometimes, and listen to tapes. We also have a video of whoever we are playing to show the things that they do against us. I sit there and look at that and listen to music before Coach Riley gets started.

Before the game, the coach and the teammates gather as the coach prepares them with the right frame of mind for the game. Positive thoughts, and the confidence of preparation fill the locker room. After the game, they gather again in the locker room, sit down for a time, shower, then go their separate ways.

This team is a very unique team. I haven't been on a team since college or high school where everyone gets along so well with each other, and there are no head problems. Nobody has a big head. Everybody talks to each other.

Experience dictates the amount of mental preparation each basketball player must make.

Some of them who have been doing this for a while don't have to go through it as much as someone who has only been here for one year, like myself. I just sit in my chair and try and visualize myself doing certain things, offense and defense, and prepare myself for the game. It usually works.

As the anticipation of the game melts into the playing of the game, the rookie player must go through the feelings of anxiousness that all rookies experience. You want to get out on that court and show what you can do. Minutes on the bench seem like hours.

In my case, I think I've put a little too much pressure on myself to get out there and perform when I should have gone out there and relaxed. Later on in the season I started just going out there and doing what I can do, in a relaxed situation. It helped a lot to do it that way.

I think a lot of rookies that don't start at the beginning of the season, want to show what they can do, and I think that is added pressure which they don't need.

In certain situations it ran through my head that I should be out there, that I could really be helping the team, I thought they needed this or that. But, it wasn't my decision.

You must wait your turn like everyone else. There is a period of adjustment required in the transition from college basketball to the pros. Media attention. Adjusting to your teammate's style. Travel.

The team traded Norm Nixon and got myself and Swen Nater, so everybody was calling it the Norm Nixon trade. Everyone was expecting this and that. I think it just comes along with the territory.

I knew it was going to be a lot of hard work. I think my misconception was that I came into the league thinking that it wouldn't take long to get used to everything. That was totally wrong. I didn't think it would take me that long to learn the plays, to adjust to where a player like Magic passes the ball. And, he has to learn where I want to catch it, and where I like to shoot it. I had to learn where Kareem likes the ball, and James Worthy and McAdoo, there was a lot of adjusting. It didn't feel comfortable until January. It's working out really well now.

Basketball season extends from October to April. The Lakers play two to three games a week and practice three to four days a week. Your body and your mind have to adjust to the constant playing, travelling, and accompanying fatigue.

You come to the pros, and you have 82 games, sometimes you are gone for 13 days on the road where you play 8 games, or you are gone for 7 days where you play 5 games. It gets to be hectic. If you're not used to it, it can be something that really wears you down. It got to me after about 50 games. I was tired mentally and physically. You have to do something to regain your strength. You play 82 games just to eliminate 8 teams.

Use the off-season to relax and regain your strength.

I had a coach at Arizona State who used to play for the Philadelphia 76ers. He told me that the worst mistake he ever made was to play basketball when the season was over. He continued to play all year round. It took it's toll on him, and he injured his knee doing it. So the best advice that he gave me, was when the season is over, let it be over. Relax, get your rest, and start back playing in September. That's what I have been doing.

Go to college. Players will only benefit from the college experience.

Don't think that you can go from high school to the professional ranks. You do need the education and the background. Do the things that you enjoy, and have fun. Once you get to the professional ranks, it's not fun, it's business. It can be very enjoyable, if you look at it as fun like our team does.

Get some kind of coach who will prepare you for the professional ranks, and hopefully, you'll do well.

EDUCATION

Americans are said to have a love affair with education. The tradition of free public education has been characteristic of American life for generations and the development of public schools was one of the first steps taken by pioneers who settled various areas of this republic.

Today, our educational system remains one of our greatest national strengths as evidenced by American leadership in literary, scientific, and other research. Additionally, a high proportion of Americans of all ages receive educational degrees. Perhaps the finest compliment to our system of higher education is the fact that record number of students from other nations come to attend our colleges and universities.

In our society, teaching opportunities are open at three basic educational levels:

- **Kindergarten and elementary education teachers** provide training up to the sixth grade and introduce children to the basics of mathematics, language, science, and social studies. In some cases, one teacher provides instruction in all subjects—sometimes aided by specialists in the areas of reading, art, or physical education. In addition, some teachers and teacher aides work in preschool settings with children between the ages of two and five. In a recent year, statistics show there were 1.4 million kindgarten and elementary education teachers at work in their field.

- **Secondary school teachers** provide instruction at the junior high and senior high school levels—grades 7 through 12. Most specialize in a single subject—such as English, French, mathematics, history, biology, or physical education. They often instruct as many as five or six classes a day. Some teachers use laboratory sessions to augment classroom discussions. Vocational teachers may use shop classes to provide hands-on experience with instruments, tools, and machinery. In a recent year, there were around one million secondary school teachers.

- **College teachers** offer instruction in junior colleges, four-year colleges, and in graduate or professional schools. They often are required to do research in their field and report in writing on their experiments through published books and studies. They often begin as instructors and move up the academic ladder through the ranks of assistant and associate professor to full professor. In a recent year, there were 730,000 college faculty members.

In addition to these fields, many people work in education as adult education teachers in evening schools, training officers in employing organizations or in the armed forces, instructors in career schools or in classes for non-English speaking people, or seminar and workshop leaders offering short courses in a variety of practical areas.

The field of education also offers jobs for administrators and support personnel working as budget officers, guidance counselors, admissions officers, career counselors, librarians, accountants, and public information officers.

The demand for teachers is obviously closely related to the numbers of students enrolled in schools. In the late 1960s a surplus of elementary and secondary education teachers developed as public school enrollments declined due to the decreased birthrate. Similarly, a few years later, the growth in college enrollment levelled off and a surplus of college professors developed.

However, yesterday's teacher surplus has turned into a teacher shortage in many areas and in many teaching fields. One result of the increased demand has been pressure to increase salaries. Over the last five years, raises given to teachers have averaged twice as much as those awarded to all professional employees.

Elementary and secondary school teachers usually start their careers with a bachelor's degree but many eventually earn a master's—in part, because salary increases are given to those with advanced training. College teachers generally must earn a doctor's degree for full professional status—but some start teaching while they hold the master's.

Women account for around 69 percent of elementary and secondary school teachers and around 30 percent of college faculty members.

Teachers are a major focus in young lives. College faculty members can be an inspiration for career choices. Many adults retain the memory of an outstanding teacher who affected their lives. Teaching can be a rewarding and responsible career at all levels of education.

MARS BERMAN

Montessori Elementary School Teacher

Nap time. An unexpected silence fills the room of preschoolers. Some children sleep. Others lie quietly on their cots gazing about a room that looks different in the darkness.

An enormous paper spider sits in the upper corner, atop a web of yarn. A long wall is filled with the children's rendition of an eastern forest in autumn. A thousand small beads are bound together in a cube to give the children an idea of how one thousand feels. The entire building is filled with fuzzy, floppy, firm and fantastic things for the children to handle.

A pretty woman with stylishly cut blonde hair slips out of the nap room to introduce herself. She is charming and personable, and speaks with immediate emotion. She has learned how to tune out noise, crawl like a snake on the floor, communicate with parents, and give the children the best of the many things she has to offer.

Mars Berman is a directrice in a Montessori school. "We are called directors, not teachers, because we direct children's activities." She has been "directing" for 12 years.

Montessori is a method. It has particular ways of approaching the child's mind. Children learn most from their eyes and their touch. When we do sound presentations, for example, we show the letter B, it's in sand paper, they see it, feel it with their hands so they get a muscular memory to B, then hear the sound. Everything has a concrete basis.

The children are very young when they first enter the Montessori school, and remain until the first or second grade. The idea behind the process is to form an unconscious foundation that later education can build on. The young children don't learn particular things as much as they learn how to learn.

They learn powers of concentration, powers of repetition. When you first start washing a chair when you are three years old, it's a mess. Everything goes wrong. It doesn't get clean and it seems to take forever. An older child starts to see that they are getting better at it. It leads to sequencing, and an ability to see a problem from beginning to end and know you can work through it.

Generally, a school year of Montessori training and an internship are required to qualify as a Montessori director. A good way to start is to apply directly to the school for a job as assistant.

We take on interns from one of the high schools. They come three times a week for a morning, as a part of their course work. A lot of people get terribly interested in it and call up a training center, apply, and devote a year's time to go through the training.

Mars' day begins at 8:30 in the morning when, with her assistant, she prepares her class activities for about a half hour. The directors have the freedom to invent activities for their class. If it doesn't work, it doesn't work, and they move onto the next thing.

You take a lot of clues from your children. For example, children are always interested in dinosaurs. Last year our dinosaur thing turned into wallpapering all the walls of the halls with giant, hand-painted dinosaur pictures. We made clay models, and it got bigger because the interest was generated from the children. You take the ball and you run with it.

At the beginning of the day, Mars runs a circle for about 20 minutes. They sing songs and see who is and isn't there. Afterwards, there is open class time for about an hour and fifteen minutes. Food preparation. Dolly washing. People are in and out doing all sorts of things. The directors make a point of developing the skills of children who need work in a specific area. For example, if a child needed hand work, he or she would spent time cutting.

As much as it is an open classroom, we do follow particular rules. There are certain ways toys are to be handled, and I show the classroom how to handle them properly. They can be creative within the rules.

By the end of open class time, it is nearly 11:00, and there is another circle, dance time, or free activity like "rolling around on the floor like a snake."

We have lunch together, and the children are expected to do a lot of the maintenance. They wash tables, lay out their lunches, clean up spills.

Storytime follows lunch, which is followed by another work period. "We have a woodshop set-up in the back. The children make things, bang on wood, things like that."
2:30 is nap time when the directors put classical music on the stereo and everyone takes a rest. A siesta.

About 3:30 or 4:00, we begin the day again with a snack, shoes on, get up. There's wood shop, art, dress-up, a lot of games outside. One day a week we have music, one day a week we have a formal dance teacher. Children are filtering out anytime from 2:30 on, but the day ends at 5:45.

The day is long, and the directors truly become a part of the children's extended family.
In a preschool setting, part of any teacher's responsibility is to remain as aware as possible of any learning disabilities or potential future problems.

You are always waiting for children to grow out of it, but there comes a time when you think that you have to intercede. That's when you start doing interjection with parents, and you start testing.

We have a speech and hearing specialist who comes in and tests all the children. I tell parents that I would much rather have these specialists tell me I am wrong than to have a seven year old child with a big problem because I didn't speak up.

Mars sees the appeal of this specific type of teaching situation in terms of the amount of freedom and self-expression that is encouraged within the system. She feels good about the fact that she can take twenty different children and have a terrific time with them.

People are shocked when they see what they perceive as a lot of stress for the directors in the classroom. There are about 27 children making all kinds of demands on you. It's just a matter of keeping balls in the air. You never really feel stress, you just feel like you are working. You are a princess in your own classroom. You do have to get over noise, however. You have to have a good screening system for noise, otherwise you will be driven crazy.

An important responsibility for the Montessori directors as well as any teacher, is the responsibility to the parents.

I think that parents are infinitely harder to deal with than children. Parents are the ones who have fears and false fronts and problems.

That is the main thing I have learned in my 12 years of teaching, and why I wasn't as good when I started. I didn't know how to glean information from parents. I didn't understand about divorces. You have to find out about these things.

I had a little kid who was limping all day. I kept asking him, 'What's the matter with your foot?' I couldn't understand it. I finally talked to his parents and found out that his mother had been in a motorcycle accident and broken her foot. The child was imitating his mother.

A successful rapport between parents and director requires a delicate balance.

On the other hand, you want them to respect you as a professional. In Montessori, they tend to respect us more because we stay in the jobs, and because the parents spend money to put their child into a private school. At the same time they will accuse you of not understanding because you are not a parent. All you can do is talk from experience and from things that you see, not value judgements. I think that the hardest thing for new teachers to learn is to put themselves aside and be diplomatic.

It takes a special kind of person to wake up each morning, arrive at work, and spend the day playing with other people's children. It has been said that Montessori orders the director's minds as much as it orders the child's mind.

When you teach children, it is a reflection of yourself. It's an adventure. What you take away from it is never a loss. Your people skills are strong. You have diplomacy skills and the ability to handle yourself in front of a group. If you can handle children, you can handle adults. There is no difference. We change in size and rhetoric, but the same motives go on.

The only thing is, to work as a teacher, you have to make some financial arrangements. If you are very young and have no financial demands, you could live off the salary. Otherwise. . . .

JOAN MOYLETT

Junior High School Teacher

In the state of Connecticut, the Glastonbury school system is rated as one of the finest. The high school students consistently score higher than the state and national averages on SAT and other standardized tests.

Joan Moylett teaches geography at Gideon Welles Junior High, the only junior high school in the Glastonbury system. In 1984, Gideon Welles was named one of the top four junior high schools in the state of Connecticut. The teaching staff plays the quintessential role in the student's success.

A petite woman with tiny feet and hands, Joan exudes confidence and ability. She always wanted to be a teacher, aimed for it in college. Before fulfilling her initial ambitions, Joan married, quit college after one year, and started a family that would eventually consist of eight children.

> *I guess it was about 25 years later, when my youngest child was in second grade, I began to get bored and said to my husband, 'I think I'm going to get a job.' He said, 'Finish school. Do what you want to do.'*

Joan returned to college and received her bachelor of science degree in history.

> *In my college, the BS means that you are going to teach. Getting the BS qualifies you for a temporary certificate. Within ten years of obtaining your temporary certificate, you have to earn a master's degree or 30 credits beyond a bachelor's degree in order to get a permanent certificate. If you don't get it within ten years, no school district can hire you. That is the law in Connecticut.*

Teachers in the state of Connecticut are paid on three pay scales. One is the bachelor's only. The other is bachelor's plus 30 hour credits. The third is master's plus 30 credits. The master's plus 30 or a PhD are both the same pay scale.

When Joan initially interviewed for a teaching job, her education had emphasized history.

> *When they told me that there was an opening for two classes of geography, I felt confident to do it. I had an advantage. All through my school years, my father had a map of the United States, the world, Europe, Asia, or Africa on the wall over our kitchen table. When we ate dinner, we would play games. 'Don't look at the map, and tell me the countries that surround France.' 'Which is further west, New York city or Brazil?' and 'What is the capital of . . .?'*

> *I also learned as I taught.*

Now, Joan has been a teacher since 1977.

> *When I was student teaching, I was sure that I wanted to teach high school. I liked the age group. I felt that the older the child, the happier I would be as a teacher.*

> *I was offered a job teaching junior high. After a year of that experience, I was surprised how much I enjoyed that age group. The kids are much more responsive. They are easier to motivate, easier to mold. You can change their behavior very readily if they like you.*

> *The flip side is that if you have a personality or teaching style that is not warm and nurturing, junior high school kids turn off, and it is very hard to get them to respond. High school kids are old enough to be more objective about their teachers. They also have other people that are important to them. High school teachers and students are more content/subject oriented, whereas, junior high school students and teachers are more 'personal relationship' oriented. They are very serious about school, and if the teacher is serious, and at the same time nurturing, they will really work hard for you.*

Joan has been teaching junior high students ever since.

There are approximately 780 students in the two grades. Each teacher works from a detailed curriculum with specifically listed behaviorial objectives. There are approximately 100 behaviorial objectives for the geography course, plus a course outline. For example, by the end of the year, students will be able to find a latitude and longitude. Students will be able to identify three different land forms and explain their impact on people. Students will be able to explain how latitude and altitude affect climate.

The teachers are responsible for composing their own exams, with the agreement that the final exam will be a unit test.

We feel that 12 year olds are too young to handle a cumulative test.

A copy of the final exam is sent to my supervisor, and she assures us that the superintendent looks through some of them. Part of the reason is that we used to have difficulties maintaining discipline in the last three or four days of school. So, they establish an exam schedule for the last four days. The other part of the reason for submitting the exams to the administration is to be sure that we are taking it as seriously as we want the kids to.

On school days, Joan wakes between 6:00 and 6:15, and leaves the house an hour later to arrive in her classroom by 7:45 a.m. Homeroom is from 7:55 to 8:24. The day's announcements are made, Pledge of Allegiance said, and attendance taken. There are seven 50 minute periods per school day.

I have an unusual schedule because I am the director of an alternative program, a little school within our school. I have three planning periods each day. Every teacher gets one planning period. I have a second for team planning with other teachers in the program, and a third as director of the program. So, instead of the normal social studies teaching load of five classes and one supervisory assignment, I teach four classes and spend the rest of the time doing things connected with the program.

There are five lunch periods during the day; each is half of a classroom period. Depending on your schedule, you will have lunch at a different time each year, with different members of the staff.

The students leave school at 2:30, and Joan is generally finished for the day sometime around 3:00.

I have an aide, too, who pretty much works for me in connection with the responsibilities I have as director. She also does clerical work for the other three teachers in the program.

Within Gideon Welles Junior High, there is a positive connection between the teachers and the principal, and among the teachers themselves. This is not always the case inside schools, but positive working relationships are always a benefit to the teachers and, ultimately, the students.

Gideon Welles is organized in such a way that similar class subjects are taught in the same area of the school. The social studies classes, for example, are situated next to each other. It provides an atmosphere which is conducive to the sharing of teaching materials, and support of faculty members for each other.

If one of the social studies teachers is absent and has a substitute, one or two of the others will help the substitute get organized, find materials, stuff like that.

We have a room where all of the audio visual materials, supplementary reading materials, desk maps, and things like that are stored. In some schools they have careful sign-in and sign-out systems. We don't do that. If I go look for something, like the filmstrip kit on earthquakes, and it's not where it belongs, I usually know which teacher is likely to be teaching with it. I'll go ask if I can use it the next day.

There is also a teacher's lounge in the building, so we get a chance to interact with teachers from other departments and visit and talk about students we share.

Occasionally, work at home is required. During the first year, there will be substantially more work required than in following years.

It's not just the first year teaching, it's the first year teaching a new subject. There is a great deal of preparation. If you watch what you do, and keep a good file on the teaching materials you use, then the second and third, and every year after that, all you have to do is refine what you've done.

After teaching for eight years, Joan brings work home when she is preparing report cards, or has given a writing assignment. It is an average of three hours a week outside of school grading or preparing.

New teachers face the moment of truth as they first stand in front of their class. All faces facing front. Eager listeners.

> *I didn't worry about having to be entertaining. I think that was maybe because I started at age 45 when most of my own children were older than the students I was teaching. I didn't feel an intimidation of the kids.*

> *I think young teachers, who are only in their twenties themselves, can be intimidated by a six-foot seventeen year old, even the girls, and feel the need to be entertaining.*

Maintain a serious attitude about what you are teaching. "I don't mean that you are grim about it, but recognize that you are doing a worthwhile thing." The teacher must get the message across that the students are there to learn, and the teacher is there to teach, and it's not a frivolous thing.

> *There are always going to be some who are goof-offs, but I think it's very important for teachers not to be flip and casual about schoolwork.*

As a professional teacher, Joan has never had any problems controlling a class. As a volunteer, however, she did encounter problems with discipline.

> *When we lived in Lancaster, they had a problem at the high school where three of my kids were enrolled. A teacher resigned in March and the principal asked me if I would teach the class. So, I went into this senior class. Looking back on it now, it was a cruel thing to do. I was teaching mostly seniors, suffering from severe cases of senioritis to begin with.*

> *I had one class that I really lost control of. They were shooting paper airplanes around the room. It was bad. Mostly, I was glad they didn't destroy anything. I didn't feel weepy or teary or like I needed help. Once or twice, the principal came in and read the riot act to them. I didn't know then how to make kids behave without threatening them.*

Joan learned from watching two good teachers teach. She was a student teacher and absorbed all she could, retaining a valuable rule to teach by: Don't humiliate or confront a student. Always give them a way out.

> *If I have two kids talking in the back of the room, I always ask if there is a problem. There could be. Some girl could be confiding to her best friend that she is pregnant or that her father just walked out on her mother last night. It could be an important conversation. If they say no, I ask them to pay attention to the lesson. If I sense that there is a problem, I ask if they want to go to the nurse, the girl's room, do they need to leave?*

> *I had a great kid who all of a sudden was going down the tubes. Two months later, his mother thought that maybe it would be a good idea if the school knew that his father had had a nervous breakdown. Usually, there is an explanation for unusual behavior.*

A big bonus inherent in teaching is the opportunity to start fresh each year. You can change any way that you want to. No one will be there to say, "Hey! That's not the way you used to do it!"

The biggest reward, however, is knowing that you are doing something worthwhile. You can make a difference in people's lives. You can help kids grow, help them realize that they have better brains than they thought they had. They can do things that they never thought they could do.

> *I am going to go back to school and tell my students that I was just on a trip to Death Valley, and ask them what they think I experienced. Once kids know that you have affection for them, I won't put them down, or allow anyone else in the class to put them down for making mistakes, they have a lot of fun with figuring things out. They stretch and think and make connections with things they learn and things in the real world.*

A teacher can tangibly see ways in which he or she has prepared a student to do something that the student could not do at the beginning of the year. It's very satisfying.

The hours and work schedule are another advantage. Two months off in the summer. Frequent breaks. Good teachers give a lot to their students, emotionally and intellectually. The breaks and time off are a time to replenish yourself.

> *Up until recently, I think the main disadvantage was the pay. I think that has changed greatly, in Connecticut. There was a time in the 50's when anyone who wanted a job teaching got one. With the baby boom, they just needed warm bodies. Now, they are seeing the need to attract good people, and the pay seems to be increasing.*

To teach at the junior and senior high school level, Joan advises majoring in the subject that you intend to teach. Grade school teachers must major in education, but junior and high school teachers really must have command over what they are teaching. You must thoroughly know your subject and be very comfortable with your material.

Secondly, do your student teaching in a good school with good teachers. Ask questions. Learn from them. Take risks and try new things. Your colleagues can be invaluable in providing hints on how to prepare lessons and prepare yourself for the realities of teaching.

As the students reach higher levels of education, such as the junior and senior high school levels, the emphasis changes. In elementary school, many teachers grade students on effort and punctuality as much as the content of their work. As the students graduate into junior high, effort counts for less, and the standard of the work produced is measured more. It is a time of change for many students, and all of the changes will affect the classroom environment.

> *The bottom line is that you really have to love kids, and love them in a way that you set high standards for them, not in a way that you let them do anything they please. Be willing to make them work hard, but you also have to have the understanding that not all of them can do the same work. That was one of the things that was hardest for me.*

> *I was always a good student in school. Most of us tend to look back on our own experience, and say well, I did this, therefore. . . I had to realize that it wasn't reasonable to expect all eighth graders to do what I had done in eighth grade. I had to understand that this kid can't do what the kid who sits next to him can.*

PETER HAMMOND

University Professor

A close friend of the Hammond family, a sociologist, had worked in Africa and returned with tales of his experiences. Peter was fascinated by Africa and its culture. The family friend provided the perfect opportunity to find out how to go about doing what he wanted to do.

Peter Hammond is a professor of anthropology at UCLA. His book-lined office overlooks the green grass of the square. He is a precise man, a man who knows his subject, a man who loves to teach.

Peter is a cultural anthropologist. Cultural anthropologists do not study human evolution, nor do they dig up buried cities.

> *We study contemporary, living people. We go out and do field work, live among the people, study them, and try and figure out how their culture works.*

In the field of anthropology, the graduate student generally chooses a department which is known to focus on the geographical area in which he or she is interested. Northwestern University was prominent in African Studies, and that's where Peter chose to further his study of the people of Africa. He was also interested in working in French speaking countries in Africa, so he completed part of his graduate work at Northwestern, and part at the University of Paris, in France.

An important part of obtaining an advanced degree is your dissertation based on field work, completed after your formal graduate work.

> *I then went out to Africa for a couple of years working on a particular problem. I was interested in the cultural problem of increasing food production. They suffer continuously from drought, overpopulation, and limited natural resources. I studied the farming people there for a year, studied their traditional farming system as it related to the other aspects of their culture. Then, I followed a sector of that population to a new area where they were adapting to a new farming system. There, the focus of my inquiry was the way in which this change in food production affected other aspects of the culture, family life, their economic and political system, and their religion.*

Peter returned from Africa, wrote his dissertation, then received his PhD. The next step is to get a job. Most often, in the course of graduate training, you work for a particular professor and he or she is your mentor. Professors have a series of contacts, and will know of people looking to hire a person with your qualifications.

> *It's very important to study with someone who is prominent themselves so that if a university thinks they want an Africanist, they know that (your mentor) is the person to ask. That's exactly what happened in my case. Two universities called him for a recommendation. I was just finishing up my PhD, and I got two job offers, and took the better one.*

Then, you are launched. In the typical university system, the entering PhD will start as an Assistant Professor. It is usually not a tenured position, but you will be hired for a maximum of three years. If you get to stay on will depend on how well you teach, and your progress in terms of research and writing.

> *You go to meetings and develop a network of contacts, and you hear about other jobs, people hear about you. I got my second job as a consequence of someone knowing about me and my work and offering me a job.*
>
> *You write as you go along. In the course of my writing, I think in the first teaching job that I had, an editor at one of the publishing houses had heard about something that I had written, came to see me, and asked me if I would be interested in editing a couple of books.*

The general standard in a university the size of UCLA is that you are an assistant professor for three years, then renewed for another three years. At that point, you will either be offered tenure, or you should begin looking for another job.

If you have published quite a lot, they promote you and you stay in the university. But, if you are a real hot shot, there is nothing to prevent you from being offered an associate professorship after one year. There are people who have moved up the ranks very quickly because they are very good.

The hierarchy follows a certain path: assistant professor, associate professor, professor. Within each of the ranks there are salary steps: assistant professor one and assistant professor two. You will be reviewed before each promotion.

Peter finds one of the nice things about his profession is that, although he works a lot of hours, he can essentially arrange his own time. In this quarter, he teaches three courses. He has two lectures a week, for an hour and fifteen minutes in the morning, then a seminar on Tuesday afternoons from 2:00 to 5:00, and a similar one on Thursdays.

The seminar is really fun because it's informal. There is a smaller group of students, and we have coffee and cookies and talk about some really interesting stuff.

Peter arrives at the University by 8:00 in the morning, five days a week, and usually leaves about 5:30. He generally works for 6 or 7 hours on the weekend. He also has three research assistants and three teaching assistants. They are all graduate students.

I have a large course, so I have to have assistants to help me with my research. I have to get money to support my research, I use that money to pay my assistants to put stuff on the computer, go to the library.

Aside from classroom time, much of the rest of Professor Hammond's time is spent on committees of various sorts. He is on the mayor's task force on Africa, for example, and time is spent in meetings. Most of the work he does is in or related to the University in some way.

If you are in a University that emphasizes research and publication, you don't get here unless you publish quite a lot, unless your name is fairly well-known, you don't get a full professorship.

There is another way to go as an anthropologist, which is very, very nice. Teach at a small college. As a professor teaching at a small school, your career path will be very different. The school expects you to spend much more time with the students, have them over to your house, guide them, give them hands-on attention as they go along. It is a very lovely, rewarding way to be a teacher. There is much less pressure for publication.

UCLA is a university that defines itself as having an important role in contributing to the generation of knowledge. The pressure to publish is in the form of expected performance. It is expected that you will make progress. You won't get fired if you have tenure, but you won't be promoted if you don't publish.

You can be an Associate Professor for the rest of your life. There are also lots of informal ways the university can punish you for not continuing to grow and make a substantial contribution.

At UCLA, for example, you are reviewed every three years. You submit a record of the things you have done during that period, the teaching, the university committees that you have served on, the number of students that you have trained, the amount of community outreach that you have participated in, and your publications. Probably of all those things, your publications are the most important things.

Most often, if you are a well-known professor in your field, a publisher will approach you to discuss publication.

Then, you try to establish a good relationship with the publisher, with a particular editor at that publishing house. If you publish a book, and that book is successful, and you make them some money, they are likely to ask you for another book. If you are doing a book that is likely to have large sales, a textbook, or trade book, they will probably give you an advance, and then your royalties, which you negotiate.

Good writing skills are essential. Without them, your chances of getting into a good graduate school are slim.

> *As a teacher, I resist very much having to teach people how to write. Usually, the first time a student gives me a paper that has some interesting ideas but is badly written, I will correct two or three pages, then tell them that they can assume there are those kinds of mistakes all the way through. I tell them that I am not there to teach English, and to find someone who will help them and bring the paper back.*

> *If they can't master the ability to write, they are not going to have a career that I am interested in. They are not going to succeed with me. I'm sorry, because sometimes they are really smart, but if they haven't learned how to write, nobody is going to know it.*

Once you have reached the level of full professor, you can decide what you want to teach. There is an expectation that you will teach one undergraduate course and two graduate courses, but Professor Hammond feels that he is essentially in control of what he wants to do.

The hierarchial structure within the department consists of a chair of the department, an executive committee, then the professor is reviewed by his or her peers.

> *These people who review you for promotion every three years are your fellow professors. You don't know who they are. You submit to the central office evidence of what you have been doing in reports and publications and so forth, and they make a recommendation. On the basis of that, you are promoted or not.*

> *You do have classroom evaluations, but really, they are not very important as far as your promotion goes. I think that I have a good reputation as a teacher, but I am very aware of the fact that it probably doesn't affect my promotion. I just have the kind of ego that would feel awful if I didn't do a good job in the classroom.*

A university gains its reputation and is rated by the number of Nobel Laureates and Pulitzer Prize winners it has. Graduate school ratings are based on the number of distinguished faculty and the quality of their publications.

> *If you don't teach well, the university is sort of sorry, but the people who suffer from that are the students.*

For men and women thinking about a career as a university professor, Professor Hammond suggests attending a small liberal arts school for your undergraduate work, and a large, research-oriented university for graduate work.

> *At the graduate level, professors will pay attention to you. As an undergraduate in a university like UCLA, Berkeley, Harvard, you are likely to have a lot of courses with teachers who do not yet have their degrees and are under pressure to finish their own writing, so are not the polished teachers they might be, or young professors who are again under the gun for publishing, and may or may not be good teachers.*

You may see full professors with established reputations, but you will be in a classroom with 300 other students.

> *It's sad. I feel badly about it, but that's the way it is. There are, however, ways to get around it. I always meet a few undergraduate students who bite and scratch and kick, and get into see me, but alot of them are lost.*

The major advantage to his profession is his ability to control his own time. Additionally, universities are stimulating environments where everyone is working with ideas, discussing theories, and staying in touch with the world.

> *In a university environment, there is always something going on that is interesting that you can take advantage of, drama series, films, wonderful athletic facilities.*

A disadvantage is the low pay scale.

You are under a lot of pressure to continue to perform at a high level. You are only as good as your last publication in a certain sense. I am very much torn with wanting to spend time with the students, and aware of the fact that I am stealing time from my own research and I will be punished for it. There are certain points at which a promotion can make as much as $10,000 difference in your salary. If you give that time to a student, and you don't get on with your work, and then you have just lost yourself money. So, you have to think twice.

There is the opportunity for a sabbatical leave every seven years, and the professor, if he can find the money to do it, can take time off to go back out in the field if he wants to, or write.

Peter advises slowing down. Don't be in a rush to make a decision as important as the decision of what to do with your life.

If you aren't sure still, go to graduate school and take a master's degree in psychology or something like that, and see if you really like it. You can always stay on for a PhD, or maybe go into something else. Resist the pressure to decide too soon.

I think travel is marvelous. I think taking a year off in college or after college is great.

BARBARA ANDREWS

Teacher for the Developmentally Disabled

The American Heritage Dictionary defines autism as, "abnormal subjectivity; acceptance of fantasy rather than reality. A form of childhood schizophrenia characterized by acting out and withdrawal." The Brentwood Center for Educational Therapy is a school serving autistic, multiply handicapped, severely emotionally disturbed, and developmentally delayed children, adolescents, and adults. Barbara Andrews is the principal.

In 1973, the executive director had a Saturday program for autistic children and young adults. Their parents came to him and said that their children were not in school, and asked if he would start a school program for them. That's what he did. The school started as a program for children who were not allowed in regular public school because of a severity of behavior problems.

Autism is a developmental delay. Autistic children don't come in any clear, packaged category, however, all autistic people have a severe communication disorder.

Their social skills are radically different from ours, different in the sense that they don't tend to relate to another person. They have to be prompted to relate. The speech is usually rote. For example, they may learn to count, but it is clearly just echoing back what they have learned over and over again. There really is no comprehension of what the number 2 looks like. They know that it comes after 1. Stereotypical behavior: you get a lot of self-stimulation. Things like rocking or rubbing their ears.

The youngest student at the Brentwood Center is seven and the oldest is forty. There are 80 students, with a staff of 10 teachers and 10 teaching aides.

Barbara Andrews received her bachelor's degree in 1978, at the State University College in Buffalo, New York. In New York, she taught severely emotionally disturbed children and adolescents in a residential treatment center. From there, Barbara moved to Stamford, Connecticut and worked as a bilingual learning disabilities teacher.

I was always interested in working with emotionally disturbed kids, more than anything else, and kids that were learning disabled, and kids that weren't fitting into school and were having a lot of problems in school. From there, my experience has just grown.

In 1979, she accepted a position as head teacher at the Brentwood Center, and continued her education, receiving a master's degree in educational administration. Soon, Barbara was principal and acting director of the school.

Barbara's working day begins at 7:30 a.m.

There are usually about 10 or 15 different problems that all have to be solved between 7:30 and 8:00. Somebody has called in sick, a bus is going to be late, a bus is too early, a kid is having a temper tantrum and got here ten minutes too early. There was a break-in this morning and we've had stereo equipment stolen. There are all kinds of things that go on from 7:30 to 8:00.

At 8:00, the kids arrive and enter their programs from 8:00 until lunchtime at noon. During those four hours in the morning, Barbara is responsible for billing, ordering necessary teaching equipment and supplies, redoing billing that has been lost by the school district, and all the different things that come up in between.

A mother can call me up and say, 'Please make sure that Stevie drinks his milk for lunch.' Each person thinks that their problem is equally as important as all the others.

The curriculum for the Center is functionally oriented. The teachers teach reading skills and math, but for the purpose of training the students to function in the world.

If you look at a normal elementary school basal reader, the book might be at the third grade level. It says, 'Mr. Frog went to see Mr. Squirrel, and they had lunch.' That's not functional for our kinds of kids. We teach them how to read stop signs, or the signs on men's and women's bathroom, or a grocery list.

Some of the students will be able to hold down paying jobs after they leave the school.

We do have students who have graduated and are making money in a workshop setting. You may get a student that you train to work, maybe two hours a day, with Coca Cola bottling company, sorting bottles or something like that. There are different kinds of jobs for which our kids can qualify with a tremendous amount of training and supervision.

In this special school, the parental involvement can be a source of special frustration.

I can imagine why it's magnified in this situation. If I had a child who was up all night screaming and hollering, and every time I did something, he undid it, there's no question that it's draining.

Many of the students in the program were abandoned and put in state hospitals when they were five and six years old. They don't have parents, but live in a group home setting.

Often, you get a Mom and a Pop agency where they've got three mentally retarded young adults, and their level of sophistication is not nearly as high as you would like. You say to them, "you know, we are really working on age-appropriate skills, and it's really not appropriate for a 32 year old woman to bring a Snoopy lunch box to school." They say, "Well, wait a minute. That's a good lunch box and I spent $8.00 on it." It's difficult to get them to understand what it is we are trying to do.

Often times parents and group care providers really do sabotage some of your work. Sometimes they think they know their child better than anyone else, and they won't cooperate with the program. It's incredibly frustrating.

The working environment in the school can vary from day to day. On some days, students will be having temper tantrums left and right, and getting work done is impossible.

It's basically a maintenance day where everyone is doing low level, independent activities. You've got a couple of people working on a hundred-piece puzzle, while someone else is doing something very simple because the level is so tense. You know that someone is going to blow, and you've got to make sure everything is very quiet.

On other days, you can hear a pin drop. The students are working very hard, the teachers are working very hard, there is a lot of work on the board, and a lot of physical work being put out. Quite often, the environment within the school is directly related to the student's environment at home.

Lots of times I get calls in the morning on the answering service, a mother will say, "Johnny had a very bad Sunday, and he didn't sleep Sunday night, so watch out Monday morning." It's very helpful. We know that when he comes in, we'll immediately give him the easiest possible working environment.

In a sense, a lot of the behavior and the classroom structure is really very normal. When you think about normal adults, every once in a while, we come to work and we've had a really bad weekend, we had a fight with our husband or our boyfriend, and we really don't want to work nearly as hard a we should be. We kind of slack off. These kids are no different and they should have that kind of respect as well.

At 2:30, the school day ends for the students. Barbara's day can end anywhere from 2:30 to 5:00, and at times, extends into the night.

I get calls at night sometimes. I have given my home phone number to some of the parents who are a little bit more needy. It's rare, but I do get them on the weekend, or parents will call and leave a message on the school's answering service with a dire emergency and they have to talk with someone.

As with the teaching profession as a whole, job burn-out is high. "Unless you've been a teacher, you don't know how difficult it is. There's so much that goes along with the job that people don't know about." One of the reasons is the tremendous amount of politics involved at the school level.

There are things that you want to do, but it's not the policy of the school district to do it. You may have something that you want to say to a parent, and the principal says, 'Don't you dare!'. You may suspect child abuse and you know that if you do something, the parent is going to sue you and drag you through the court system.

Although it is Barbara's experience that most school districts pay special education teachers more money than teachers within regular public schools, it is a negligible amount.

It's about $500 a year more, nothing to write home about. But, what that also tends to create is a sense of animosity between regular teachers and special ed teachers. Regular teachers say, 'Wait a minute. I've got 28 kids in my class. You've only got 7, and you make $500 a year more than I!

Work in the field while you are in school. Try and do some field work for each class you take.

On my resume, I've got a list of about 20 different field placements before I even graduated. If you are taking a class, and there is no field placement, go to the instructor and tell the instructor that you really want to do two hours a week of field placement. It's a heck of a lot of work, but it gives you a tremendous amount of exposure and it prepares you so that when you do graduate college, you are ahead of someone who never worked in the field. Go to a school district and ask them if you can volunteer. Volunteer in a psych hospital. Volunteer in a behavior management program.

There is the potential for violence in a special education school such as the Brentwood Center. There are students in the school that the teachers are afraid of. The fear is perhaps more with the female teachers than the male.

We tend to give the more difficult students to the male instructors. Whenever a student goes off, there are plenty of male aides and teachers available to give assistance. No one here gets away with anything, and the kids know it, which I think is one of the reasons there is a significant decrease in the behavior problems here. When they do go off, they know that someone is going to handle it.

The best defense for violence is a well-trained staff that is watchful and knows when someone is going to blow. "When you know someone is going to have a really bad day, you take precautionary measures so that they don't break windows or something else."

With the recent publicity over sexual abuse in schools, teachers everywhere have felt the pressure. While Barbara feels glad that sexual abuse is out of the closet, it's sad that because of a bad program, the good programs suddenly find themselves on the defensive. Many teachers refrain from patting children on the back and hugging them for fear of misinterpretation as fondling.

I wouldn't say that I have stopped being affectionate with the kids. I was always hugging them and patting them on the back, stuff like that. It's important with any kid. Initially, when the publicity about molestation in schools broke, there were a lot of phone calls that came in. Parents were saying, "I saw a bruise on so and so's right leg." We say look, you know that your kid throws herself on the ground, she gets bruised like that all the time. Why are you suddenly bringing this up. We did see that kind of panic.

The status of teachers has changed.

When I went through school, teachers had a very high status in the community. You didn't do anything bad to a teacher. Now, if a kid tells a parent that they want to be a teacher, the parents try to talk him out of it.

It's my feeling that kids don't have a strong sense of values and ethics. When I was in school, you were in Girl Scouts so that you could become the best American citizen. There was a sense of pride, and pride in your school and commitment and citizenship, high ethics and values. We really need to bring those things back.

At our school, we try and instill this pride by having a real sense of pride in our kids and the work they are doing. We'll take them out in the community and show them off in a sense. I'm not afraid to take these kids into a grocery store. People will look and stare, but we will take them in a store because we are proud of the work we have done here. They can go into a store and not run up to a cookie box and rip it open.

MILITARY

Over the past three decades, public attitudes toward the military services have fluctuated greatly. Different administrations, international events, and societal pressures have directly affected men and women in the armed forces and how the public views them.

In the 1980s, with an era of peace and a pro-defense administration, enlistments have increased and military services have attracted recruits—some for one or two enlistments, others for their career.

The basic mission of the armed forces is national defense. Members of the armed services are stationed in this country as well as a number of overseas locations. Together, the military services constitute our largest single employer.

Much of the time in the service is spent in training. This may include unit training such as field exercises or maneuvers. Or it may include individual training whereby thousands of service persons receive instruction in occupational skills useful in service as well as civilian employment.

There are five basic services—Army, Air Force, Navy, Marines, and Coast Guard. Unlike civilian employers, persons who join one of the armed forces sign up for a definite term, an enlistment. These may vary from two to six years. Generally those military programs which offer the most training also require the longest enlistment. The Navy's highly regarded nuclear program requires an enlistment of six years for the combined training and service. Some of the shortest enlistments are offered for combat arms where shorter training may be required.

The following is a sampling of the types of occupations commonly found in the military:

- **Administrative and office** which includes accounting, public affairs, office and clerical work, computer operation, instruction, social work, and counselling.

- **Professional and technical** which utilizes scientists, operations research analysts, historians, psychologists, photographers, and topographic surveyors.

- **Health** which includes medical and dental jobs such as medical laboratory technician, dental assistant, pharmacist, nurse, and veterinary assistant.

- **Engineering and mechanical** which involves a wide range of occupations such as aeronautical engineer, mechanic, ordnance specialist, electronic technician, lithographer, or communications specialist.

- **Service and supply** such as cook, postal worker, motor vehicle operator, procurement officer, and military police officer.

- **Combat occupations** which are found in infantry, artillery, tank, rocket, airplane, and ship units.

Military occupations require formal dress and a discipline not found in many civilian fields. One of every seven persons on military duty is a comisssioned officer. Most officers tend to be career personnel, staying in for more than a single enlistment. Women now serve in 95 percent of all military specialties—excluded only from fields which involve combat duty. Around 10 percent of those on current military duty are women.

In a recent year, the Air Force reported over 600,000 persons on active duty including 105,000 officers. The Army had 780,000 with 109,000 officers. On active duty with the Navy were 571,000 of which 71,000 were officers. The Marines has 198,000 with 20,000 officers.

Though enlistment in the military is not for everyone, there are wide opportunities for those who seek this type of unique experience.

SERGEANT TURNER[1]

Tank Commander, US Army

He laughs and promises to try not to sound like a commercial for the Army. He loves it. He married a German woman while stationed overseas and they had a baby together. Now, back in the States, Sergeant Turner is anxious to return to Germany and retrieve them. He has a few things to settle before he is ready to live with his family on the army base.

Sergeant Turner has been in the Army for five years. He re-enlisted after four, and is currently a tank commander. A tank commander's job is to run and maneuver his tank and tank crew. He identifies targets and makes the decision when to engage the tanks. He is the link between his tank and the platoon leader. Sergeant Turner displays the kind of confidence and determination that indicates he can do just about anything he sets his mind to.

A tank commander is in charge and responsible for two or three people. It's his responsibility to insure that the maintenance of the vehicles is done, and the vehicle stays in good shape. He is a personnel manager, and handles their problems at his level if he can.

When Sergeant Turner first enlisted in the Army, his goal was to advance his career. He was told that the best method for rapid advancement was in the combat arms field, such as an infantryman or a tanker. He is mechanically inclined, and was looking for a hands-on, physically rewarding job. Tank commander was perfect. He made the rank of E5 in two years.

I went to Germany right away and always displayed a positive attitude. I never complained. That's one thing in the Army that will really be a benefitting factor.

As an E3, I went to different boards, like 'Soldier of the Month' board. There are Senior Non-Commissioned Officers, Sergeants, Majors, and the like, and they ask you different technical questions. The questions are not only in your field, but in general soldiering skills. The way you answer the questions and carry yourself will reflect on whether you will become soldier of the month for your level. I went on to be a division level soldier of the year. It really had a positive influence as far as an Army career went.

I put in the extra effort to make sure that I looked good. I always pressed my uniform, shined my boots, and did my job to the best of my ability.

Sergeant Turner has a high school diploma and two years of trade school in auto mechanics. He enlisted in the Army when he found himself in a dead-end job. He was working as a manager trainee in a restaurant that has subsequently gone bankrupt.

The hours were long. I worked sometimes 18 hours a day, depending on how business was. You don't make any overtime. You get a salary, and that's what you get. I was looking for something more exciting.

Sergeant Turner had a friend in the Army who had gone overseas to Germany. His friend told him of his lifestyle. He saw Europe, and found that the Army gave him the self-discipline to go out and strive to achieve different things.

I wanted to be on a tank. I wasn't into all that walking to be an infantryman. I said that I would like to be on a tank, and I'd like to go to Germany. They stationed me about 35 miles from Frankfurt.

---

[1] Sergeant Turner never indicated his first name. Shortly after this interview he was transferred and unable to be reached.

Sergeant Turner is currently stationed at Fort Irwin in Barstow, California. On a typical day, he rises at 5:30 in the morning, three days a week, and has physical training. PT involves calisthenics and a two mile run. For the remaining days of the week, the first formation is at 7:30 a.m.

From the time we wake up to the first formation, we have to clean up our rooms, sweep, mop, make sure that our beds are made, put a shine on our floors.

At Fort Irwin, there are four people per room, two desks and four lockers similar to a standing closet. Two sets of bunk beds line the walls, and each man has his own small chest of drawers.

If you are married they have quarters like two, three or four bedroom apartments depending on the size of your family. You don't pay anything for them. They aren't furnished but the Army pays for utilities and most of them are air conditioned. They have recreational facilities for the dependents on post. It's like its own little city.

After the rooms are cleaned in inspection order, Sergeant Turner has breakfast, then lines up for the first formation.

We have a training schedule, and by looking at the training schedule, you know what is going on for the day. Maybe we'll have class on how to give CPR, or we'll have common task testing, which involves different skills.

The tankers train together. As a tank commander, Sergeant Turner has a gunner whose responsibility is to know his gunner's station, how to engage tanks at different ranges, precision fire, and such. The gunner must also know the tank commander's job.

In the event of a war, everyone on the tank needs to know every position on the tank, how the tank works. If I get blown away, the next ranking man on the tank would take my position.

The training lasts until about 11:30, when they are released to lunch. After an hour and a half, there is another formation for announcements, and the afternoon is spent continuing training or on maintenance.

It's not always training. Sometimes you go down and do the maintenance on your vehicle. We have a technical manual, and you go through and check all the different portions of it, then you can order your parts, or repair or fix it.

The day usually ends about 4:30 or 5:00. Normally, evenings are your own, but occasionally evening work is required.

If something is wrong with your tank, and your parts come in, you work and fix your tank. Those times are the exceptions, not the rule. Evenings are pretty much free.

While overseas in Germany, Sergeant Turner's lifestyle was similar, with the exception of tighter controls on the personnel. "You are in a foreign country, and the Army needs to know where their people are."
If out in the field, the work week extends through Sundays.

When you are in the field, they bring you back and you can take a shower, and see the family. You have a day off or two in the middle of the field time. You may go out for two or three days, and then come back for a day, go out for two days, and come back for a couple of days, then you have a day off and one day of training or maintenance.

Sergeant Turner found that, although life in the Army required some adjustment, it was easier than he had expected.

They work you hard, but you are fed well. You have plenty of time to sleep. They make sure you get into bed by 8:00 p.m.

Basic training is all day. They train you to work as a team. A lot of people are 'me, me, me' but they teach people how to act as one.

There is complete medical and dental coverage and 30 days paid leave each year. The Army provides emergency relief, where they will loan you money at no interest with small repayment installments.

The military wants to make sure that their people are taken care of, and that's one thing you won't see in many jobs.

A disadvantage is that you might be required to stay out in the field for long periods of time and that takes away from time with your family.

Some people don't like the training, it's hard, and there's a lot of pressure put on you sometimes. There is stress involved because there is pressure put on you to perform.

It's not all like the commercials you see on TV where you jump out of a plane, land on the ground, and say, 'Good morning, First Sergeant!' It's more realistic. When you know you are doing your job, you can feel good about it. And you are rewarded for it, too. You make rank faster.

At Fort Irwin, they believe that they have the most proficient Army in the United States Army.

We train to know the Soviets. At the National Training Center, it's our mission to train other units on Soviet tactics. We act like Soviets, we wear different uniforms, Soviet-looking uniforms. We have American tanks with fiberglass visual modification. In other words, we put fiberglass on our tanks to make them look like Soviet tanks, Warsaw Pact nations.

I feel that the people here know their jobs. They know what is going on. When units leave here, they have improved at least 100 percent. They have seen, sometimes for the first time, what 100,000 tanks coming at you looks like. The Soviets fight in masses, so it's something to train for.

As far as preparation for civilian life, Sergeant Turner believes that he can transfer his skills easily. "There are a lot of similarities between a tank and heavy equipment."

Advice to potential recruits: strive to be the best you possibly can be. Have the self-discipline to work hard, and the rewards will be great.

PRIVATE MELISSIA BARBERA

Specialist, US Army

Her hair is short and styled, with one long tail of hair falling from behind her ear to her chest. Energy bursts forth in abundance. She is eager to talk about her experiences as a Private in the Army. Wearing a black and white sleeveless tee shirt with Japanese printing, Melissia is most definitely an individual, and prides herself on the ability to remain so in an atmosphere of uniformity and conformity.

Melissia was in the Army for two years, beginning as a Private, E1, when she entered and ending her tour of duty as a Specialist E4.

Melissia chose the Army after checking out the other branches of the service. The Army offered a two year plan, as opposed to four years with the other branches, and she enlisted.

The way my life was going, I felt like I was in a rut. My friends weren't going anywhere, I wanted something different, a change. I needed to become a stronger person, which I did. They dehumanize you so much that you have a lot of respect for yourself for making it through. I thought that if I could go through this, I can make it through anything.

In the recruiting office, Melissia asked a lot of questions to prepare herself for what lay ahead.

I asked them if I had to cut my hair, if my earrings would be a problem (I have three holes in my ear), if I would go through all these changes. They said no, but the whole time I was in, they gave me a hard time verbally about getting my hair cut, and you couldn't wear any jewelry anyway.

Basic training begins at the reception station where each individual is issued a uniform. It is a processing stop where the new recruit fills out information, is taught about saluting and respect for officers, then given shots and a physical.

In basic, I got up at 3:30 a.m., had to have my bed made, dressed in uniform to my boots, 50 pounds of gear on, and be downstairs anywhere between 4:15 and 4:30.

The first thing in the morning is formation. The formation consisted of 4 groups of 50 women in 4 different areas. It is a time for roll call and physical training before breakfast.

For the first week or so, they pamper you, train you, and see how many push-ups and sit-ups you can do. Then you get into the routine. At about 5:30, or a quarter to 6, we finish physical training and have breakfast.

We march everywhere. We march to breakfast, and it's about a 15 minute walk. Your company has a certain time to get in and out of the mess hall. Our breakfast was at 6:30. There was a choice of mushy scrambled eggs, bacon, sausage, pancakes. It depends on the cook, and what mood he was in. If the cook was in a bad mood, or sleepy, or just didn't care, the food tasted like it. They also had cereals and fruit and juice.

The first few weeks of basic training are called "total control." The Army presents its requirements for proper behavior. In formation, you stand in a position of parade rest, silent, with your feet still and head straight forward.

There is a motto in the Army called 'hurry up and wait' because that's what you do. We hurry, hurry, hurry, then get to the destination and wait.

After breakfast, the group goes into an auditorium for an hour and a half of classes. You are taught how to march, for example, though there is something different to do each hour of the day. You sit and listen in some classes, do things with your hands in others. There are smoking breaks.

Someone told me that I would be glad that they had smoke breaks even though I'm not a smoker because I could sleep for nine and a half minutes.

Time after class is reserved for a return to the barracks to clean.

You'd be amazed how dusty the barracks can get. We used to come back and think that they had to be throwing dust in our rooms, I don't know where it was coming from. It seemed like we were cleaning up the same stuff over, and over again.

Lunch consists of hamburgers, grilled cheese sandwiches, and basic cafeteria-styled food.

During basic, when it's time for those meals, you are ready to eat. You have burned off a lot of calories.

We marched everywhere. When we went out to play war, which is like camping to a civilian, we'd march in sand and it would be boiling hot.

After lunch there is an opportunity to spend some time back in the room, reading, writing letters, and relaxing.

They come and get you. Everywhere you go, you have to run. You have to run around the building and get in formation. If they catch you walking, you have to do push-ups. That's the punishment. Push-ups, push-ups, push-ups. Believe me, fear makes you do push-ups very well.

After a dinner of roast beef, steak, fish, etc., the group of women gather in formation, then return to the barracks for a shower.

You have an hour, or an hour and a half to shower. You have to share a bathroom of three stalls with 50 girls. You take a shower then, or you lose until the next time you are allowed to take a shower. You have to clean the bathroom up, and they want you in bed by nine.

At night, each person has a chore such as buffing and waxing the hallways, scrubbing the wall lockers, or wiping down the bunks. The beds must always be made to inspection standards.

There is an inspection in the morning while we are at breakfast or physical training. If the inspection went badly, we have to go back upstairs sometimes during the day and clean.

Each platoon is in competition with each other. When one person does badly, her platoon gets 'dogged out' and you have to clean, they yell at you and make you do push-ups in front of everybody. They really make you feel bad. I left my locker open a couple of times. I thought it was locked and it wasn't, so I had 49 girls plus the sergeants mad at me. It's so humiliating that they got a certain number of points taken off because my locker was open.

During the night, each person is responsible for one hour of guard duty. If your hour is at 10:00 p.m., you go to sleep afterwards. If your hour is at 2:00 a.m., you must wake up, and return to bed at 3:00 a.m.

The majority of the people that you deal with have a certain mentality. A lot of them are from places where they didn't get much education. It's almost like jail because you are dealing with different walks of life. Different lifestyles are being thrown together in one organization to work together.

There were a lot of people in charge who were really good to me and there were a lot that I liked. There were many who had less of an education than I did, maybe 8th or 9th grade, and because they have been in for so long, Vietnam, or whatever, they are in charge of you. That's what is really frustrating. I could see easier ways of doing things, but they judge your intelligence by rank, so they wouldn't listen to me.

After the two months of basic training, there is schooling for your Army job for two months, then you are assigned to a base where they need the job skills you learned.

After basic training, there are some changes in lifestyle. "They weren't on you as much. I got up at 5:00 a.m. instead of 3:30."

Melissia's job was in the motor pool, driving trucks. She was the only woman, and found problems of prejudice among the men.

> *They feel you don't work, or can't work as hard as they can. But, I did. I pulled my weight. There were some things that I couldn't do. I couldn't change a tire by myself, and I had to ask for help, and they would laugh at me. But, realistically, some men couldn't change those tires either.*

> *Since I was the only girl in the motor pool, they were giving me all the jobs that they thought were women's jobs. I was sweeping out garages, painting tailgates. I finally got out of the motor pool and started to work in the office.*

Melissia feels that the Army is a good place for certain people. For example, if you are just out of high school and don't know what you want to do, the Army can give you direction and teach you skills. There are also advantages and opportunities available to a veteran once you get out of the Army.

> *I appreciate my life more. When I first went into the military, I felt like I really didn't have anything. Now, I realize how much I have. It does build your self-esteem because you feel that if you can get through that, you can get through anything.*

A negative aspect to life in the Army, for Melissia, is the fact that the Army is too concerned with your personal life.

> *You are always owned by Uncle Sam. After you spend a certain amount of time in the military, there's nothing else you can do. Everything you do in the military is nothing like what you do out here. It's like a world within a world. They have their own laws, judicial system, police force, shopping marts, everything.*

> *For example, if you were a mechanic in the military, you would have to go out and learn how to work on civilian vehicles. They say, 'Be all you can be, learn a skill'. It's a joke. You can't use anything.*

As a woman in the Army, Melissia found that procedures and facilities were basically set up for men, and not women.

> *When you were out in the trucks, you couldn't stop to go the bathroom. We would have these breaks, and the guys would just go right beside the truck, but we would have to go find a tree, and they wouldn't want to take the time to wait for you.*

Basic training and life in the military is a process of learning how to succumb to authority, and conform to rules, whether you agree with them or not.

> *In the military, they would never be outright prejudiced, or treat you badly, but they can make you do things. If you ever brought it up to someone else, they could cover it by saying it was part of the training. They can make you dig holes and say that it is extra training, but it could be just that they don't like you. I was going to make it, because they all said that I wasn't. They made it extra hard for me. But, later on, I learned the tricks of the trade. There are ways that can make it easier for you.*

CAPTAIN RICH PETERSON

Pilot, US Air Force

"Freedom and Flight Limited by Nothing At All." The embroidered sampler hangs on the wall of his Air Force office next to crayoned pictures bearing the message, "I love you, Daddy." His own father's friend had taken him up in an airplane when he was in the eighth grade. He knew then that he wanted to fly. The vision of a young man remained. The sky was the limit. To fly, the goal.

Rich Peterson enrolled in the Air Force ROTC program at Iowa State University in 1969, during the height of the Vietnam conflict.

When you go through ROTC, you take a month long summer camp after the first two years, and before the last two years. That's not a real boot camp, it's a camp where you learn a little more about intense military, an officer training situation.

You have enlisted folks in the service, and you have officers. Normally, you either start out enlisted and stay enlisted, or start out officer and stay officer. For some folks, they start out as enlisted, finish their school while they are in the Air Force, and then compete for officer training school, which is a 12 week leadership and management school. Then they are commissioned as officers. You must have a four year degree to be an officer.

After completing the ROTC program, you are commissioned as an officer, a Second Lieutenant. You spend two years as a Second Lieutenant, two years as a First Lieutenant, then start the long road as a Captain, usually about 8 years.

I'll plan on Major when it's my turn. With the rank of Major and above, Congress controls the number that you can have at any particular time. Someone needs to retire at the top end for someone to move up.

Rich Peterson is currently a Captain. As a Second Lieutenant, fresh out of college, he graduated with a degree in computer science, and headed straight for Moody Air Force Base in Georgia to begin pilot training.

Pilot training lasts a year. Upon completion, I was selected to become an instructor pilot, and basically given my choice of staying at Moody and flying jets, or going into the Air Force academy and flying the T-41's, teaching cadets how to fly.

Captain Peterson chose to spend two years in Colorado teaching cadets how to fly. Following those two years, he headed for Vance Air Force Base to teach students going through undergraduate pilot training in the T-37's. After a year at that, the next two years were spent as a flight examiner administering test rides.

It's testing the other pilot's capabilities. Every pilot has to re-qualify at least twice a year to show that he can do the job.

Captain Peterson is a lifetime Air Force Officer.

I had to make a decision. I initially came into the Air Force to learn how to fly and then go and be an airline pilot. I took a look at what I would be doing with the airlines, and what I would be doing in the Air Force, and decided that the Air Force was really the right place for me.

First of all, the most boring flying for me is to take off, point the airplane someplace, and then just drone off into infinity and land when I get there. What is fun for me is flying traffic patterns, aerobatics, spins, stalls, formations, and teaching other people how to do that.

The Air Force made me an instructor pilot right away, after just a couple of months of extra training, and put me in charge of a bunch of students, and turned me loose. In the airlines, you are going to spend 8 or 10 years as a flight engineer never even touching the controls, and another 10 years as a co-pilot before you finally make it to aircraft commander.

Flight training is a year of 12 hour days, basically five days a week. The day begins at 4:00 or 5:00 in the morning, and ends at 4:00 or 5:00 in the evening.

The regulations state that the students must be released 12 hours after they get in. You have so much to learn, that you can't afford to be released any earlier.

The students are male and female, with the only congressional limitations on women being the exclusion of flying combat aircraft. Eight to nine hours of the day will be spent at the flight line, where, with the instructor pilot, the students will fly one or two missions in the actual aircraft or the simulator. The flight training for those hours will mean approximately an hour and twenty minutes in the air.

The remaining day is spent in academic classes, mixed in with physical training like soccer, basketball, or raquetball.

About six weeks before graduation from pilot training, the student pilots list their preferences for flying airplanes. The top 10 percent of the class get exactly what they ask for. It's a carrot that the Air Force dangles in front of the students to encourage them to excel in their training.

For the rest of the class, the air training command picks the students they would like to keep on as instructor pilots. The remaining students are matched up with Air Force needs and their desires. "About 85% of the students get their first or second choice."

The days following pilot training are as varied as the airplanes. A mission is the process of taking off, flying, and landing. The details of the mission depend on the type of aircraft.

A typical day in bomber aircraft would involve a lot of mission planning. They fly fewer missions, but longer ones, for example, 10 to 12 hour missions, three or four times a month.

For a bomber, a typical mission might be to take off, fly across country, maybe from North Dakota to Texas, link up with a tanker down in Texas, take on gas, drop down to a low level training route where they might fly 500 feet off the ground, climb back up, hook onto another tanker, fly back to the home base, and fly some traffic patterns and landing approaches. The training is designed to prepare the pilot for all the types of missions necessary in an actual combat situation.

One week out of the month, they sit on alert. Their job during this week, 24 hours a day, seven days, is to be on alert, ready to go. They stay on the alert facility, unless they are going out to some base area, as long as they are within five minutes of their airplane. When the alert is over, they have four or five days off to spend with their families.

The day of the tanker pilot is similar. They will fly shorter missions, but more during the three weeks that they are not on alert.

For a transport pilot, flying C-141's or C-5's, it's going to be a very erratic schedule.

They go on a two-week trip, maybe to South America or Africa or Europe, come back home for three or four days, be gone on a two-day trip, come back for two-weeks, be gone on a five-day trip, and so on. Normally, our east coast transport bases cover South America, Africa and Europe. The west coast bases cover all of Asia, Australia and that area.

Normally there is a crew rest time when they reach another country. Depending on the mission, they will have anywhere from two to four days to spend in the country.

It depends on whether it's just a stop-over for gas, or whether that's where we are leaving cargo or picking up new cargo.

The schedule of a fighter pilot averages about one mission per day throughout the month.

About 60–70 percent are going to be local missions, where you come in early in the morning, maybe 6 o'clock for the daily briefing, and plan your mission. It may be an air to ground mission where you go out and practice dropping the bombs, or practice in the target area, or it could be an air to air mission.

There is an extensive amount of pre-planning and pre-mission briefing before you go out. You fly about an hour and thirty minute mission and afterwards come back in to a three to four hour debriefing among the other pilots who were out there flying. This is so that everybody learns the absolute maximum so that they can maximize their dollars. It is fairly expensive to go out and fly an hour and twenty minute mission in a fighter. And then you do the whole thing over the next day with a different kind of mission. Maybe on the weekends, you take the aircraft to build up your cross-country experience.

In a fighter aircraft, you may be gone three months in a year on temporary duty, a war games exercise, or practice such as moving the entire squadron to Europe.

The lifestyle of an Air Force pilot can be condusive to raising a family. It depends on your job.

As an instructor pilot, I am home all the time. I'm gone maybe one or two weekends a month. The other folks are gone more, but when they're home, they are working shorter days.

Rich feels that the most important aspect of maintaining a positive family enviornment in the Air Force, like in any other business, is receiving support from your spouse and family for what you are doing.

They need to love what you do as much as you do. Especially when you are talking about flying. Pilots have a tendency to become very dedicated to flying to the point where that's the only thing they can talk about. You get together with your friends who are all pilots and all you talk about is flying, and it's very easy for a wife to become alienated if she isn't interested in talking about it also.

It is an intense business. There are no 40 hour work weeks, you work until the job is done.
Plan on moving every three or four years.

The government pays for your household goods to be moved, and $50 a day, plus mileage for the time you are going to be moving. But, they don't pay for real estate brokerage fees to sell your house, the inconvenience of possibly having to sell your house on short notice. It comes with the territory.

The advantages to the career center around the respect Captain Peterson feels is inherent in the job.

People realize that in order to protect what we have here, we need to have some sort of defense.

To be successful in the Air Force, you have to have confidence and a firm belief in what you are doing. The "right stuff."

There is a thing in the Air Force called 'fighter pilot attitude'. It's something that you look for in everyone. 'I am the best, and if I'm not the best, dammit, I'm going to learn how to be the best. I'm going to work hard until I do everything better than everyone else to be the best. And I am going to put out the extra effort to do it because I know it's important, and I want that feeling.'

In the Air Force, you have to have a certain amount of 'devil-may-care' attitude. You know it's a dangerous business but you love it, and it's exciting. When I am up there flying formation and doing aerobatic maneuvers and I'm sitting there on the wing, I always find myself saying, 'I can't believe I get paid to do this.' It's so much fun, and such a good feeling.

Examine your long range goals. Where do you see yourself in 10 years? 20 years?
If you want to be a pilot, enroll in an ROTC program in a top university, or compete for selection in the Air Force academy. If your goals are to own an auto mechanics business, for example, enlist in the Air Force and get involved with auto or aircraft mechanics, and continue your college education to prepare you for the business aspects.

I think everybody should go to college. But, not everybody can leave high school and afford college right away, not everybody has parents that can support them in college, and not everybody has the maturity to start in college. There are kids who need a couple of years break before they start college.

Maybe the right thing is to get in the Air Force, get some skills, and then start working into college and use those skills to build on. For the folks that can afford to go to college and hit it straight, I would say, sure, go right to college. The more education you have, the more marketable you are going to be on the outside. The service is not right for everybody, it needs to be something that fits in to the direction you are going.

STAFF SERGEANT JENNIFER ANDREWS

Personnel Specialist, US Air Force

She is a mother. Her husband is also in the service. Staff Sergeant Jennifer Andrews loves her life as a woman in the Air Force, and is into her seventh year.

The ranking structure for enlisted persons in the air force ranges from E1 to E9. Staff Sergeant is middle management, Jennifer is an E5. Promotion is initially based on time served, but after the grade of E5, the enlisted person must pass an exam to move forward.

> *It's called the WAPS (Weighted Airmen's Promotion System). You get a certain number of points for time in service and time in grade. Then you take two tests. One test is on basic military knowledge and the other is specifically on your career field. There is a certain Air Force-wide score that you have to meet to get promoted. For Staff Sergeant, which is E5, you take it twice a year. If you are E6, you take it once a year.*

Staff Sergeant Andrews is a personnel specialist, in charge of the separations unit. The unit deals with voluntary and involuntary separations, retirement, and any other type of officer or enlisted separation from the Air Force.

> *When I first came in, I wanted to get into word processing, but they didn't have any openings, so I came in open general. I got a cook's job. I did that for three years and as soon as I could, I retrained. A lot of it is your attitude. Even though I didn't like the job, I did it well, and got promoted very quickly. I made E5 in three years.*

Basic training was essentially a "mind game". You are put through various stringent requirements, folding your clothes in a certain way, maintaining your locker in inspection order.

> *They want to make sure that you can handle the stress of military life because it is different than civilian careers. You are under a lot of different types of pressures. They want to be sure that you will be able to handle it and not break in a stressful situation.*

Air Force basic training is not as physically demanding as some other branches of the service. You may begin with running a quarter of a mile, and work your way up to a mile and a half. There are calesthenics, but the physical stress is not unmanageable.

> *The Air Force is more into intellect. They are gradually stressing physical fitness more, but it's not as physical as the other services. That's why you have to have a higher intelligence to come into the Air Force than you do for the other services.*

Staff Sergeant Andrews is stationed at Norton Air Force Base, her husband is stationed a few hours away. They live halfway between the two and commute.

> *I usually get up about 4:30, get dressed, get my little girl up and dressed, and take her to school. I like to come in early because I would rather work early than stay after 4:15. Our normal duty hours are from 7:30 in the morning to 4:15 in the afternoon, Monday through Friday.*

The actual work within the office is similar to a civilian job, with the exception of the possibility of being called at any time, day or night. Air Force personnel are at the mercy of what is going on in the air force, and are essentially on the clock 24 hours a day.

The office environment is much like a civilian office also, with the exceptions of the uniforms worn by the employees. There are some options in clothing, however, as long as it falls within the required dress. The office space is large and partitioned.

I think for a woman, the office environment is much better in the military than in civilian life. We're more protected, I think. The Air Force really stresses equal opportunity and they do not tolerate sexual discrimination or sexual harassment. There are different agencies on base that are specifically there in case you do have a problem of that nature.

Staff Sergeant Andrews has found her lifestyle in the Air Force to be more stressful than she had imagined. There are a lot of demands on your time, and your time must be managed effectively to get everything done. As a supervisor, she finds that she is often at the office longer than her regular shift, writing reports, and finishing up the day's work.

When I came into the Air Force, I was coming in blind. I came in primarily for the educational benefits and for the travel. The travel and the benefits are better than I thought they would be. I was over in Europe for two years before I came here. In what other job can you get to stay in Europe for two years? You have 30 days of leave a year, and can utilize it in any way you want to. I've been all over. So far, I have really enjoyed it.

There are enormous educational benefits. "It's so expensive on the outside." The Air Force will basically pay 75 percent of your tuition, and it can move up to 90 percent.

Also, I like the promotion system. It's based on your merits, how well you do. They take various things into consideration in the promotional system, and don't discriminate if you are a woman. I think in the civilian community, women are held back at times from management positions because they are a woman.

Military personnel must live with the vulnerability of being on call at any time. You may be sent on a temporary duty away from your home whenever the Air Force needs you.

You have to have provisions made for your children. They can tell you at a moment's notice that you are gone, and you could be gone for 60 days, 80 days, whatever. You sign a paper saying that you have things set up to take care of your child in case this happens. Sometimes you aren't stationed near anyone that you really know, so the vulnerability can sometimes be very frightening.

There are occasions when you are placed on stand-by. The Air Force may not call you in, but you must remain within the limited responding distance.

Be absolutely certain that you know what you want. The Air Force is a very structured environment. If you have a problem accepting authority and having someone tell you what to do, the Air Force isn't for you.

I would say, also, that if an individual likes to smoke pot, the Air Force is not for them at all. It is totally not tolerated. We see a lot of discharge cases for people who smoke marijuana.

SERGEANT LAURA JAROS

Recruiting Service, US Marine Corps

A guard stands watch near the parking garage, standing erect and still for an undetermined duration. The men and women inside the government building are sharp and clean, the scrubbed masses of the military.

An ease and humanism filled the office air.

Sergeant Laura Jaros is a pretty, blonde woman in her twenties. Her posture is straight, hair flawlessly combed, uniform pressed. She is a Marine, right down to the shine on her shoes.

The perfect Marine is totally squared away. He's in great shape, his uniform is neatly pressed, total military alignment down the front. There are no wrinkles, no dust, no lint. His shoes are shined. He has edge dressing around the edges to make them shiny. He has all his ribbons and everything on nice. He carries himself well. His head is always up. He does his job, and more than he's supposed to. And he goes home and goes to bed. He's always in control.

Sergeant Jaros exemplifies her description and remains a woman, warm and loving, and very proud to be a Marine. She enlisted seven years ago.

A girlfriend that I went to high school with talked me into going in with her. We went in and talked with a recruiter. I thought it sounded good. I went and she didn't.

Laura began by enlisting in the reserves, afraid to commit herself to a full four years. In the reserves, she went through recruit training and formal schooling for one weekend a month, and two weeks in the summer. She found out what life as a Marine was all about, and joined. "I decided on the Marines, first choice, only choice."

Most females either grow up and get married, or they go to school. They really don't know what they want to do. So, instead of wasting my time going to school, I decided to try this out.

The entrance test for all the armed forces is call ASVAB (Armed Services Vocational Aptitude Battery). The test results indicate your best abilities for a particular job. Many times, you qualify in several different areas and have the choice. Laura works in the recruiting service, and lives in an apartment off the base.

I get up in the morning about 6 or 6:30, iron my uniform, take a shower, have a cup of coffee. I get to work by eight. My apartment is about four blocks from where I work, and I get paid extra money for living off the base.

Once in the office, she spends a lot of time making phone calls talking to possible recruits about the Marines. The names and phone numbers come from high school lists or cards of people that the recruiting office has already spoken with. Her goal is to set up four recruiting appointments a day.

Sometime during the day, I may go out on the street and do area canvassing, looking for qualified men and women who really don't know what they want to do.

Laura's working day generally ends after 6:00 in the evening. In the service, you are paid for 24 hours a day and make yourself available to work until the job is done.

The pay scale is based on rank, and promotion is based on a combination of time in service and merit. Women in the Marine Corps will never be in a combat situation.

Our job would be to free the men to fight. Nowadays, women in the Marine Corps go through training with M-16 rifles. They are more physical, they go out in the field for three days. Basically, if things got really bad, at least we would have the knowledge of what to do with a rifle.

I think everybody should be trained, whether you are in the military or not. If you are in the military, you have an understanding of what it's really all about, how important the military really is. It's because of the military that you can walk down the street and not fear being gunned down by a terrorist. There is a lot of blue sky out there because the military has made it possible.

Again, the working style within the military requires that you adjust to accepting authority and control.

Just like anywhere else you go, you get angry, and frustrated. People make you angry. One of the disadvantages is that you can't just tell someone to take a walk. It's good, though because you have to learn to control yourself.

Once you adapt to the environmental change and take advantage of the opportunities that are available, Laura believes that life as a Marine is very satisfying, and a positive contribution to the country.

I keep my work here, and my personal life separate. That's not always easy, but it has to be done.

I'm just like everybody else, I'm no different. I still have the same feelings, and the same outlook on life as everybody else. Just because I am in the military doesn't mean I am a strange, unusual, or vicious person. I'm not.

LANCE CORPORAL TED PAYNE

Rifleman, US Marine Corps

Ted Payne enlisted in the Marine Corps in 1980 and was released in 1983.

They were overcrowded and had a waiting list. If you had a clean record, and you were getting out, I think between December and August, you could qualify for the early-out program. It makes room for other people to come in.

He appears the typical image of a Marine; muscular, stocky, and physical. The kind of guy who wouldn't mind crawling through the mud in the heat if it was for a good cause.

I was short of credits because I messed around too much in high school. I was six credits short, and I knew I wasn't going to graduate so I went and signed up.

Ted's job as a Marine was rifleman, which is basic infantry, machine gunner, and assault team leader.

I had a party lifestyle, pretty much. I would stay out until 5:00 a.m., and have to get up at 5:30 a.m. Usually, we were off around 3:00 in the afternoon.

At about 5:00 or 5:30 in the morning, Lance Corporal Payne would get up, shower, and go to breakfast. His days were divided between time in the field, and time on base.

We were in the field sometimes twice a week, sometimes two or three times every two weeks. It was for three, four, sometimes five days at a time. The most we were gone was two weeks at one time. We would set up tents, dig holes, and attack other battalions, a lot of war games. Those are fun, I was good at them.

If the destination were more than 20 miles, they would take trucks. If less, many times they would walk.

You load up your pack of everything that you have to take out there. I carried on the average about 55 pounds, a machine gun, my own pack, my M-16 cartridge belt. When we were out, we had to take turns guarding and sleeping and would only get about two hours. We would watch for the other battalions to come up and pull a sneak attack on us. They were trying to set-up a wartime situation.

On days when he was not out in the field, Ted would wait for orders, or continue his previously prescribed tasks.

A lot of it was so slow, there wasn't any work. When you're not in the field, they try and figure out something for you to do like, go clean your weapons. A lot of times, they would tell us at 9:00 a.m. that we're going to do something at 11:30, so we all just sit around until then.

Lance Corporal Payne found the Marines easier than he had expected, after he finished boot camp. Boot camp was a rough experience, both mentally and physically.

Everything is strict. You can't say nothing, you can't get out of line, you are like robots. It's for 12-16 weeks.

As a Marine, Ted enjoyed the opportunity to travel and see the world.

I've been to Okinawa, Japan, Hong Kong, Philippines, Hawaii, Guam, Tokyo. We stayed in Mainland Japan for six weeks, Hong Kong for one week, Philippines for two weeks.

After exiting the Marines with an honorable discharge, Ted has found his enlistment to be an asset on employment applications. While in the Philippines, he received Top Secret Clearance, and could, if he chose to, use that clearance to work for the FBI.

As he remembers his time in the Marines, one piece of advice jumps to the forefront of his mind: "If you can't take orders, you are not going to last."

PETTY OFFICER (3RD CLASS) NOEL BOYLES

Fire Control Technician, US Navy

A guard stands at the entrance gate to the naval harbor. Strict parking limits are enforced. Registration and identification are checked. An officer escort arrives to insure safe passage onto the ship.

Once inside the huge gray bulkheads of the vessel, the atmosphere changes from one of tight security to friendly human exchange. A seaman exists the galley with a grilled cheese sandwich and onion rings. Another ducks into a tiny office to allow an officer to pass.

Narrow vertical stairways lead down narrow gray hallways. It is a world within a world, a floating city.

Noel Boyles is a Third Class Petty Officer in the United States Navy. He has just entered his third year as an FTM (Fire Control Technician Missiles).

It's on the seaman rating. The seaman rating is everything above, the fireman rating are usually the guys that work below. Fire control are the guys that are in charge of the missiles, and the launches. We make sure that the system, the equipment, is working properly.

An easy-going, contented young man, Noel joined the Navy right after high school graduation. He was a part of the delayed entry program.

The delayed entry program is a waiting period that the Navy is offering right now. It's good up to one year. You don't have to go into the service for up to one year after you enlist. I wanted some time for summer vacation.

Noel's father was in the Navy, and young Noel had a fairly good idea of the lifestyle involved. As a kid, he was travelling with his family to the various places the Navy sent his father.

I wanted to go into the Navy and check out all of the available fields. After I got out of boot camp I trained for about a month to learn basic seamanship. Then I switched from deck division to fire control technician. One of the reasons I picked that is because they work on electronic gear, and it's very useful on the outside.

His day begins at 6:00 a.m. At 6:30, the men have breakfast in the galley until quarters at 7:00.

You have to be up and ready for inspection. They take roll call, and stuff like that. There is a chart where they have planned each day of the week what you are supposed to be doing. Usually, you go at your own pace, as long as it's done by that day.

The racks (beds) have a mattress that is about three and a half to four inches thick. It's got hinges so that in the morning you can put it up and clean under it. It's about 7 feet long, three feet wide. This ship has better living conditions than most ships. Most ships have more people than we do.

The environment in the Navy, as Noel sees it, is as easy as you make it. It's a matter of having the right attitude, especially in the close quarters of a ship.

Some people on the ship like to jump on people just for the heck of it, and they usually don't make it on a ship.

I try and keep it cool all the time. When people argue with me, I don't yell back. You have to go with the system, and not go against it.

Enlistment in military service provides the benefits of financial and medical security. There is a complete health care package with everything provided. There is an opportunity to save money, and relieve yourself of financial worries while you are enlisted.

The Navy can be a good place to receive mechanical and technical training for jobs later in civilian life. You must be at least 17 years of age to join, or enter boot camp before your 35th birthday.

A disadvantage can be the long hours out at sea.

The longest we have gone out is 20 some days. It gets lonely out there. You miss all the luxuries of land. You can't get all the food you like.

Sea sickness is an experience that each person in the Navy deals with in one way or another.

I remember the first time I came on ship, I didn't know if I was going to get sick or not. When we first went out, I was so excited when the ship started moving. I didn't get sick. The ship was barely moving. We went from San Diego to Long Beach.

Then, we went in the open ocean, no land within 20 or so miles. I looked out, and I couldn't see anything. The swells looked like a rollercoaster ride. They started getting really big. I was in deck division then, and I got to drive the ship and was a lookout. That's when I started feeling sick. I started seeing double vision, two horizons. My stomach started telling me something that I didn't want to know. It happens to everybody once or twice.

While in port, you can leave the ship every day but your duty day. You can stay out all night if you want to. Duty is every four days, and if it doesn't fall on a weekend, you are free to do whatever you want.

Each month, the Navy offers two and a half days of leave. You can accumulate it up to 90 days. "After 90 days, if you don't use it, you lose it."

There are adjustments to be made upon entering a military life. Noel's experiences in boot camp marked his first steps in adjusting to the four years that were to follow.

I went down to San Diego, and had to travel from my home in Hawaii to San Diego. I was by myself the whole time. I had just come out of high school, and I had never gone away from my family for any length of time. I was scared.

I went in and looked at all these people marching. There was no expression on their faces. The Navy started doing things like cutting my hair and giving me shots. That was the first time I saw myself bald. I had expected it to be cut, but not that short.

Noel warns that you can't enter boot camp expecting everyone to treat you nicely. You have to be ready to take whatever they throw at you and maintain a positive attitude.

You don't have to be in real outstanding physical shape because you don't do that much running. The Army and the Marines are all physical work.

My father was so proud. He drove from San Francisco to San Diego, 10 hours straight, for my graduation day.

After boot camp, be prepared to work hard.

A lot of people see television and think they can join the Navy and see the world on a cruise. They think they can kick back and relax, get a lounge chair on the deck, just like the Love Boat. It doesn't happen that way. You have to work.

It's a good way of life for some, but not for all. The people who can adjust will make it a lot easier. People who are used to an easy life, and come in expecting too much won't make it in the service.

SEAMAN BROWN[1]

Communications Specialist, US Navy

A loud intercom announcing the Captain's orders resounds through the steel room. It is the communication for the ship, the channel of organization. Seaman Brown is one of the men whose job is to keep the interior communications going.

I work on the phones. It's anything to do with phone communications, the intercom system. My job is good for the outside. I can do what I do in here the same as outside. It's all the same wires.

Seaman Brown asks to be called, "just Brown." He is a soft-spoken, gentle young man, ending his first year in the Navy. Brown enlisted after a Navy friend told him what it was all about.

I had always wanted to be in the military. A friend who had been in the Navy for two years came home on leave and gave me a first hand view. I could take it from him that what he said was true. He told me to make sure that they gave me a job that I could use on the outside, so I picked communications. It's everywhere.

The wake up call at 6:00 in the morning rings forth through the intercom. "It's a mad rush to the showers." Each person had a certain section with other people who work in similar jobs.

I am with the electricians. There are different places where different groups muster. We get all the information, and go back to the berthing, the room where we sleep, until 8:00 when the day starts.

In Brown's berthing compartment, there are about 40 to 50 men, all electricians. Each week, a certain number are required to stay down and clean up the compartment.

At quarters, we get inspected. They tell us if we need a haircut, and this and that. At 10:00 a.m., the room gets inspected.

Brown starts work at 8:00 a.m., and does something different everyday. "Anything could happen. There has never been a case where all the communications are working perfectly."

In my rate, we have a lot of people who can do the same thing that I do, so basically, there's not too much to do at times. It's relaxed. As long as the job gets done, nobody is going to be hassling you.

We work on everything that has to do with communications or tracking. My rate mostly keeps up the equipment that is used the most. We keep the system up so that the captain can carry out his orders and people can hear what is going on.

There are breaks during the working day for coffee and sodas, much like a civilian job. At about 3:15, the working day is over. "Unless I have duty, I can do anything I want until 7:00 the next morning."

Brown feels that, unlike the other branches of the service, the Navy gives you the chance to think for yourself. Friends and family are allowed on the ship and can watch movies or eat with the men.

When out at sea, it's more relaxed, with less time restraint. The ship pulls out whenever it has a mission or an exercise. Frequency of sea duty is determined by the type of ship you are assigned to. Each member of the ship is notified when they will be leaving, and when they will be back in port.

Time at sea is a time for the peace of solitude.

---

[1]Seaman Brown preferred to just be called Brown so his first name is omitted.

You don't have traffic, you don't have people bothering you. You can just go out and enjoy being out there.

Conversely, long periods at sea are a grim reminder of how important interpersonal interaction is. Aside from the men on the ship, there is little chance to build relationships with people in one area because you will be in and out all the time.

This is a nice ship. Everybody takes care of everybody, everybody knows everyone. It's a small ship.

On a big ship, like an aircraft carrier, you may be on the ship for two or three years, and you meet some dude for the first time who has been on the ship as long. I like this ship. Everybody is close, there isn't too much stealing, if anything goes on, everybody knows about it.

Hitting port is another advantage. It's not the travel experience that many recruiters speak about, because there is often little chance to stay where you have landed for very long. But, there is the chance to see different parts of the world, for however brief a time.

One of the main reasons I am here is that I have been at home. I haven't had a chance to do too much. I wanted to come here and know that I don't have to depend on anybody.

It's not the Navy, it's the people that work for the Navy. Some people think that just because they are so much, they have to treat you like you're nothing. It's just people. I have worked with the chiefs on this ship, and all of them treat me like I am a person. They have a lot of responsibility, but they treat me like an equal.

Finish high school. Realize that enlistment is a big decision that will affect the next four years of your life. Then, if you are sure, and want something different, go for it. You only live once.

PROTECTIVE SERVICES

They save lives, fight fires and other disasters bravely, place their own safety second to a strangers, know no fear. Members of the various protective services who handle the natural and unnatural tragedies of life are a special breed, indeed. However, with the advent of "television truth" some delusions about the protective services are diminishing. Yes, they do fight bravely and save lives, but a big part of the job is learning how to cope with the stress of a potentially dangerous job.

Protective services include these occupations:

- **Police officers** protect cities, towns, and highways by controlling traffic and preventing and investigating crimes. They also are moving into the area of instructing the public on how to reduce their risk of becoming a victim.

- **Detectives** are specialized members of police departments whose job is to investigate crimes which have occurred and, hopefully, arrest and bring to trial the guilty parties.

- **State troopers** are highway patrol officers who work directly for a state government, in contrast to police officers who are employed by cities or counties. In a recent year, there were around 520,000 police officers, detectives, and state troopers in the United States.

- **FBI agents, federal marshalls, and secret service police** work for the federal government and are concerned with protecting public officials and working on crimes which are national in scope, covering more than one state.

- **Firefighters** provide information to help prevent fires from starting, they fight fires when they occur, and provide continuous staffing ready to swing into action at any time. In a recent year, there were around 308,000 firefighters, almost all of whom worked for municipal fire departments. Backing up these firefighters are numerous volunteers who leave their regular work or activities to respond to fire alarms when sounded. Many firefighters are also trained paramedics, able to handle medical emergencies on the scene.

- **Guards** patrol, inspect, and help safeguard property against fire, theft, vandalism, and illegal entry. They protect such buildings as banks, stores, hospitals, and offices. They are stationed at airports, ports, and railroad yards. Because of the nature of their work, guards often work nights and weekends.

- **Corrections officers** are concerned with the safekeeping of persons who are incarcerated—either because they have been arrested and are awaiting trial or because they have been sentenced to serve time in a correctional institution. They maintain order, enforce rules, and often provide work supervision or job training. Most work in local jails or federal or state prisons. In a recent year, there were around 130,000 corrections officers—roughly half were employed by state governments.

Firefighters, police officers, and other protective service workers are placed together in this section of the book due to their shared classification as protective service workers. However, they are quick to point out that their duties are quite different and should not be thought of as one. What they do have in common, however, is the sense of service to their communities and the sobering reality that their jobs involve substantially higher risks of death or injury than most do other occupations.

Protective service jobs are becoming more professionalized. The applicants are well-educated and the training more stringent. Women are making strong headway into these professions. Around 10 percent of some protective service forces are women and the ratio is increasingly yearly.

For people seeking a career where every day is different, protective services occupations can provide excitement mixed with physical challenge.

DAN MARSHMAN

Fire Fighter, Paramedic

Quiet strength and confidence characterize him. He is a father and a husband. Should the need ever arise, he relaxes with the knowledge that he can administer emergency assistance to his family. Fire fighter Dan Marshman is also a paramedic. In his particular department, he is not isolated as strictly a fire fighter or strictly a paramedic, but vacillates where he is needed.

> *Today, I am a fireman first and a paramedic second. I ride the second rescue. For example, today I'll go out on a fire call. If we get a rescue call, like a heart attack or something, then I'll take that.*

Like most men and women entering fire departments today, Dan has a college degree, a bachelor in business. Different departments stress education to varying degrees. Education, however, is always an asset.

> *My degree is not applied specifically to this field, but it certainly was a plus when I was applying for a fire department job. For the written test, it gave me a background in reading, and it also gave me a background when it came to the oral because I know about administrative management.*

In the city where Dan works, there are five portions to the fire fighter test. The tests vary from city to city, and state to state, but the general content is the same.

The first portion of the exam is written—testing anything from your aptitude for mechanical application, to your reading ability and comprehension, to actual mathematics. Once you pass, you move on to the physical agility test which can vary dramatically from department to department. The agility test is designed to test your strength, size, agility, and overall physical performance. Normally, you either pass or fail, determined by the standards set forth for each task.

The next step is the oral interview. It may be conducted by other fire captains, firemen of the station you are applying for, personnel officers, or a combination.

After passing the oral interview, there are two further steps: a medical physical and a psychiatric evaluation. The medical physical determines if you have any hearing loss, heart disease, or anything that might be detrimental to your performance as a fire fighter. The psychiatric evaluation is an attempt to determine if you have the personality to adjust to the working conditions of a fire fighter. The test is designed to evaluate your ability to deal with stress, and to get along with others in a working unit that operates under life and death conditions.

There is also a polygraph (lie detector) test administered in the final stages of the hiring process.

> *The lie detector test is given when you are at the point where you are about to be hired. They do a total background check to make sure that you haven't been involved with drugs, or had criminal offenses.*

Dan was a fire fighter for eight years before going through paramedic school, and has been a fire fighter/paramedic since 1982.

For Dan, paramedic school consisted of five months of training, two months in the classroom, one month in the hospital, and two months of actually doing the job under the supervision of two licensed paramedics. As a working fire fighter, his department sent him to the school with full pay. After his licensing, he received a monetary bonus for the additional training and responsibility he would be using on the job.

The working day for a fire fighter is 24 hours long.

> *An easy way of looking at it is, there are 24 hours in the day, and there is someone required to be here every hour of the day, so we work for 24 hours, then we are off for two days. It's a little more complex than that, but that's basically it.*

The shift change is at 8:00 a.m., and the fire fighter is required to arrive on time to relieve their co-fire fighters and begin their shift. In the morning, there is about half an hour of conversation regarding the events of the previous day, which equipment was used, if anything didn't work correctly, if anything was broken, and what type of calls they had.

We do this so you don't walk in cold. You depend on your equipment to work right, so it's important to know if there were any problems.

They go on the floor at about 8:30 in the morning, and then physically check the equipment. The inventory is checked to insure that everything is in place and in the proper order. As a paramedic, Dan must also make sure the ambulance is in perfect working order—he starts it and checks it. The remainder of the morning is spent repairing anything that needs it, studying, or doing whatever needs to be done. Unless, of course, a call comes into the station.

On the average, we have between seven and eight rescue calls a day. Relatively, we're a moderate-level station. Some of the busy stations can run up to 20-25 calls on a shift, which means you don't get any sleep at night—you're up for 24 hours straight.

The average call takes approximately one hour, including transportation to the hospital and medical first aid. "Dispatch," where the emergency calls come in, determines whether the call is an actual emergency or not.

An emergency to us would be life threatening or property damaging. For example, in the case of a water leak, the property would be damaged, therefore, it would be of concern to us.

At times, the fire fighter him or herself must determine out in the field what must take place.

In most cases, people are just excited. We settle them down, and get them on the right path of travel. We do a lot of directing—telling them what to do to solve their problem.

Specifically on a paramedic call, like a heart attack, for example, there are certain steps to take. The primary step is to check to see if the patient is breathing. You put the oxygen mask on and do the basic assessment of the patient, vital signs, a medical history, if possible, and any medications that the person may be taking.

At that point, you contact the hospital and relay all the information you've been able to extract from the patient. With that information, the hospital will determine what course of action should be taken, whether the patient should see his own doctor, whether he needs to come to the hospital, or needs emergency intervention right there.

If emergency intervention is required, the paramedics start an I.V. (intravenous—injection directly into the vein), administer drugs as ordered, and prepare to transport the patient to the hospital. This is the basic procedure, but the many variables that occur when dealing with human life can change the process.

An important aspect of the working style of a fire fighter is the fact that the fire station is the home of the men and women in the department while they are on duty. It must be maintained, meals must be prepared and the kitchen must be cleaned up afterwards.

We have one man assigned to cook dinner (per shift). It's his responsibility, but if we're running behind that day, everyone pitches in and helps out just as if you were in your own home. This is your family away from home and you have to learn how to live together. If you don't live together and work together well, you won't make it in the fire department.

In this particular fire department, the fire fighters are required to do work around the station, as well as respond to calls, until 5:00 p.m. Occasionally, though, they work until 8:00 or 9:00 at night, and occasionally the work is completed early in the day.

It depends upon the amount of calls that come in. There is usually about three hours of work that needs to be done each day.

The initial anticipation of being called out at any moment passes quickly for the rookie fire fighter. The calls become merely part of the job. On the average, Dan is wakened for a paramedic rescue call two to three nights a week. The purely non-medical calls average once a night. Statistics indicate that a fire fighter fights fire, or is actually in the field doing emergency work only between three and five percent of their total working time—that leaves a lot of idle time to fill. "I have only missed a few meals over the years."

After dinner, the fire fighters have the option of watching television, studying for a class, or whatever else they may want to do. It's a time to relax and recreate. There is a standing rule that the fire fighters don't go to bed until 9 o'clock. "It's really not a problem, most guys stay up past 9 anyway." In cases where someone is not feeling well, permission will be granted for him to retire early for the night.

The Captain of the station sleeps in the station also.

> *The Captain is still a fireman. We look at everyone as being firemen here. A Captain just has a different job to do. He's in charge of the station or the engine, but he's still a fireman. We are all equal as far as the living goes.*

The sleeping facility at this station provides separate rooms. There are two people to a room.

> *It's the new mode of fire department building because eventually more women will be on the job and they'll need private rooms.*

The separate rooms allow for privacy as well as reducing the passage of illness that occurs when everyone sleeps in the same room. If one fire fighter has a cold, everyone will get it.

> *However, the guys are pretty considerate. If they're sick, they usually stay home.*

Personal visitors are allowed in the station, but only until 9:00 p.m. Consideration and cooperation are the name of the game.

> *Again, it's a lot like a fraternity would be in a college. The camaraderie, the practical jokes, the lifestyle, it's really a necessity to the job. If you don't work together as a successful unit, you can't work together at a fire.*

> *It's like anything. You have to work at it. It's not always congenial. There can be a lot of friction created when you are forced to stay with someone for 24 hours. They may do something you don't like, you do something they don't like. You work it out. You can't just get up and leave.*

If you are a person who has problems dealing with people in a close working and living environment, the fire department is not for you. In a big department, you can transfer to another station if you have problems with someone in particular, but Dan sees transfer as avoidance rather than a solution to a problem.

> *If you have a problem working with people, you'd better look at the fact that maybe it's you, not them. You have to work the problems out. One of the worst things you can do is move away from a problem.*

Good communication skills are essential. "That's probably the hardest part of a fire department's everyday living, just getting along with everyone. It's not as easy as it may seem."

The advantages to the fire fighting profession include a satisfying pay scale, though pay scales fluctuate from department to department, and lots of time off. Another advantage is the work itself—you'll be outside a lot and very active physically.

> *It's rewarding in the sense that you are doing your community some good. You feel good that you could do something with your own family if an emergency arose.*

The disadvantages are the other side of the advantages. The time off is great, but you also must spend 24 hours at a time away from home.

The divorce rate can be high because of that. That's a problem that a lot of the men and a lot of the wives can't handle. It's a consideration when you are considering the career. You want to make sure your family unit can take it.

The profession of fire fighting is extremely competitive. A person may take tests for four or five years to get on a department.

I think the last test we gave, we had four openings for new recruits—2,000 people applied.

Aside from a basic college degree to give you an edge against the competition, educational preparation for the job can include courses at the junior college level in fire science. However,

Fire science is great if you will definitely be working in the fire department, but it's not very useful if you are going to be working in a warehouse. I would take courses that are relevant to fire service, but also get a general background that could be used in other areas. Pursue more than one job, because you may not be fortunate enough to get onto a fire department. And if that was the case, strictly fire science courses wouldn't look good on your resume.

Some fire departments have a volunteer program where you can learn about the specifics of fire fighting by joining a summer work crew. You'll be involved in fire fighting only to a small degree, but you will get a hands-on feeling for what the job entails.

When asked what the single most important qualification responsible for his hiring was, Dan replied, "Luck." He then added, "But, I did have a good image of what the job actually entailed."

CINDY FRALICK

Fire Fighter, Paramedic

Truly a woman in a man's world, Cindy Fralick spends her working day in the company of men. They share meals, share the dorm space, share the responsibilities and stresses of a physically demanding occupation. Some men say women can't do it, some say let them try. All agree that there should be no weakening of the stringent physical testing for female applicants. The women wouldn't have it any other way.

Cindy is physically fit and strong. She takes pride in her job, and her ability to do it well, proving herself deserving of the fire fighter/paramedic uniform she wears.

She has been a fire fighter since early 1983, and was certified as a Paramedic in 1984. After receiving a bachelor of science degree in kinesiology, she landed a job working for a large university writing parking tickets. In keeping with the policy of the university, Cindy joined the other parking officers in EMT (Emergency Medical Technician) training.

The training course was her first exposure to the fire department. The paramedics who taught the class spoke of their working environment. Other students in the class who were familiar with the Fire Department spoke to her. Cindy made the decision to pursue a career as a fire fighter. It sounded like an interesting and worthwhile job.

The process of applying to the fire department was a process of mass appeal.

I sent out about 40 or 50 3 x 5 cards with a little message saying that I was interested in working for the department. I asked them to send me information on tests, and any other information they had.

Many of the departments informed her that they were not testing, but would keep her name on file for the period of one year. Others responded with their next available testing date.

It's very competitive. If you want to be a fire fighter, you can't really be specific about where you want to work. You try and get on anywhere. They only have testing once a year or once every two years.

The competition is equally as stiff for women as it is for men.

When I first started the training, I didn't know a lot about the job. People were pretty skeptical about a female coming onto this job. Since there aren't many females, you more or less have to prove yourself. Proving yourself just means doing your job. Most people, after seeing you do your job, are pretty fair in their evaluation.

Once they hired a woman, the station made only minor changes to accommodate the female fire fighter.

We do what works for everyone. We have ten people per shift, and one dorm room. Everyone sleeps in the dorm. There is one main locker room and one smaller area. The only thing we have done to adapt the station is put a sign up on one door and a lock on the other door. It's just so that you know who's in there. When you're done, you swing the doors open, and it's free for anyone. There are individual showers just like at home.

A typical shift for Cindy is to work a day, off a day, work a day, off two days, work a day and off a day, and work a day and off four days.

After the morning line-up where the Captain informs the crew of the happenings for that day, the fire fighters are given an hour to exercise.

Each station has their own designated running area. We drive (to the running area) in the piece of apparatus that we are on that day, along with our turn-out clothes. One person will run with the radio in their hand so if we get a call, we can respond from the exercise area.

In 1983, Cindy's station, in the Los Angeles County Fire Department, averaged 15 paramedic and fire calls per day. The day is active, though a common misconception among rookie fire fighters is that they will be fighting fires much more than they do.

Cindy would extend the same advice to a woman wanting to work for the fire department as she would a man:

> *Get involved in the programs that are available. You learn almost everything that a fire fighter is going to learn in the Explorer program (of the Boy or Girl Scouts of America), so that when you go to the fire training tower, you will know what is going to happen. Fire sciences classes always help on your resume.*

If a woman hasn't been athletic in the past, she should consider some kind of weight training program rather than aerobic types of training.

Cindy smiles when thinking about the advantages of her profession. She is paid to stay in shape and live an active existence, something she would do anyway. She is with men all day, and occasionally misses female exchange, however, she loves her job and is surrounded by people who feel the same satisfaction.

> *Fire fighters are about the only group I know who say that they wouldn't ever want to do anything else.*

JACK BECHT

Police Sergeant

In a bedroom community of the state of New York, with a population close to two million people, the Nassau County Police Department proudly protects its citizens. For the past 32 years, Jack Becht has proudly worn the badge of a police officer. "I'm a cop," he says, with a voice full of grit and good humor.

At the time of his application to the department, the requirements were a high school diploma and some psychological testing "to make sure you weren't an out and out nut."

We've gone into educational emphasis since then. We either demand college, or ask that you continue your education while you are on the force. A greater part of our younger police officers now have their degrees.

After spending the majority of his career on the streets, Jack is now a desk Sergeant. He is in charge of 11 police officers and spends his day dealing with parents, wives, lawyers, judges, and bail.

We are charged with booking procedures, fingerprinting, working at the records bureau. We prepare a "previous" on a person who is booked in the precinct if he has been locked up before.

My job entails a lot of humanness and paperwork. If court is open, we send him right over with the necessary paperwork. If court is closed, I have 19 detention cells for males, three for females. We lock up fifty people a night, hence, people get doubled up. At 8:00 in the morning when court is open, we bring a paddy wagon over, send them all over to court with paperwork.

Typically, the day for a street officer begins at 7:00 a.m. The officers gather together for "turn-out" where the Sergeant briefs them on the events that occurred during the night, and what they might expect during the day.

Each officer has an area that he or she patrols. In the Nassau County Police Department, nearly every officer has a patrol car. There are very few walk-in posts.

Contact with headquarters is through radio.

People that need police assistance will call 911. Assistance could mean that a kid is locked in the bathroom, a cat is in a tree, someone lost their senile grandfather, a purse was stolen, or a bank was robbed.

For the next eight hours you respond to whatever happens. You take an hour for lunch, if you're lucky to get it, and you sign out with headquarters so they know that you are not going to be in your car. That's it.

Sergeant Becht works out of police headquarters. Nassau County Police Department is divided into eight precincts, with nearly 200 officers, sergeants, and lieutenants to a precinct.

Police headquarters is always busy. You have constant investigation. You have the medic running through. There has always been a kidnapping or a murder or something sensational. You see the hand-held cameras. The precincts are going. With a population of almost two million people, you get a lot of activity.

As a police officer for the last three decades, Sergeant Becht has had a first-hand, specific view of societal changes. Crimes have changed, criminals have changed, violence has increased. The police force is always in the center of all the action.

Going back to the 50's—it was a nice calm time. There was parental discipline. You believed what your teachers said. You wouldn't get caught by your father doing anything. The policeman on the corner had authority. I think that's what we liked about the job. It was like, 'There goes God.' They thought we knew everything. If a big boom went off in the sky, they'd say, 'Hey, call the cops! Find out what that was!'

Because they thought we knew everything, we were very inquisitive and it ended up that we did know everything.

The 60's. The years of the Beatles. Long hair. It was horrible then. All the bums and the scuzzes had long hair. All burglars had long hair. All trespassers had long hair. We started to gear up in the turbulent 60's. If your kid wanted long hair, well, naturally you threw him out of the house.

The 70's. Vietnam. We were all confused about that. All the cops were wearing American flags. Woodstock was certainly taboo. Kids were wearing flags on the seat of their pants. It was almost like one cult against another.

Then we started to grow up along with them. All of a sudden, we were anti-Vietnam. But, we wouldn't admit it to anyone out loud.

The violence started and we started to swing with it. As movies started to say bad words, we started to hear bad words on the streets and walking through shopping centers. People were getting knocked off in the afternoon. Horrendous things were happening to human beings. We more or less expected it and went with it.

It's gruesome now. Criminals think nothing of dismemberment, while you are alive. Cops are fair game. More and more policemen are getting shot.

Going with the societal flow is merely a part of the job. Danger. It's there and always will be. Few police officers allow themselves to dwell on it though they must maintain a constant awareness of their vulnerability.

About 7 years ago, everyone got a bullet proof vest. They were a little uncomfortable to wear, but when you make a vehicular stop at night, you like to know that you are wearing it.

You think that it's always going to happen to somebody else. Like landing barges. Second World War. Everybody hitting the beaches. The Commanding officer said, 'You know, we are going to have a 30 percent casualty rate here.' They were all thinking, 'Gee, I'm going to miss the other guy.'

The daily working hours of a police officer are varied. One week you work days, one week afternoons, one week midnights.

In this particular department, we work four midnight tours, and get a swing of 96 hours, four days. So, you get off one morning at 7:00, and you are off the rest of the day.

I've rolled over in bed and seen the clock say 4:00 and not known whether it was morning or night. When you get up you don't know if you are going to have eggs or if your wife is waiting for dinner. It gets confusing.

Additionally, many police officers find it difficult to turn off their profession once they go home. You are trained to be alert at all times. Even in social situations, it's hard to divorce yourself from your profession.

You go to a party and someone says, 'Oh, Jack is a cop.' Well, all of a sudden, Jack the cop has become Jack the lawyer, Jack the judge.

The cop stories start. One time or another, everyone has had something to do with a cop. 50 percent were good experiences, 50 percent bad. And you can believe that you are going to hear it all at this party.

Though salaries vary from department to department, careers in law enforcement are becoming more professionalized and the pay scales are rising accordingly. When Sergeant Becht started with the department in 1953, he was earning $3,600 a year. He has been a Sergeant now for 10 years, and earned $54,000 in 1984.

Additionally, police departments offer substantial benefits. Sergeant Becht enjoys 27 working days of vacation per year. In his department, an officer who has put in 20 years can retire on half pay. Although the working schedule is erratic, and officers are required to work on holidays, the average working week consists of 37 to 40 hours, with a substantial amount of quality time with the family.

We were home during the day when the kids were home. It's true I might be sleeping, but the kids would get up and daddy was in the house. When they were sleeping, daddy was out of the house.

Choose the department that you want to work for and it's location. "The weather in the east coast is horrendous. You are outside whether it's snowing or not."

Police Departments have self-study programs and schools to help you fit into civil service work. If you want to be a police officer, find out about them.

You have to prepare yourself for it, and not complain. You see a lot of bad things, and you've got to say to yourself, 'It's not happening to me.' Stop his bleeding. Put him in the ambulance. Then go home to your wife and kids and see that nothing has happened to them.

Go to school, get yourself a decent education, then be prepared to handle every nut that comes down the pike.

KAREN PEREGOY

Police Detective

A call comes in through dispatch. The owner of a convenience market, his voice shaken and angry, tells the officer he has been robbed. Two men had entered, picked up a six-pack of beer, and pulled a gun instead of a wallet. He can describe them perfectly. One man wore the cologne that his son wears. The other had peculiar stains on his fingernails. Hair dye? Both were under 6 feet and over 30.

The patrol officer responds. Arriving on the scene, he tries to calm the man. He asks questions, writes the report, cites each detail. He assures the man that they will do all that is possible to catch the thieves.

The case is turned over to the Detective Bureau. One of the detectives will do the follow-up work, make the arrest, do the case filing, and see it through to the district attorney's office. Normally, if the case goes to trial, the detective will sit as witness during the trial.

Slightly over 20 years ago, a young woman in junior high school decided that she wanted to be a police officer. "I'm not really sure why. I just decided that's what I wanted to do, so I went to college with that intention." She continued her education and received a four year degree in police science.

Technically, police science is a bachelor of arts degree which covers police administration, patrol techniques, state law, vice investigations, crime scene investigations, and all different types of (police work).

Karen Peregoy is now a detective with the Littleton, Colorado Police Department. June of 1986 will mark her thirteenth year in law enforcement.

I think that having a degree is what gave me an advantage towards getting on the force, not so much having a degree in police science. Police work is not, from what I have been able to determine, something that you can learn about in school. It's very difficult to translate what you do on the street to something that is relevant in the classroom.

To obtain employment on the Littleton Police Department, Karen completed a written general intelligence test, an oral interview, a lie detector test, and a psychological test. The hiring decision is made only after the applicant passes each of the tests.

They don't have a physical test. Some of the major departments have their own training, or their own academy. Physical requirements are a part of the academy, and if you can't keep up, I suspect you would flunk out of the academy.

When I joined, I was trained by the Colorado Law Enforcement Training Academy, a metro-wide, state-run organization that a lot of different departments send their people to. At the time I attended, it was four weeks long, six days a week, and you had to stay there because you had classes almost all of the time. We had a firing range program, we played volleyball at night, and had self-defense as a part of our physical program.

Now, the school has been expanded to three months.

Littleton is a primarily residential city with a population of 30,000. A typical suburban community. In her 13 years on the department, Karen has seen a change in the types of crimes.

When I first started, we never had a homicide. In the last two years, I've been involved with six or seven. We always have had all types of crimes, we just haven't had the amount that we have today.

For her first six and a half years on the department, she was a street officer in a patrol car.

In every department that I know, you cannot be a detective before you've spent time on the streets. If you can't survive the streets, you won't make it as a detective.

One of the differences between a detective and a patrol officer are the hours. Normally, a detective in the Littleton department works from 8:00 in the morning to 4:00 in the afternoon, Monday through Friday. There are six detectives in the department, so once every six weeks, one detective is on call for the evening and weekend hours. That detective will be called out for anything that happens. "You can't go too far because you are required to respond if they do call you."

8:00 a.m. in the detective room—it's basically one large room with nine desks. An investigator sits at one of the desks, a secretary at another, and the six detectives at the others. There are no room dividers. Phones ring and resound throughout the room. It is, at times, difficult to concentrate with the distractions. Other times, the detectives exchange information based on snatches of overheard conversation.

In the morning, the detectives gather at a large table in the lieutenant's office to go over the reports that have come through in the last 24 hours. They read the cases to insure that everyone knows what is going on. Afterwards, they return to their desks, and from then on, each day is different.

> *Sometimes we have scheduled interviews all day with witnesses or victims. Sometimes we have housekeeping types of things to do with the cases. We may have to go to Denver to pick up a photograph to run a photo line-up. We may have to go to a jail to interview someone in jail. We may spend half a day writing up a case filing.*

> *A lot of our time is spent on the telephone interviewing people, trying to find people.*

> *This week, I am looking for this guy so that I can issue him a ticket for joyriding. However, he already has two warrants out on him, so I don't know if I'll be able to find him. I've got a guy that I arrested for sexual assault on a child. We are trying to get him served so we can start the court processing.*

Although the lieutenant is in charge of the bureau, each detective is fairly autonomous. They do what they have to do to complete and close their cases.

> *They like to know where you are, of course, so we have a check-out and check-in board. If we are going on an interview, or to some jail or other police department, we check out and let them know where we are going to be. If they need us, they can call us.*

Lunchtime. If a detective is having lunch within the city limits, he or she must remain on call, available to respond. They are still considered on-duty. If he or she leaves the designated area to have lunch outside the city, they must take themselves off-duty for that hour, and instead of working from 8:00 to 4:00, will work until 5:00.

The Littleton Police Department has six detectives, all with a heavy caseload. They work without partners.

> *We coorperate with each other. I have a case right now, a forgery ring that consists mostly of juveniles. Some of the checks that were forged came out of a burglary that one of the other detectives is working on. So, we are trying to set up an interview with one of the suspects and will do that interview together.*

On major cases, a homicide for instance, each detective will be pulled off the case they were working on to work together intensively for a week or two. If there is no solution after that time, the detective who had the original assignment will continue with the case alone.

There is no average time it takes to solve a case. Some can be solved in a day, others require months, still others are never solved.

> *I have cases where I know who did it, but I don't have enough for an arrest warrant. If I could talk to the guy I might be able to do it, but I don't know where he is.*

Although there is no partner situation, the detectives will never make an arrest alone. Detectives face danger just as patrol officers do. The only difference is the fact that detectives work in plain clothes, there is no police uniform to immediately identify them.

> *Normally we don't respond to immediate life-threatening situations that patrol does. Often times we make arrests in people's home, we go to speak with people that we know are burglars, or whatever, and they know we are police officers. But, if they choose not to cooperate, they always have the option of resorting to violence.*

Fear is dealt with by remaining on guard at all times.

We tend to relax a little more because we are not in uniform, and that has proven fatal for some detectives. You begin to think that you are invisible.

Still, I am more relaxed in plain clothes than I was in uniform. There are always times when I am frightened, but you get used to it and learn to deal with it.

As the first woman on the Littleton Police Department, Karen and her fellow officers had to make a few adjustments. "If we're out there and there is something dangerous, I might have to remind (the male officers) that I am there to do the same job that they do." After the initial awkwardness, it wasn't a problem. Karen does her job just like everyone else.

Speaking as a woman, Karen does see some difficulty in successfully combining her personal and professional life.

There are a lot of times when I'll come home on a Monday night and say, 'Well, for the rest of the week, I'll be working swing shift, make yourself a sandwich for dinner.' If I get called out, I get called out. If it's in the middle of something, that's too bad.

The personal life of a police officer often revolves around a small circle of law enforcement friends. There can be communication problems when dealing with people outside of your business.

I have a couple of friends who are outside of law enforcement. Sometimes when I get to talking about what I do, I see this look on their face. They cannot believe what I deal with everyday.

This job really does affect your life more than most other types of jobs. You have to make an adjustment.

Detective Peregoy admits, however, that there is nothing like the elation and satisfaction she feels at having done her job thoroughly, backed a criminal into a corner, and sent him to jail. The challenges and stimulations are unlike any found in another profession.

One thing that good officers never lose is anger when they see someone get hurt. After all of these years of police work, I don't have a whole lot of ideas left, but everytime I see a victim, I get angry and I am going to do something about it. I feel good about having an avenue to do something about it.

It's difficult for someone on the outside to truly understand what it's like to be a police officer.

You don't know what it feels like until you do it. It's an extremely frustrating job, and you need to know how to deal with that.

I knew that I would be dealing with victims, with people that were hurting, but there is a big difference between sitting in a classroom and hearing that you must be sympathetic and empathetic to a victim of a sexual assault, and actually sitting in front of the victim and dealing with how they feel. Reality— that's the big difference.

APPENDIX A

Organizations Which May Provide Additional Career Information

COMPUTER FIELDS

American Federation of Processing Societies
1899 Preston White Drive
Reston, VA 22091

Data Processing Management Association
505 Busse Highway
Park Ridge, IL 60068

Association for Systems Management
24587 Bagley Road
Cleveland, OH 44138

BUSINESS

Alliance of American Insurers
1501 Woodridge Road, Suite 400W
Schaumberg, IL 60195

American Society of Women Accountants
35 E Wacker Drive, Suite 1026
Chicago, IL 60601

American Association of Advertising Agencies
666 Third Avenue
New York, NY 10017

Insurance Information Institute
110 William Street
New York, NY 11038

American Bankers Association
1120 Connecticut Avenue
Washington, DC 20036

National Management Association
2210 Arbor Road
Dayton, OH 45439

American Institute of Certified Public Accountants
1211 Avenue of the Americas
New York, NY 10036

ENGINEERING

Accrediting Board for Engineering and Technology
345 E 47th Street
New York, NY 10017

American Society of Mechanical Engineers
345 E 47th Street
New York, NY 10017

American Ceramic Society
65 Ceramic Drive
Columbus, OH 43214

Institute of Electrical and Electronic Engineering
1111 19th Street NW, Suite 608
Washington, DC 20036

American Society of Agricultural Engineers
PO Box 410
St. Joseph, MI 49805

National Society of Professional Engineers
1420 King Street
Alexandria, VA 22314

American Society of Civil Engineers
345 E 47th Street
New York, NY 10017

Society of Mining Engineers
Caller Box D
Littleton, CO 80127

LAW

American Bar Association
750 N Lake Shore Drive
Chicago, IL 60611

Association of American Law Schools
1 Dupont Circle NW, Suite 370
Washington, DC 20036

National Association for Law Placement
440 First Street NW, Suite 307
Washington, DC 20001

WRITING

Accrediting Council on Education in Journalism
and Mass Communications
c/o University of Missouri
PO Box 838
Columbia, MO 65201

American Society of Magazine Editors
575 Lexington Avenue
New York, NY 10022

Public Relations Society of America
845 Third Avenue
New York, NY 10022

Society for Technical Communication
815 15th Street NW, Suite 576
Washington, DC 20005

Women in Communications
PO Box 9561
Austin, TX 78766

ACTING

American Theatre Association
1010 Wisconsin Avenue NW
Washington, DC 20007

League of Professional Theatre Training Programs
1860 Broadway, Suite 1515
New York, NY 10023

Theatre Communications Group
355 Lexington Avenue
New York, NY 10017

MUSIC

American Federation of Musicians
1500 Groadway, Suite 600
New York, NY 10023

American Guild of Musical Artists
1841 Broadway
New York, NY 10023

American Guild of Organists
815 Second Avenue, Suite 318
New York, NY 10017

American Symphony Orchestra League
633 E Street NW
Washington, DC 20006

National Association of Schools of Music
11250 Roger Bacon Drive
Reston, VA 22090

DIRECTING

American Theatre Association
1010 Wisconsin Avenue NW
Washington, DC 20007

League of Professional Theatre Training Programs
1860 Broadway, Suite 1515
New York, NY 10023

Assistant Directors Program
14144 Ventura Boulevard
Sherman Oaks, CA 91423

Theatre Communications Group
355 Lexington Avenue
New York, NY 10017

JOURNALISM/REPORTING

American Newspaper Publishers Association
PO Box 17404 Dulles Airport
Washington, DC 20041

Dow Jones Newspaper Fund
PO Box 300
Princeton, NJ 08543

American Society of Magazine Photographers
205 Lexington Avenue
New York, NY 10016

National Association of Broadcasters
1771 N Street NW
Washington, DC 20036

Broadcast Education Association
1771 N Street NW
Washington, DC 20036

National Cable TV Association
1724 Massachusetts Avenue
Washington, DC 20036

MEDICINE

American Hospital Association
840 N Lake Shore Drive
Chicago, IL 60611

Association of American Medical Colleges
1 Dupont Circle NW, Suite 200
Washington, DC 20036

American Medical Association
535 N Dearborn St
Chicago, IL 60610

International Chiropractors Association
1901 L Street NW, Suite 800
Washington, DC 20036

American Osteopathic Association
212 E Ohio Street
Chicago, IL 60611

National Health Council
622 Third Avenue
New York, NY 10017

SPORTS/ATHLETICS

American Alliance for Health, Physical Education,
   and Recreation
1900 Association Drive
Reston, VA 22091

Women's Sports Foundation
625 Madison Avenue
New York, NY 10022

EDUCATION

American Federation of Teachers
555 New Jersey Avenue NW
Washington, DC 20001

American Association of School Administrators
1801 N Moore Street
Arlington, VA 22109

American Association for Counseling
and Development
5999 Stevenson Avenue
Alexandria, VA 22304

American Vocational Association
1410 King Street
Alexandria, VA 22314

National Council of Teachers of Mathematics
1906 Association Drive
Reston, VA 22091

MILITARY

Air Force
USAF Recruiting Command
Randolph AFB, TX 78180

Army
US Army Recruiting Command
Fort Sheriden, IL 60037

Coast Guard
Commandant (G-PMR)
US Coast Guard
Washington, DC 20593

Marine Corps
Director, Personnel Procurement
USMC
Washington, DC 20380

Navy
Navy Opportunity Information Center
PO Box 5000
Clifton, NJ 07011

US Military Entrance Processing Command
2500 Green Bay Road
North Chicago, IL 60037

HOTEL AND RESTAURANT

American Culinary Federation
PO Box 3466
St. Augustine, FL 32084

American Hotel and Motel Association
888 Seventh Avenue
New York, NY 10019

Council of Hotel, Restaurant,
and Institutional Education
Harrison Building Room S 208
University Park, PA 16801

National Institute for the Food Service Industry
20 N Wacker Drive, Suite 2620
Chicago, IL 60606

National Restaurant Association
311 First Avenue
Washington, DC 20001

PROTECTIVE SERVICES

American Correctional Association
4321 Hartwick Road
College Park, MD 20740

CONTACT
PO Box 81826
Lincoln, NE 68501

International Association of Chiefs of Police
1329 18th Street NW
Washington, DC 20036

International Association of Fire Fighters
1750 New York Avenue NW
Washington, DC 20006

National Fire Protection Association
Batterymarch Park
Quincy, MA 02269

APPENDIX B

Selected Books on Careers

COMPUTER FIELDS

Computer and Mathematics Related Occupations Pueblo, CO: Consumer Information Center, 1985.
Engineering, Science and Computer Jobs Princeton: Peterson's Guides, Annual.
Ledick, Julie *Opportunities in Computer Science Careers* Lincolnwood, IL: VGM Career Horizons, 1984.
Mitchell, Joyce Slayton *Your Job in the Computer Age* New York: Scribners, 1984.
Staia, Lila B. *Careers in Computers* Homewood, IL: Dow Jones, 1984.
Stone, Jack and Stephen S. Roberts *You Don't Have to Be a Genius to Land a Computer Job* New York; Bobbs, Merrill, 1984.

BUSINESS

Business and Management Jobs Princeton: Peterson's Guides, Annual.
Farley, Jennie *Women in Management: Careers and Family Issues* Ithaca, NY: ILR Press, Cornell University, 1984.
Fields, Daisy *A Woman's Guide to Moving up in Business and Government* Englewood Cliffs, NJ: Prentice Hall, 1983.
Fischgrund, Tom *The Insider's Guide to the Top Business Schools* Boston: Little, Brown and Company, 1983.
Guide to Graduate Business Schools Woodbury, NY: Barron's, 1986.
Marrs, Wanda J. and Texe W. Marrs *Secretary Today, Manager Tomorrow* New York, ARCO, 1984.
O'Brien, Mark *The MBA Answer Book: A Career Guide for the Person Who Means Business* Englewood Cliffs, NJ: Prentice Hall, 1984.
Rosenthal, David W. and Michael A. Powell *Careers in Marketing* Englewood Cliffs, NJ: Prentice Hall, 1984.
Salzman, Marian and Nancy Marx *MBA Jobs: An Insiders Guide to Companies That Hire MBAs* New York: AMACOM, 1986.

ACTING

Careers in Radio Washington: National Association of Broadcasters, 1986.
Reed, Maxine K. *Career Opportunities in TV, Cable, and Video* New York: Facts on File, 1985.
Smith, Dian G. *Careers in the Visual Arts: Talking with Professionals* New York: Julian Messner, 1985.
White, Virginia L. *Grants for the Arts* New York: Plenum Press, 1980.
Zernick, Theodore *Careers in the Visual Arts: Options, Training, and Employment* Reston: National Art Education Association, 1980.
Henry, Mari Lyn and Lynne Rogers *How to Be Working Actor* New York: M Evans, 1986.

MUSIC

Busnar, Gene *Careers in Music* New York: Julian Messner, 1982.
Career Guide for Young American Singers New York: Metropolitan Opera, 1986.
Careers in Music Skokie, IL: American Music Conference, 1985.
Dagnal, Cynthia *Starting Your Own Rock Bank* Chicago: Contemporary Books, 1983.
Dearing, James *Making Money Making Music* Cincinnati: Writers Digest Books, 1987.
Directory: National Association of Schools of Music Reston, VA: National Association of Schools of Music, 1985.
Feder, Judity *Exploring Careers in Music* New York: Richards Rosen, 1982.
Field, Shelly *Career Opportunities in the Music Field* New York: Facts on File, 1986.
Gerardi, Robert *Opportunities in Music* Lincolnwood, IL: VGM Opportunities, 1984.
Guide to Business of Music Schools Chicago: Charles Suber and Associates, 1984.
Siegel, Alan H. *Breaking into the Music Business* Chicago: Charles Suber and Associates, 1984.

ENGINEERING

Beakley, George *Careers in Engineering and Technology* New York; Macmillan, 1984.
Engineering, Science, and Computer Jobs Princeton: Peterson's Guides, Annual.
Goldberg, Joan Rachel *High Tech Career Strategies for Women* New York: Collier Books, 1984.
Shanahan, William F. *Engineering Career Guide* New York: ARCO, 1982.
Women in Engineering Washington: Business and Professional Women's Foundation, 1986.
Women in Engineering: Directory of College-University Programs Washington: American Society for Engineering Education, 1983.

LAW

Careers in Patent Law Chicago: American Bar Association, 1971.
Gillers, Stephen *Looking at Law School* New York: New American Library, 1984.
Law and Legal Information Directory Detroit: Gale Research Company, 1984.
Legal Careers: Choices and Options Washington: National Association for Law Placement, 1985.
Miller, Saul *After Law School; Finding a Job in a Tight Market* Boston; Little, Brown & Company, 1978.
National Law Journal Directory of the Legal Profession New York; National Law Journal, 1985.
Paralegal Career Guide Doylestown, PA: National Paralegal Association, 1984.
Williams, John W. *Career Preparation and Opportunities in Law* Chicago: American Bar Association, 1984.

WRITING

Goldin, Stephen and Kathleen Sky *The Business of Writing of Being a Writer* New York: Carroll and Graf, 1985.
Guiley, Rosemary *Career Opportunities for Writers* New York: Facts on File Publications, 1985.
Hensley, Dennis E. *Writing for Profit* Nashville: Thomas Nelson, 1985.
Writing Careers Cincinnati: Writer's Digest Books, 1986.

DIRECTING

Information Packet Sherman Oaks, CA: Assistant Directors Training Program, Annual.
Katz, Judith A. *The Business of Show Business* New York: Harper and Row, 1981.
Langley, Stephen and James Abruzzo *Jobs in Arts and Media Management* New York: Drama Books Publishers, 1986.
London, Mel *Getting Into Film* New York: Ballatine Books, 1977.
Lukas, Christopher *Directing for Film and TV* New York: Doubleday, 1985.
Mikes-Brown, John *Directing Drama* Atlantic Highlands, NJ: Humanities Press, 1980.
Robertson, Joseph F. *The Magic of Film Editing* Blue Ridge Summit, NJ: TAB Books, 1983.
Sievers, David et al. *Directing for the Theater* Somewhere: William C. Brown, 1974.

JOURNALISM/REPORTING

Broadcast Programs in American Colleges and Universities Washington: American Women in Radio and TV, 1984.
Career Directory of Publishing New York: Career Publishing Company, 1986.
Career Guide for Minority Journalists Princeton: Dow Jones Newspaper Fund, Annual.
Index Directory of Women in Media Washington: Women's Institute for Freedom of the Press, Annual.
Journalism Career and Scholarship Guide Princeton: Dow Jones Newspaper Fund, Annual.
Women on the Job: Careers in Electronic Media Washington: Women's Bureau, US Department of Labor, 1984.

MEDICINE

Ablow, Keith R. *Medical School: Getting In, Staying In, Staying Human* Baltimore: Wilkins and Williams, 1987.
Barron's Guide to Foreign Medical Schools Woodbury, NY: Barron's, 1984.
Chiropractor Information Kit Washington: International Chiropractic Association, Annual.
Medical School Admissions Requirements Washington: Association of American Medical Colleges, Annual.
Minority Student Opportunities in US Medical Schools Washington: Association of American Medical Colleges, Annual.

Rucker, T. Donald and Martin D. Keller *Planning Your Medical Career: Traditional and Alternative Opportunities* Garrett Park, MD: Garrett Park Press, 1986.

Schmolling, Paul Jr., William R. Burger and Merrill Youkeles *Careers in Mental Health: A Guide to Helping Occupations* Garrett Park, MD: Garrett Park Press, 1986.

SPORTS

Athletic Scholarships for Women San Francisco: Women's Sports Foundation, Annual.

Career Opportunities in Sports and Athletics St. Paul: Athletic Achievements, 1985.

Figler, Stephen and Howard Figler *The Athlete's Game Plan for College and Career* Princeton: Peterson's Guides, 1984.

Green, Alan *Directory of Athletic Scholarships* New York: Facts on File, 1987.

High School Planning for College Bound Athletes Skokie, IL: National Association of College Admissions Counselors, 1986.

McGonage, Bob and Marguerita McGonage *Careers in Sports* New York: Lothrop, Lee, and Shepard Books, 1975.

Your Rights and Responsibilities as a Student Athlete in Higher Education Columbus: National Association of Student Personnel Administrators, 1986.

EDUCATION

Beard, Marna and Michael J. McGahey *Alternative Careers for Teachers* New York: ARCO, 1985.

Ortiz, Flora *Career Patterns in Education* New York: Henry Holt and Company, 1981.

Overseas Employment Opportunities for Educators Alexandria, VA: Overseas Dependents Education Program, Annual.

Rice, Robin *The American Nanny: A Comprehensive Guide* Washington: TAN Press, 1986.

Teacher Supply-Demand Report Madison: ASCUS, Annual.

MILITARY

Aim High: Air Force College Commissioning Program Maxwell AFB, AL Air Force ROTC, Annual.

Be All You Can Be (packet) Fort Monroe, VA: Army ROTC, Annual.

Betterton, Don *How the Military Will Help You Pay for College* Princeton: Peterson's Guides, 1985.

Bradley, Jeff *A Young Person's Guide to Military Service* Boston: Harvard Common Press, 1983.

Marrs, Texe and Karen Read *Every Women's Guide to Military Service* Cockeysville, MD: Liberty Publishing, 1984.

Military Career Guide Washington: US Department of Defense, Annual.

Parent's Guide to the Five US Service Academics Harrisburg, PA: Stackpole Books, 1986.

HOTEL AND RESTAURANT

Burns, Jim and Betsy Ann Brown *Women Chefs of California: The New Culinary Pioneers* Berkeley: ARIS Books, 1986.

Career Packet Washington: National Restaurant Association, Annual.

Cavallalo, Ann *Careers in Food Service* New York: Lodstar Books, 1981.

Course List East Lansing, MI: American Hotel and Motel Association, Annual.

Directory of Hotel and Restaurant Schools University Park, PA: Council on Hotel, Restaurant, and Institutional Education, Annual.

Miller, Daniel *Starting a Small Restaurant* Cambridge: Harvard Common Press, 1983.

Westbrook, James *Aim for a Job in Restaurant and Food Service* New York: Richards Rosen Press, 1978.

PROTECTIVE SERVICES

Fire Fighter Professional Qualifications Quincy, MA: National Fire Protection Association, 1974.

Horne, P *Women in Law Enforcement* Springfield, IL: C Thomas, 1985.

Miller, George W. *Police Employment Guide* Huntsville, TX: National Employment Listing Service, 1982.

Saniers, William B. *Detective Work: A Study of Criminal Investigations* New York: Free Press, 1979.